RESILIENCE AND WELLBEING IN YOUNG CHILDREN, THEIR FAMILIES AND COMMUNITIES

Resilience and Wellbeing in Young Children, Their Families and Communities unpicks the theme of resilience and wellbeing through diverse contexts, circumstances, populations and life stories in order to explore its complexity globally.

Current societal events have brought forward a need for understanding how to best support and create environments with conditions that promote children's holistic wellbeing. Violence in all its facets, poverty, political conflict and the recent pandemic are among the major realities threatening children, and this demands attention to how resilience can be supported to effectively safeguard children's lived experiences. This book explores resilience from a range of perspectives, research projects and practical support mechanisms for young children, families, educators and communities. It starts with theoretical conceptualizations and goes on to present specific research projects and applied initiatives and how these can be used in application to praxis for young children and their families.

Being of interest to educators and human services striving to advocate for and enhance young children's wellbeing, this book will serve as both a useful overview of the many approaches to supporting resilience in young children, while providing a sound theoretical perspective that is accessible for all.

Zoi Nikiforidou is Associate Professor in Early Childhood Pedagogy at the University of Ioannina, Greece.

Babs Anderson retired as Principal Lecturer in Early Childhood at Liverpool Hope University, UK.

Wilma Robles-Melendez is Professor of Early Childhood Education at the Abraham S. Fischler College of Education & School of Criminal Justice of Nova Southeastern University, USA.

Towards an Ethical Praxis in Early Childhood

Written in association with the European Early Childhood Education Research Association (EECERA), titles in this series will reflect the latest developments and most current research and practice in early childhood education on a global level. Feeding into and supporting the further development of the discipline as an exciting and urgent field of research and high academic endeavour, the series carries a particular focus on knowledge and reflection, which has huge relevance and topicality for those at the front line of decision making and professional practice.

Rather than following a linear approach of research to practice, this series offers a unique fusion of research, theoretical, conceptual and philosophical perspectives, values and ethics, and professional practice, which has been termed 'Ethical Praxis'.

Other titles published in association with the European Early Childhood Education Research Association (EECERA):

Science, Technology, Engineering, Arts and Mathematics (STEAM) Education in the Early Years
Achieving the Sustainable Development Goals
Edited by Weipeng Yang, Sarika Kewalramani and Jyoti Senthil

Resilience and Wellbeing in Young Children, Their Families and Communities
Exploring Diverse Contexts, Circumstances and Populations
Edited by Zoi Nikiforidou, Babs Anderson and Wilma Robles-Melendez

For more information about this series, please visit: www.routledge.com/education/series/EECERA

RESILIENCE AND WELLBEING IN YOUNG CHILDREN, THEIR FAMILIES AND COMMUNITIES

Exploring Diverse Contexts, Circumstances and Populations

Edited by Zoi Nikiforidou, Babs Anderson and Wilma Robles-Melendez

LONDON AND NEW YORK

Designed cover image: Credit goes to Elia Leontari for the cover image of the book

First published 2024
by Routledge
4 Park Square, Milton Park, Abingdon, Oxon OX14 4RN

and by Routledge
605 Third Avenue, New York, NY 10158

Routledge is an imprint of the Taylor & Francis Group, an informa business

© 2024 selection and editorial matter, Zoi Nikiforidou, Babs Anderson and Wilma Robles-Melendez; individual chapters, the contributors

The right of Zoi Nikiforidou, Babs Anderson and Wilma Robles-Melendez to be identified as the authors of the editorial material, and of the authors for their individual chapters, has been asserted in accordance with sections 77 and 78 of the Copyright, Designs and Patents Act 1988.

All rights reserved. No part of this book may be reprinted or reproduced or utilised in any form or by any electronic, mechanical, or other means, now known or hereafter invented, including photocopying and recording, or in any information storage or retrieval system, without permission in writing from the publishers.

Trademark notice: Product or corporate names may be trademarks or registered trademarks, and are used only for identification and explanation without intent to infringe.

British Library Cataloguing-in-Publication Data
A catalogue record for this book is available from the British Library

Library of Congress Cataloging-in-Publication Data
Names: Nikiforidou, Zoi, editor. | Anderson, Babs, editor. | Robles-Melendez, Wilma, editor.
Title: Resilience and wellbeing in young children, their families and communities : exploring diverse contexts, circumstances and populations / edited by Zoi Nikiforidou, Babs Anderson and Wilma Robles-Melendez.
Description: Abingdon, Oxon ; New York, NY : Routledge, 2024. | Series: Towards an ethical praxis in early childhood | "Written in association with the European Early Childhood Education Research Association (EECERA)." | Includes bibliographical references and index.
Identifiers: LCCN 2023051243 (print) | LCCN 2023051244 (ebook) | ISBN 9781032385693 (hardback) | ISBN 9781032385709 (paperback) | ISBN 9781003345664 (ebook)
Subjects: LCSH: Resilience (Personality trait) in children—Europe. | Early childhood education—Europe. | Community and school—Europe
Classification: LCC BF723.R46 R474 2024 (print) | LCC BF723.R46 (ebook) | DDC 362.2083/094—dc23/eng/20240126
LC record available at https://lccn.loc.gov/2023051243
LC ebook record available at https://lccn.loc.gov/2023051244

ISBN: 978-1-032-38569-3 (hbk)
ISBN: 978-1-032-38570-9 (pbk)
ISBN: 978-1-003-34566-4 (ebk)

DOI: 10.4324/9781003345664

Typeset in ITC Galliard Pro
by Apex CoVantage, LLC

*To my parents and my two little sunrays who remind me
of life and goodness.
– Zoi Nikiforidou*

*To my amazing, loving, supportive family, who have
encouraged me to do my very best.
– Babs Anderson*

*To my mother, whose example, caring words, and
resilience continue today to inspire my work and efforts.
– Wilma Robles-Melendez*

Special dedication to Babs
*Honoring the memory of Dr. Babs Anderson, a resilient
and distinctive professional and friend*

*It was during the summer of 2023 when we last met and
chatted with our dear colleague Babs about the last steps
of the project that became this book. With the wisdom,
enthusiasm and optimistic ways that always described
her, Babs was radiant and smiling as we talked about
the final steps for this book about resilience. Though she
left us before this book was published, her strong presence
and resilient example will always be treasured in our
memories and hearts. We honor her today for her legacy,
passionate dedication to children and to early childhood
excellence that will always be remembered.*

CONTENTS

List of Contributors   *x*
Series Editor Foreword   *xv*
Preface   *xix*

PART 1
Research-Based Views on Resilience   1

1 Resilience and Children: Introducing Concepts, Notions, and Tensions   3
   Wilma Robles-Melendez, Zoi Nikiforidou and Babs Anderson

2 Resilience and Wellbeing in Children: A Meta-Synthesis   10
   Esra Akgül and Dila Nur Yazici

3 Risk, Rights, Responsibilities and Resilience: Considering Practical Ways of Supporting Children's Resilience   35
   Samantha Hoyes

PART 2
Theoretical and Practical Perspectives — 49

4 "The Children Are Grand!": Educators' Perspectives on Educator and Child Wellbeing During the COVID-19 Pandemic — 51
   Maja Haals Brosnan, Rhona Stallard and Natasha O'Donnell

5 How to Create a More Open-Listening Climate in Early Years Settings: A Multi-Professional Perspective When Supporting Children's Wellbeing — 71
   Alison Moore

6 Resilience and Children With Disabilities: The Role of Positive Relationships and Friendships — 95
   Kyriakos Demetriou

PART 3
Applied Practices and Initiatives With Young Children — 111

7 The Compassion–Resilience Connection: Their Place in Early Childhood Education in a Global Arena — 113
   Harriet Broadfoot

8 Towards a Pedagogy of Hope: Creating a Listening Culture for Nurturing Children's Wellbeing — 130
   Naomi McLeod, Diane Boyd, Catrina Luz Aniere and Suzanne Axelsson

9 Play in the Education and Care of Young Autistic Children — 147
   Jenny Louise Gibson and Sinéad Máire McNally

10 Holistic Education as Support for Wellbeing and Resilience — 159
   Tansy Watts

11 Building a Circle of Caring Support for Our Children With Diverse Roots: Nurturing Young Children's Resiliency — 176
   Wilma Robles-Melendez, Berta Capo and Eric G. Robles

12 A System in 'Fight Mode'?: Resilience and Social
   Capital in a Community Emerging From Conflict   195
   Clionagh Boyle

PART 4
Connecting Ideas   **211**

13 Reflecting on What We Know and Beyond   213
   *Zoi Nikiforidou, Wilma Robles-Melendez
   and Babs Anderson*

Index   *220*

CONTRIBUTORS

Esra Akgül is Associate Professor in Early Childhood Education at the University of Hasan Kalyoncu, Türkiye. Her research interests focus on multicultural education, culturally responsive pedagogy, cultural differences, early interventions and children at risk.

Babs Anderson was Principal Lecturer in Early Childhood at Liverpool Hope University in the UK. She was a co-convenor of the Holistic Wellbeing Special interest group of EECERA. She had over 20 years of experience as an early years practitioner. Her research interests included young children's wellbeing, outdoor learning and early years leadership. She taught on undergraduate, postgraduate and doctoral programs at Liverpool Hope University with a particular interest in the ethics and methodology of research projects. She was the editor of *Philosophy for Children: Theories and Praxis in Teacher Education* (Routledge).

Catrina Luz Aniere is CEO of Millennium Kids Inc, a youth led environmental, not for profit organisation, where young people can tackle the big issues. Catrina has a passion for 'youth voice and engagement' and has 26 years experience working with young people to change their world.

Suzanne Axelsson works as a pedagogical consultant using experience, inspiration and research in listening, philosophy with children and Indigenous Knowledge to guide creating democratic learning and play spaces in early childhood education. She holds seminars on intersectional approaches to inclusive play as part of the Preschool Teacher Programme at BUV, Stockholm University, which continues to inform her research and published work.

Diane Boyd specializes in early childhood education for sustainability with a particular focus upon the Sustainable Development Goals and Indigenous ways of thinking and being. Diane has been at LJMU since 2005 and is on the Executive Committee and is Sustainability Lead for the Early Childhood Studies Degree Network. Her latest project is to develop an early years resource based on the SDGs which will be printed with four Home Country versions. She is part of the Department of Education action groups for early childhood sustainability moving forward from the strategy published at COP 26.

Clionagh Boyle is Head of Early Childhood in the School of Education at Liverpool Hope University. Her interest is in the political dimension of Early Childhood, and her research problematizes the ways in which dominant policy discourses intersect with the lived experience of children, families and communities. She has over 20 years of experience in policy and advocacy in children's rights working with children, parents, practitioners, schools and communities in Northern Ireland and internationally in areas impacted by war and conflict.

Harriet Broadfoot is currently an ESRC doctoral researcher and Education Studies tutor at Durham University. Her research interests center on compassion, sustainability, wellbeing and global citizenship in Early Childhood Education (ECE), as well as early environments and experiential learning. With a background as a qualified Early Years Teacher and in Montessori education, she has experience working across the ECE sector in teaching, mentoring and management roles. Harriet is also the director of The Children's Voice, which aims to promote children's voices on how we can co-create a more compassionate and sustainable world.

Maja Haals Brosnan has a PhD degree in social anthropology in the area of childhood adversity. She is Program Director for and Senior Lecturer in Early Childhood Education in Marino Institute of Education, Dublin. Her experience is in the area of child and family policy and in the last seven years specifically in early childhood education policy and research. Her research interests include early childhood policy, cultural and linguistic diversity and socioeconomic disadvantage in early childhood education.

Berta Capo, EdD, is Associate Professor of Science Education at the Masters and Doctoral levels at the Abraham S. Fischler College of Education & School of Criminal Justice (FCESCJ). She has been a veteran Miami-Dade County Public School (MDCPS) science teacher for 22 years. She holds a Bachelor of Science in Animal Science from Florida Agricultural and Mechanical University, a Master of Science Education from the University of Miami, and a Doctor of Education in Information Technology and Distance Education from Nova Southeastern University. Dr. Capo's research is on STEM and technology as an equity issue and on student resiliency.

Kyriakos Demetriou is Assistant Professor in Inclusive Education at the University of Nicosia, Cyprus. His research interests relate to special educational needs, inclusion, inclusive policy and practice, assistive technologies, social aspects of disability such as friendship and disability, cultural representations of disability, and disability stigma.

Jenny Louise Gibson is Professor of Developmental Psychology at the Faculty of Education, University of Cambridge and Chief Scientist at Nesta, the UK's social innovation agency. Jenny's background is in Speech and Language Therapy and Psychology; she completed her PhD studies at the University of Manchester before taking up postdoctoral posts at Cambridge and UEA. She joined the Faculty of Education in 2014 and was part of the team that founded the center for research on Play in Education, Development and Learning (PEDAL). Her research focuses on the role of play in the development of social, emotional and linguistic skills in children.

Samantha Hoyes is Senior Lecturer at Bishop Grosseteste University, teaching on the Early Childhood Studies degree program. Prior to this, Samantha worked in the Early Years sector, undertaking a variety of roles, including owning and managing her own Early Years Settings. Samantha's research interests include Early Years professionalism and the role of risk play. She is currently undertaking her PhD which explores how working mothers make sense of their identities.

Naomi McLeod is at Liverpool John Moores University and teaches across Early Childhood and Education Studies. Her research focuses on working creatively and respectfully 'with' people to promote young children's participation and agency, through critical reflection as a tool for continued professional development for transformational change. This focus and the importance of listening have informed her most current research.

Sinéad Máire McNally is Associate Professor in Psychology and Early Childhood Education at the School of Language, Literacy and Early Childhood Education at the DCU Institute of Education. Sinéad's research investigates the ways in which early inclusive and playful educational environments contribute to young children's development and learning. She is currently leading a national study of the school experiences of young autistic children in Ireland, funded by the Irish Research Council.

Alison Moore is Professional Practice Placement Manager at University College Cork, Ireland. Until recently, she led a group of Children's Centres in Birmingham, England, managing multidisciplinary teams and delivering support to children under five and their families, including early years care and education, family support and health services. Alison's roots lie within early years, and she has over 40 years' experience in the sector. Her doctoral thesis, awarded by Birmingham City University as part of a combined program at the Centre for Research in Early Childhood (CREC), explored parent and practitioner perspectives on how an open-listening climate in early years settings can facilitate child voice.

Zoi Nikiforidou is Associate Professor in Early Childhood Pedagogy at the University of Ioannina, Greece. Her research interests focus on children's cognition and wellbeing as well as on aspects of pedagogy, risk, technology and rights. Zoi is a co-convenor of the European Early Childhood Education Research Association (EECERA) Special Interest Group 'Holistic well-being', a member of the World Organisation for Early Childhood Education (OMEP) UK Executive Committee, and Senior Fellow of the Higher Education Academy UK.

Natasha O'Donnell is a lecturer in Early Childhood Education at Marino Institute of Education. Her doctoral thesis was on The Identities of Early Education Teachers (Educators). Tasha has 25 years of experience as an early childhood educator. Her research interests include policy pertaining to early education; children's perspectives of their experiences in early education; the role of educator identity in practice; children's rights; special education and inclusive practice.

Eric G. Robles, BA, is a graduate student in the School Psychology program at Interamerican University of Puerto Rico (San Juan, PR). He graduated from Universidad del Sagrado Corazon (San Juan, PR), where he received a bachelor's degree in Secondary English Education with high honors. He has engaged in researching equity issues related to the impact of social trauma on children.

Wilma Robles-Melendez is Professor of Early Childhood Education at the Abraham S. Fischler College of Education & School of Criminal Justice of Nova Southeastern University (Fort Lauderdale, USA). Being an experienced early childhood educator and teacher educator, she served as a school principal and state early childhood general supervisor. Her research focuses on multicultural and social justice issues with attention on children's immigration issues and equitable and culturally responsive practices for children and families. She is a co-convenor of the Holistic Children's Wellbeing Special interest group of EECERA. Being an advocate for children and families, she has several publications on diversity issues and is an active member and presenter at state, national and international organizations.

Rhona Stallard is a lecturer in Early Childhood Education at Marino Institute of Education. Her research interests relate to early childhood education pedagogy and curriculum, the professional practices and experiences of ECEC educators and contextual issues impacting ECEC in Ireland and beyond. Rhona has a background in psychology and in ECEC practice.

Tansy Watts is a lecturer at Canterbury Christ Church University and teaches across Early Childhood and Education studies degrees. Tansy has 13 years of experience in diverse forms of early education, including reception class teaching, voluntary-independent setting management and work in the Steiner kindergarten movement. Tansy's recent research with The Froebel Trust has explored the contemporary contribution of a holistic educational paradigm in developing an education for sustainable development. Tansy's current interdisciplinary research is with The National Institute of Christian Educational Research and Tansy investigates support for young children's spiritual flourishing.

Dila Nur Yazici is Assistant Professor at Hacettepe University, Turkey. Her research interests are inclusive education, children-at-risk, bilingualism, early intervention, transition to school and in-class transitions.

SERIES EDITOR FOREWORD

Reflections on the Focus

We have seen the negative impact of global crises on children and childhoods. Many of us are living through a series of global crises which include the COVID-19 pandemic, rising poverty, diminishing health and mental wellbeing, mass population movements through war and climate breakdown, changing and increasingly diverse family structures, the creation of digital childhoods and the growth of AI, increasing surveillance and privacy intrusion and the dominance of metrics and big data. These changes shift the nature of childhood and family life, and the evidence is that they have impacted more heavily on the young than any other section of society. Reflecting on the current state of children's wellbeing and mental health, and the quality and nature of the early experiences that are shaping their life chances, causes us to re-think our priorities in ECE policy and practice.

This scholarly and reflective book titled '*Resilience and Wellbeing: Children, Families, Communities and Societies*' edited by Zoi Nikiforidou, Babs Anderson and Wilma Robles Melendez provides the 13th book in the EECERA Ethical Praxis book series and offers a timely and very important agenda for our re-thinking. Its focus on building resilience and wellbeing in young children offers a much-needed stimulus for reflection on how the ECE sector might better understand

> the nature of resiliency and the factors supporting its development as well as practices to guide practitioners and parents. Because of the importance that resilience has in promoting positive developmental outcomes, there is a need for further knowledge on how to enable and support it.

As the authors point out, this is of particular importance and urgency and has resonance and value for all cultures and societies who face global and local adverse realities and conditions. We believe this book provides a valuable contribution to transforming the quality of early education as we move to consider a new post-pandemic and post-Anthropocene world in which all involved in ECE need to carefully consider how to progress towards achieving the Sustainable Development Goals where resilience and wellbeing are seen as central to this agenda.

As the Editors point out, the *'aim of the book is to unpick the theme of resilience and wellbeing through diverse contexts, circumstances, populations and life stories'*. And

> at the centre of this work is the search for practices that will better inform efforts of early childhood professionals in a time when many diverse challenges heighten the need to empower children with skills and abilities to cope with difficult events and circumstances.

This opportune book contains a wealth of new knowledge and theoretical thinking about resilience and wellbeing, in which ideas and concepts to integrate resilience into the praxis of early childhood education are explored and exemplified. This book's editors and chapter authors are experienced and active researchers and practitioners committed to contribute with their views and work to the need for resilience-oriented practices to support children's wellbeing in times of greater societal challenges. Collectively, the contributions of each chapter provide an excellent fusion of theory, research and practice which lives out the intent of the EECERA Praxis Series and should stimulate critical and deep reflections and actions to transform and improve current ECE policy and practice.

Underpinning Aspirations

The EECERA Book Series titled *'Towards an Ethical Praxis in Early Childhood'* offers an innovative and exemplary vehicle for the international early childhood sector to develop transformative pedagogy which demonstrates effective integrated praxis. The EECERA Book Series is designed to complement and link with the European Early Childhood Education Research Journal (EECERJ), which is primarily a worldwide academic platform for publishing research according to the highest international standards of scholarship. The EECERA **Ethical Praxis** Book Series aims to highlight pedagogic praxis in order to demonstrate how this knowledge can be used to develop and improve the quality of early education and care services to young children and their families.

Pedagogic Approach

The approach taken in the book series is not a linear one, but rather a praxeological one focused on praxis, meaning a focus on pedagogic action impregnated in theory and supported by a belief system. It is this fusion of practice, theoretical perspectives, ethics and research which we term **'Ethical Praxis'**. This fusion is embodied in all EECERA research and development activity, but we anticipate that the book series will have a stronger focus on the development of pedagogic praxis and policy. In addition to offering a forum for plural, integrated pedagogic praxis, the series will offer a strong model of praxeological processes that will secure deep improvements in the educational experience of children and families, of professionals and of researchers across international early childhood services.

The book series acknowledges pedagogy as a branch of professional/practical knowledge which is constructed in situated action in dialogue with theories and research and with beliefs (values) and principles. Pedagogy is seen as an 'ambiguous' space, not of one-between-two (theory and practice) but as one-between-three (actions, theories and beliefs) in an interactive, constantly renewed triangulation. Convening beliefs, values and principles, analyzing practices and dialoguing with several branches of knowledge (philosophy, history, anthropology, psychology, sociology, among others) constitutes the triangular movement of the creation of pedagogy. Pedagogy is thus based on praxis, in other words, action based on theory and sustained by belief systems. Contrary to other branches of knowledge which are identified by the definition of areas with well-defined frontiers, the pedagogical branch of knowledge is created in the ambiguity of a space which is aware of the frontiers but does not delimit them because its essence is in integration.

Praxeological Intentions

There is a growing body of practitioner and practice-focused research which is reflected in the push at national and international levels to integrate research and analysis skills into the professional skill set of all early childhood practitioners. This is a reflection of the growing professionalism of the early childhood sector and its increased status internationally. The development of higher-order professional standards and increased accountability are reflective of these international trends, as the status and importance of early education in the success of educational systems are acknowledged.

Each book in the series is designed to have the following praxeological features:

- strongly and transparently positioned in the socio-cultural context of the authors
- practice or policy in dialogue with research, ethics and with conceptual/theoretical perspectives
- topical and timely, focusing on key issues and new knowledge
- provocative, ground breaking, innovative
- critical, dialogic, reflexive
- euro-centric, giving voice to Europe's traditions and innovations but open to global contributions
- open, polyphonic, prismatic
- plural, multidisciplinary, multi-method
- praxeological, with a concern for power, values and ethics, praxis and a focus on action research, the learning community and reflexive practitioners
- views early childhood pedagogy as a field in itself, not as applied psychology
- concerned with social justice, equity, diversity and transformation
- concerned with professionalism and quality improvement
- working for a social science of the social
- NOT designed as a text book for practice but as a text for professional and practice/policy development

This 13th book in the series exemplifies these underpinning philosophies, pedagogical ethics and scholarly intentions beautifully. We believe it is topical and timely, focusing on key issues and new knowledge, and also provocative and critical, encouraging and opening polyphonic dialogue about our thinking and actions in developing high-quality early childhood services internationally.

Tony Bertram and Chris Pascal

PREFACE

This is the first collective work of the 'Holistic Wellbeing' EECERA SIG. We are really excited to share this interdisciplinary international collaboration that derives from a common interest – that of resilience under the spectrum of wellbeing. As EECERA SIG co-convenors and co-editors of the book, we believe that this edited book will showcase and problematize contexts, experiences, realities of young children, their families and communities, where resilience plays a key role in wellbeing and well-becoming. It is our hope that this book will contribute to bring attention to the ongoing need for practices to support and empower children to build their resilience growing up in a society of change and challenges. This book has also been a personal journey for each of us, facing life in a post-pandemic world and navigating many life challenges while learning about our own resilience.

We would like to thank all the authors who contributed to the book with their valuable chapters, knowledge and enthusiasm. We would also like to thank the EECERA book series editors Dr. Chris Pascal and Dr. Tony Bertram for their support and guidance, and the Publishers for their invaluable efforts.

Zoi Nikiforidou, Babs Anderson
and Wilma Robles-Melendez

PART 1
Research-Based Views on Resilience

1
RESILIENCE AND CHILDREN

Introducing Concepts, Notions, and Tensions

Wilma Robles-Melendez, Zoi Nikiforidou and Babs Anderson

Establishing happy and healthy early experiences and preparing children for life at present and in the future is at the heart of efforts and practices in early childhood programs. This is what guides and leads early childhood professionals and advocates of children to defy undesirable realities and embrace actions for the future of new generations. Consciously aware of our interconnected realities, the world of childhood is always intricately tied to the context of society and its advances and challenges (Bronfenbrenner, 1979; Drerup & Schweiger, 2019; Darling-Hammond et al., 2020). The notion that their present and future are dependent on the array of circumstances and events they face, both personal and societal, raises awareness to the ongoing interest for ways to care for and take care of young children.

It has been long understood that contextual factors, whether individual or community based, play a fundamental role in how children are and become – grow, thrive, and develop (Copple & Bredekamp, 2009; Corsaro, 2018). This brings attention to the influence and impact of ecologies, interactions, and conditions experienced by children, many times becoming confounding factors for the young child. Given the multiple disruptions many children may experience and encounter in their communities, highlights the search for concerted efforts and practices centered on their wellbeing. A way to respond is through what is called resilience, what inspires hope and shines through now (Nearchou & Douglas, 2021), even in times of unusual and difficult adversities.

In the Best Interest of the Child

The overarching principle of "*in the best interest of the child*" that frames the Convention on the Rights of the Child (1989) and the call for developmentally

DOI: 10.4324/9781003345664-2

appropriate and responsive support (National Association for the Education of Young Children, 2020), inspires and guides practices and efforts in early childhood. The aim is to promote and nurture in the child the abilities needed to effectively face the challenges of a world and time denoted by multiple uncertainties. The goal is to ensure that "every child [is] resilient" (UNICEF, 2022). Resilience is what many consider as that shield and individual capacity that protects children and adults whenever faced with challenging, many times difficult, and stressful circumstances (Dvorsky & Langberg, 2016; McLaughlin et al., 2020; Masten et al., 2021). Today, it is what is much needed, as society continues to face greater complexity. Thus, making possible for children to become resilient is a call for everyone working for what is in the best interest for children.

A Focus on Resiliency: Concepts and Notions

The recent events experienced with the 2020 pandemic made evident the need for placing attention on efforts to ensure children's wellbeing. In particular, it has created interest in aspects that contribute to supporting children's capacity to handle stress and overcome challenges through resiliency. Studies on resilient children show that this is a capacity that can be supported and developed during the early years (Masten, 2014; Sorrells, 2015; Center on the Developing Child, 2023). Contrary to the notion that resilient individuals are born with that capacity, research today has shown that many factors are known to empower children and build their resilience. Among those factors, caring relationships are crucial in fostering a child's ability to face and adjust to adverse events and challenges (Ungar, 2011; Sorrells, 2015; Slone & Peer, 2021). Considerations of the influential role of relationships on children raise attention to the role of early childhood practitioners and how their interactions and caring actions contribute to enabling children to become resilient. Implications for practitioners, particularly for early childhood educators and social services, call for considerations to the nature of resiliency and factors supporting its development and to needed practices to intentionally guide efforts for children. Because of the importance that resilience has in promoting positive developmental outcomes, serving as a mitigating factor when children are faced with threats and risk factors clearly establishes a need for furthering knowledge on how to support it. Contributing to understanding its meaning, educational implications of resilience, and applications in practice is what guides and defines the goals for this book.

Defining Resilience: A Multidimensional Construct

Recent and ongoing research continues to unveil the power of resilience on individuals when faced with adverse realities throughout life (Masten et al.,

2021; Senger, 2023). As a concept, resilience has been defined as a capacity individuals develop to process realities and successfully adapt to challenges (Herrmann et al., 2011; Masten, 2014; American Psychological Association [APA], 2023; Center on the Developing Child, 2023). It is a process with outcomes that progressively unfold as individuals continue to adjust to realities. This dynamic ability is what reveals the empowering capacity that supportive experiences and people's relationships exert on the child to build their power to adjust and adapt (Masten, 2014). From this perspective, resilience casts a light of hope in early childhood practices and on preparing children to face the hardships life may bring. Therefore, resilience offers a window of opportunity to build and equip children with the skills and abilities that can help them face and overcome challenges (Erdman et al., 2020; Masten et al., 2021).

Some of the views and notions about resilience are outlined in Figure 1.1.

Resilience is a construct with multiple conceptual dimensions that continues to be explored and defined. Several dimensions with implications for early education are drawn from current research on resilience (Ungar, 2012; Masten, 2014; Erdman et al., 2020) (Figure 1.2). One of these dimensions brings attention on the role of the network of relationships and their influence on the child's ability to become resilient (Wolmer et al., 2016; Center on the Developing Child, 2023). Relationships have also been described as part of the conditions and components deemed to be protective factors that in turn also foster individual wellbeing (Centers for Disease Control and Prevention, 2019; Child Welfare Information Gateway, 2020). Central is the notion of emotional security and of feeling and knowing that someone cares (Masten,

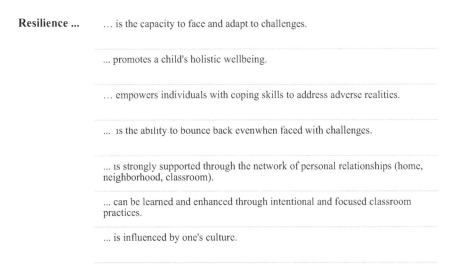

FIGURE 1.1   Views and concepts about resilience

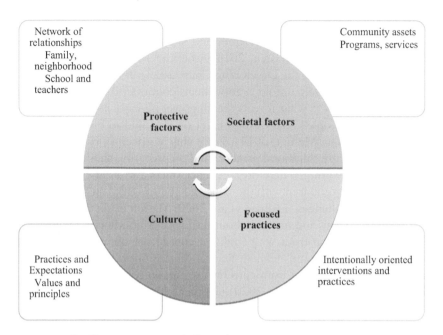

FIGURE 1.2 Resilience: conceptual dimensions

Source: Ungar et al. (2012); Masten (2014); Wolmer et al. (2016); Center on the Developing Child (2023)

2014; Erdman et al., 2020). Among these relationships, focused interactions and caring practices from educators are vital to enhance resiliency.

Societal components also emerge as another key dimension where programs and services targeted at providing support for children and families play a significant role in contributing to resilience. The presence and intersectionality of culture are undeniably the other factors that influence the emergence of resilient behaviors. How we cope with setbacks is impacted by our cultural values and principles, experienced from birth in the context of our interactions with families and caregivers (Clauss-Ehlers et al., 2006). Connectedness to one's culture furthers the child's social network providing the support needed in times of challenges.

Exploring Resilience: A Practice-Oriented Focus and the Scope of the Book

With efforts anchored on what is best for and in the interest of children, the aim of the book is to unpick the theme of resilience and wellbeing through diverse contexts, circumstances, populations, and life stories (Masten, 2014). The mission of the book is to explore the complexity of resilience globally

(Clauss-Ehlers, 2004, 2008; Wu et al., 2013), to investigate the discourse and construct of resilience within varied environments, and to record research involving policy and practice. In this direction, resilience is approached through pedagogical, developmental, rights-based approaches highlighting strong links to wellbeing and "good quality of life" (Statham & Chase, 2010). At the center of this work is the search for practices that will better inform efforts of early childhood professionals in a time when many diverse challenges heighten the need to empower children with skills and abilities to cope with difficult events and circumstances.

This book is anchored on the need for informing and learning more about the role and power of resilience to confront and navigate challenges in early childhood. It is aimed at contributing to the integral and intentional praxis of resilience in early childhood education programs and services for young children. In this practice-oriented book, reactive and proactive ways of supporting resilience in young children, families, and communities are discussed – referring to trauma-informed care; risk; advocacy; legal implications; socio-cultural aspects of resilience, within ECEC and beyond.

Topics in this book are organized into four parts, where issues and ideas are brought into practice (Figure 1.3). Chapters in each section examine ideas and

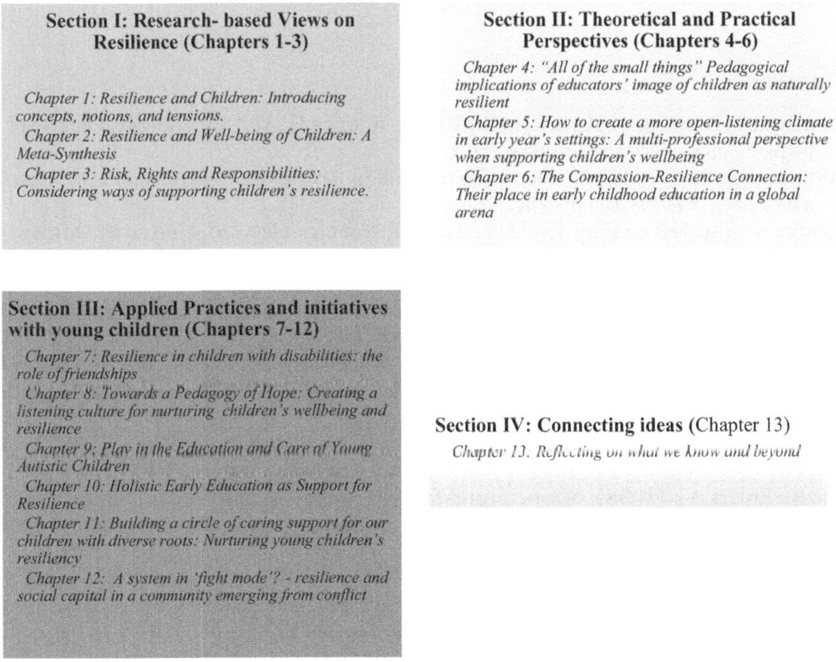

Section I: Research-based Views on Resilience (Chapters 1-3)

Chapter 1: Resilience and Children: Introducing concepts, notions, and tensions.
Chapter 2: Resilience and Well-being of Children: A Meta-Synthesis
Chapter 3: Risk, Rights and Responsibilities: Considering ways of supporting children's resilience.

Section II: Theoretical and Practical Perspectives (Chapters 4-6)

Chapter 4: "All of the small things" Pedagogical implications of educators' image of children as naturally resilient
Chapter 5: How to create a more open-listening climate in early year's settings: A multi-professional perspective when supporting children's wellbeing
Chapter 6: The Compassion-Resilience Connection: Their place in early childhood education in a global arena

Section III: Applied Practices and initiatives with young children (Chapters 7-12)

Chapter 7: Resilience in children with disabilities: the role of friendships
Chapter 8: Towards a Pedagogy of Hope: Creating a listening culture for nurturing children's wellbeing and resilience
Chapter 9: Play in the Education and Care of Young Autistic Children
Chapter 10: Holistic Early Education as Support for Resilience
Chapter 11: Building a circle of caring support for our children with diverse roots: Nurturing young children's resiliency
Chapter 12: A system in 'fight mode'? - resilience and social capital in a community emerging from conflict

Section IV: Connecting ideas (Chapter 13)

Chapter 13. Reflecting on what we know and beyond

FIGURE 1.3 Scope and organization of topics

concepts to integrate resilience into the praxis of early childhood education. Chapter authors are researchers and practitioners committed to contribute with their views and work to the need for resilience-oriented practices to support children's wellbeing in times of greater societal challenges. Discussion of fundamental ideas about resilience is presented in Part 1, *Research-based views on Resilience*. Here, resilience is examined with attention to its main conceptualizations. Part 2, *Theoretical and Practical Perspectives*, addresses views and conceptualizations derived from research about the nature of resilience. Emphasis is placed on the practical considerations and ideas about resilience. Part 3, *Applied Practices and Initiatives With Young Children*, directly bring ideas about resilience into practices for young children. Six chapters are included in this section all guided at offering practitioners with an array of strategies and concepts for classroom application. Finally, Part 4, *Connecting Ideas*, links together ideas presented throughout each of the sections and leads reader to see the implications of resilience on children's development and the scope of associated practices.

Every effort for children is always an effort for the future. This work is guided by the goal of empowering children and by the inherent responsibility that inspires early childhood educators to join and pursue practices in the best interest of the child. Every effort for children matters, and it is with that confidence that we invite you to read and reflect on the ideas, practices, and strategies presented in the chapters in this book.

References

American Psychological Association. (2023). *Resilience*. APA Psychology Dictionary. https://dictionary.apa.org/resilience

Bronfenbrenner, U. (1979). *The ecology of human development. Experiments by nature and design*. Harvard University Press.

Center on the Developing Child. (2023). *Resilience*. Harvard University. https://developingchild.harvard.edu/science/key-concepts/resilience/

Centers for Disease Control and Prevention. (2019). *Essentials for childhood: Creating safe, stable, nurturing relationships and environments for all children*. https://www.cdc.gov/violenceprevention/pdf/essentials-for-childhood-framework508.pdf

Child Welfare Information Gateway. (2020). *Protective factors approaches in child welfare*. U.S. Department of Health and Human Services, Administration for Children and Families, Children's Bureau.

Clauss-Ehlers, C. (2004). Re-inventing resilience. In C. S. Clauss-Ehlers & M. Weist (Eds.), *Community planning to foster resilience in children* (pp. 27–41). Springer.

Clauss-Ehlers, C. (2008). Sociocultural factors, resilience, and coping: Support for a culturally sensitive measure of resilience. *Journal of Applied Developmental Psychology, 29*(3), 197–212.

Clauss-Ehlers, C., Yang, Y., & Chen, W. (2006). Resilience from childhood stressors: The role of cultural resilience, ethnic identity, and gender identity. *Journal of Infant, Child, and Adolescent Psychotherapy, 5*, 124–138.

Copple, C., & Bredekamp, S. (2009). *Developmentally appropriate practice in early childhood programs serving children birth through age 8* (3rd ed.). National Association for the Education of Young Children.

Corsaro, W. (2018). *The sociology of childhood* (5th ed.). SAGE Publications.

Darling-Hammond, L., Flook, L., Cook-Harvey, C., Barron, B., & Osher, D. (2020). Implications for educational practice of the science of learning and development. *Applied Developmental Science, 24*(2), 97–140. https://doi.org/10.1080/1088691.2018.1537791

Drerup, J., & Schweiger, G. (2019). Global justice for childhood. Introduction. *Journal of Global Ethics, 15*(3), 193–201.

Dvorsky, M., & Langberg, J. (2016). A review of factors that promote resilience in youth with ADHD and ADHD symptoms. *Clinical Child and Family Psychology Review, 19*(4), 368–391.

Erdman, S., Colker, L., & Winter, E. (2020). *Trauma and young children. Teaching strategies to support and empower.* National Association for the Education of Young Children.

Herrmann, H., Stewart, D., Diaz-Granados, N., Berger, E., Jackson, B., & Truen, T. (2011). What is resilience? *The Canadian Journal of Psychiatry, 56*(5), 258–265. What is resilience? sagepub.com

Masten, A. (2014). Global perspectives on resilience in children and youth. *Child Development, 85*(1), 6–20.

Masten, A., Lucke, C., Nelson, K., & Stallworthy, I. (2021). Resilience in development and psychopathology: Multisystem perspectives. *Annual Review of Clinical Psychology, 7*(17), 521–549. https://doi.org/10.1146/annurev-clinpsy-081219-120307

McLaughlin, K., Colich, N., Rodman, A., & Weissman, D. (2020). Mechanisms linking childhood trauma exposure and psychopathology: A transdiagnostic model of risk and resilience. *BMC Medicine, 18*(1), 96. https://doi.org/10.1186/s12916-020-01561-6

National Association for the Education of Young Children. (2020). *Developmentally appropriate practice. Position Statement.* NAEYC.

Nearchou, F., & Douglas, E. (2021). Traumatic distress of COVID-19 and depression in the general population: Exploring the role of resilience, anxiety, and hope. *International Journal of Environmental Research and Public Health, 18*(16), 8485. https://doi.org/10.3390/ijerph18168485

Senger, A. (2023). Hope's relationship with resilience and mental health during the COVID-19 pandemic. *Current Opinion in Psychology, 50*, 101559. https://doi.org/10.1016/j.copsyc.2023.101559

Slone, M., & Peer, A. (2021). Children's reactions to war, armed conflict and displacement: Resilience in a social climate of support. *Current Psychiatry Report, 23*(11), 76. https://doi.org/10.1007/s11920-021-01283-3

Sorrells, B. (2015). *Reaching and teaching children exposed to trauma.* Gryphon House.

Statham, J., & Chase, E. (2010). *Childhood wellbeing: A brief overview. Briefing paper 1.* Childhood Wellbeing Research Centre.

Ungar, M. (2011). The social ecology of resilience: Addressing contextual and cultural ambiguity of a nascent construct. *American Journal of Orthopsychiatry, 81*(1), 1–17. https://doi.org/10.1111/j.1939-0025.2010.01067.x

Ungar, M., Ghazinour, M., & Richter, J. (2012). Annual research review: What is resilience within the social ecology of human development? *Journal of Child Psychology and Psychiatry, 54*(4), 348–366. https://doi.org/10.1111/jcpp.12025

UNICEF. (2022). *GP2022. Every country protected; every child resilient.* https://www.unicef.org/documents/gp2022-every-country-protected-every-child-resilient

United Nations. (1989). *Convention on the rights of the child.* https://www.unicef.org/child-rights-convention/convention-text

Wolmer, L., Hamiel, D., Margalit, N., Versano-Eisman, T., Findler, Y., Laor, N., & Slone, M. (2016). Enhancing children's resilience in schools to confront Trauma: The impact on teachers. *The Israel Journal of Psychiatry and Related Sciences, 53*(2), 25–31. PMID: 28079034

Wu, G., Feder, A., Cohen, H., Kim, J., Calderon, S., Charney, D., & Mathé, A. (2013), Understanding resilience. *Frontiers in Behavioral Neuroscience, 15*(7), 10. https://doi.org/10.3389/fnbeh.2013.00010

2
RESILIENCE AND WELLBEING IN CHILDREN

A Meta-Synthesis

Esra Akgül and Dila Nur Yazici

Introduction

Early childhood experiences have an extremely important place in the later lives of all individuals. Successful completion of this period depends on certain factors. In this section, meta-synthesis findings of studies on resilience and wellbeing, which are two of these factors, will be shared.

What Is Resilience?

Historically, the origins of resilience have deep roots in the field of medicine; however, research on resilience in the behavioral sciences began to emerge around 1970. According to Masten, pioneering scientists contended that critical aspects of human function and development, crucial for understanding and promoting prevention of, resistance to, or recovery from psychopathology, had been profoundly neglected. Four decades of resilience research followed as scientists took to the challenge of this phenomenon. There have been three waves of research on resilience in development. The first wave of research came from scientists wanting to understand and prevent the development of psychopathology. These pioneer researchers acknowledged the importance of children who seemed to progress well under risky conditions. The second wave of resilience research concentrated on detecting the processes and regulatory systems that accounted for protective factors associated with resilience. The third wave arose due to a sense of urgency for the welfare of children growing up with adversities focusing on promoting resilience through prevention, intervention, and policy (Zolkoski & Bullock, 2012, p. 2295).

Resilience is a concept derived from the Latin word "resiliens", which means "to bounce back" (Hunter & Chandler, 1999). In the American Psychological Association's Psychological Resilience initiative study, it is defined as the ability to adapt in the face of all kinds of stressful events, such as difficulties, trauma, and threats (Newman, 2005). On the other hand, Rutter focuses on people who can overcome difficulties and move forward without falling down in the face of difficulties, while defining psychological resilience (Rutter, 1987). In another definition, the concept of resilience is explained using risk and protective factors. Psychological resilience is defined as the positive adjustment that a person can maintain due to the presence of protective factors against risky events encountered in any of their developmental stages (Bernard, 1991). Winfield, like Bernard, defined resilience as a structure that includes protective factors that are effective in critical points of life, causing a person to change his behavior in the face of a threatening situation based on the concepts of protective and risk factors (Winfield, 1991).

The researchers underlined two important points to talk about psychological resilience. The first important point is stated as the fact that people have faced a risk situation, while the second point is that the adaptation they show after encountering the risk situation is effective (Masten & Coatsworth, 1998). When the literature is examined with all these different definitions, a common definition has been created for the concept of psychological resilience with three basic points by considering the risk situation and the importance of the adjustment afterwards. These three main points can be listed as risk factors, protective factors, and positive adaptation (Gizir, 2007).

What Is Wellbeing?

Generally, wellbeing is a physical, psychological, and cognitive process. Being physically, spiritually, and mentally healthy means leading a whole and happy life. Bradburn (1969; cited in Ryff, 1989) defines wellbeing as the emergence of a feeling of happiness resulting from life satisfaction. Wellbeing is defined as subjective wellbeing according to individuals being life satisfaction and happiness-centered, and as psychological wellbeing according to being self-actualizing functional individuals. Therefore, the fact that people experience more positive, less negative, and high satisfaction with life means that they have a high level of subjective wellbeing. Ryff and Keyes (1995) defined psychological wellbeing as a person's positive perception of himself, his ability to create his environment to meet his needs and desires, to know his limitations and integrate with himself, to be independent and assertive, to be aware of his abilities, and to try to develop them.

Over time, two basic perspectives on the concept of wellbeing have been put forward: (1) hedonism and (2) eudemonism (psychological functionality). According to the hedonistic perspective, wellbeing is defined on the basis of life satisfaction and happiness. The importance of experiencing positive emotions more than negative emotions and providing satisfaction in various areas of life (work, family, school, etc.) is emphasized. In this perspective, the individual evaluates his/her wellbeing according to the standards he/she has determined. There is only one criterion, and that is the individual and the subjective values that the individual imposes on their own life (Keyes et al., 2002).

Purpose of the Study

It is essential to make children happy by providing the necessary attention and care for the body and mind in raising healthy individuals (Russell, 2001, p. 28). A strong sense of wellbeing allows children to deal with their environment positively and safely and therefore to take full advantage of learning opportunities (Marbina et al., 2015). In addition, children and their psychological resilience are also essential. For this reason, in this research, it is aimed to reveal a general framework by making a meta-synthesis of the research studies that deal with the psychological resilience and wellbeing of children.

Method

Research Model

This research was patterned with the meta-synthesis model. Meta-synthesis is a method of interpreting and synthesizing qualitative findings in individual studies. In qualitative research, meta-synthesis is not simply a summary of previous findings or "collecting" all available data; rather, meta-syntheses offer new perspectives on issues by interpreting findings from different qualitative studies to generate "level three" findings for the advancement of both knowledge (Nye et al., 2016).

Sandelowski and Barroso (2003), especially by naming it as "qualitative meta-synthesis", offer a six-step way to do research: (1) formulate the investigation question, (2) perform a systematic literature review, (3) search and select appropriate research studies, (4) analysis and synthesis of qualitative results, (5) ensure quality control, and (6) present results. In this study, we completed each stage meticulously, and we concluded our study by following up this six-step research design (quoted by Ozturk ve Ozer, 2021, p. 4). We followed these six steps respectively. First, we developed our research questions focused on the issue of children's wellbeing and resilience. Second, by using search terms, we conducted a systematic literature review in certain databases to identify studies for potential inclusion. Third, we selected the studies that explored children's wellbeing and resilience. Fourth, we proceed with coding and organize themes according to our research questions. Fifth, to establish the trustworthiness and credibility of this study, we employed a three-stage strategy including a clear statement of purpose, preset research protocol, and detailed data processing and analysis. Finally, we present themes and core ideas related to our research issue according to the data analysis procedure.

Inclusion Criteria and Screening Process

The following criteria were sought in the determination of the study group in this study, which aims to metasynthesize the studies on resilience and wellbeing in early childhood with parents and/or children: (1) the study group was composed of parents and/or children, (2) it was published between 2016 and 2022, (3) qualitative or mixed pattern, and (4) published in one/more of the Web of Science, ERIC, Scopus, and ProQuest databases. Figure 2.1 shows the process of scanning research articles.

The literature review was carried out between 15 February 2022 and 20 July 2022. The literature search was carried out in the databases mentioned earlier. Topics and keywords used in searches are "early childhood, child, wellbeing, resilience, parent". In databases, "AND" and "OR" connectors are used

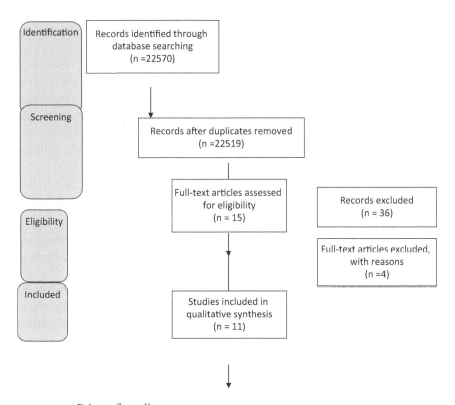

FIGURE 2.1 Prisma flow diagram

to combine concepts. Responsibility for conducting the literature review is shared between researchers.

Scan Result

The screening process was started by separating the repetitive and independent publications according to the titles of the articles; the abstracts of the articles were reviewed; and the topics that would not be included in the study were determined. The literature review results are detailed in the flow diagram (PRISMA) proposed by Moher et al. (2009) to report the meta-synthesis processes (Figure 2.1). As a result of the screening, 15 full-text articles that were determined to be suitable for the study were completely read. These studies were reviewed according to inclusion and exclusion criteria. Four articles were omitted due to repetition. Researchers worked independently at the beginning of the screening process and then came together to reach consensus on suitable articles. Studies will be included in the meta-synthesis. The purpose, method, inclusion criteria, and study value of the study were taken into consideration.

Data Extraction and Synthesis

At this stage, the articles included in the analysis process were read repetitively by the researchers. The characteristics of the articles included in the analysis process are presented in Table 2.1. In the following stage, the researchers analyzed the independently selected studies and determined the codes, categories, and subcategories. Then, they agreed on the determined category and subcategories. The inferences obtained through the synthesis of the findings are discussed together with the literature.

Findings and Discussion

As a result of the research, it was determined that the factors affecting children's psychological resilience and wellbeing focus on two main categories: risk factors and protective factors as shown in Figure 2.2.

Risk factors are divided into six themes: radical changes, poverty, social life barriers, family structure disorder, not meeting the child's basic needs, and parental issues. Protective factors were positive classroom climate, strong communication between teacher and family, social structure, close family relationships, addressing the child's special needs, family's attitude towards risk factors, and bilingualism. Table 2.2 presents the categories, themes, and sub-themes.

TABLE 2.1 Summaries of studies included in the review

Article Code	Author, Year	Database	Purpose	Participants	Method	Data Collection Way/Data Analysis	Summary of Findings
A1	Beers, C. (2021)	WOS-ERIC	To document the transition practices of a preschool as it moved to a new location and to understand effective practices in transitions.	Two early childhood teachers and three parents	qualitative	Interviews and supported by video recordings of classroom activities, photographs, and children's drawings.	Children who have a positive transitional experience are more able to adapt to new situations and develop resilience for further transitions. The teachers' behavior and the transitional procedures were both to blame for the kids' successful acclimatization. The factors that enable this are familiarization with the new school through open houses and artifact displays, encouraging the kids to take ownership of their environment

(Continued)

TABLE 2.1 (Continued)

Article Code	Author, Year	Database	Purpose	Participants	Method	Data Collection Way/Data Analysis	Summary of Findings
							by asking them to design their new playground and give tours of their school, teachers acting in responsive ways throughout the transition process with a focus on creating a positive classroom climate, and home-to-school collaboration, which is to increase families' sense of belonging in the school community.
A2	Distefano, R. et al. (2022)	WOS-ERIC	To understand whether families in emergency housing endorse or reject autonomy-supportive parenting strategies	21 parents (15 biological mothers and six biological fathers) residing in a large urban shelter for families experiencing homelessness in the midwestern United States	qualitative	Brief interview about parenting and self-regulation development	With their young children, homeless parents promote a number of autonomy-supportive parenting techniques during a critical period of plasticity for self-regulation development. These results are significant because young children who are homeless often lack adequate self-regulation, and one way they could acquire these skills is through parenting practices that foster autonomy. Therefore,

encouraging autonomy-supportive behaviors in this setting could aid in the development of self-regulation in kids before they start formal schooling. One crucial component of parenting strategies that enhance children's autonomy is highlighting their ability since it gives them the assurance they need to succeed. The study also found that parents can serve as mentors. Parents acknowledged that they play a crucial role in teaching their kids how to control their conduct.

(*Continued*)

TABLE 2.1 (Continued)

Article Code	Author, Year	Database	Purpose	Participants	Method	Data Collection Way/Data Analysis	Summary of Findings
A3	Woods-Jaeger, B. A. et al. (2018)	WOS	To understand (1) parents' experiences of ACEs, *(2) the perceived impact on parenting, (3) protective factors that buffer ACEs potential negative impact, and (4) supports and services that can reduce the number and severity of ACEs and promote resilience among children exposed to early adversity.	11 low-income, urban parents of young children who had experienced ACEs	Qualitative	In-depth qualitative interviews	By highlighting the lived, transgenerational experience of ACEs, early life trauma and adversity histories increase understanding of multigenerational trauma. In addition to describing how the weight of ACEs emerges in an intergenerational cycle, the data presented here also indicate parental strategies and familial strengths that can be used to break the cycle. These in-depth interviews revealed several resilience-promoting characteristics, including open communication, displays of love, and close familial ties.

			*Adverse childhood experiences (*ACEs*), including trauma exposure, parent mental health problems, and family dysfunction.			
A4	Jennings, M. et al. (2020).	WOS	To investigate the effectiveness of the Octopus watch in promoting purposeful ADLs (activities of daily living) for children living with spina bifida and/or hydrocephalus (SB&/H) (<8 years).	Four children and parents	Mixed-methods Quantitative pretest–post-test experimental	Semi-structured interview, childhood executive functioning inventory (CHEXI) and the Canadian occupational performance measure (COPM)	The innovative Octopus watch, which can be customized to meet each child's needs, offers a suitable setting for promoting intentional activity. The individuals' compensatory mechanisms for executive impairment were apparent. While working memory remained constant across all subjects, inhibition control increased. The Octopus watch is one practical tool for boosting independence and routines, which may support family resilience.

(*Continued*)

TABLE 2.1 (Continued)

Article Code	Author, Year	Database	Purpose	Participants	Method	Data Collection Way/Data Analysis	Summary of Findings
A5	Baker, J. R. et al. (2019)	WOS	To identify refugee children's health/wellbeing strengths and needs, and the barriers and enablers to accessing services while preparing for primary and secondary schools, in a low socio-economic multicultural community in Australia.	Arabic-speaking, 11 parents of preschool-aged children, 22 parents of adolescents, and 16 adolescents	Quantitative	Focus groups	Strengths were found to include family unity and individual resiliency. Although there were challenges with migrants knowing how to seek resources, mental health was highlighted as a complex key need. Unmet needs for adolescents were identified as opportunities for play and socialization. The merging of "old" and "modern" cultural values was mentioned by adults. Parents said that the community helps newcomers transfer their health knowledge, but stakeholders thought this was a barrier when systems changed. The majority of parents reported having trouble getting their children medical treatment and being unaware of early childhood services. Parents of preschoolers cited their

						"GP" as the primary source of healthcare advice, whereas parents of teenagers placed a high priority on their child's education. English-language-written health communication was a major barrier.
A6	Miljevic-Ridicki, R. et al. (2017).	WOS-ERIC	To explore how parents, teachers, and children in early years education understand the concept of resilience.	Three focus groups with ten parents, nine teachers and 11 children, 116 children for quantitative section	Qualitative and quantitative research	Scale of Socio-Emotional Wellbeing and Resilience in Preschool Children	What resilience is defined differently by parents and instructors. Both groups view resilience as a positive trait, but while parents place more emphasis on personal qualities like activity rather than passivity and realistic expectations of oneself and others, which could aid in increasing resilience, teachers are more context-oriented (cooperation, concrete help and support, etc.). Children find that adult assistance and direction greatly enhance their capacity for resilience. Our quantitative findings demonstrate that parents rate a child's resilience across the board more favorably than teachers do.

(*Continued*)

TABLE 2.1 (Continued)

Article Code	Author, Year	Database	Purpose	Participants	Method	Data Collection Way/Data Analysis	Summary of Findings
A7	Wright, T. et al. (2021)	WOS-ERIC	To explore how parents experiencing homelessness understand their children's participation in Head Start and publicly funded 4 K programs.	17 parents experiencing homelessness and had a child enrolled in either Head Start	Qualitative	Semi-structured interviews	According to the findings, families experience homelessness in a variety of ways and deal with a number of issues, including stigma against parents and kids. Parents noted both needs for improvement, such as more extensive transportation and lunch services, as well as many strengths in their children's educational programs, such as instruction and faculty assistance. Overall, these findings imply that securing secure housing is difficult for families who are homeless. Additionally, despite still concerned that their child may face stigmatization and prejudice in school, parents of homeless children value their education and their access to resources there.

A8	Jarrett, R. L. and Coba-Rodriguez, S. (2018).	WOS-ERIC	To Explore how 20 urban, low-income African-American mothers facilitated the transition of Head Start preschoolers to kindergarten	20 mothers from urban, low-income African-American backgrounds	Qualitative	Interviews	Mothers monitored and assessed their children's academic and socioemotional school ready skills, boosting readiness competencies while resolving readiness weaknesses, despite having parental/family risk factors linked to unsuccessful kindergarten transitions. One-on-one interactions with preschoolers were one of the ways mothers encouraged their kids' readiness for transition.
A9	Lin, K. L. (2017)	WOS	To identify the perceived influential macrosystem elements within the two preschoolers' narratives, and to understand how the elements influence the two boys' resilience development	Two preschoolers, their parents and preschool teachers	Qualitative	Observing and interviewing	The usage of the media, grandparenting, and Taiwan's many religious traditions all had an impact on one participant's ability to overcome his fear of the dark, which served as a barrier to his ability to develop resilience.

(*Continued*)

TABLE 2.1 (Continued)

Article Code	Author, Year	Database	Purpose	Participants	Method	Data Collection Way/Data Analysis	Summary of Findings
A10	Erdemir, E. (2022)	WOS-ERIC	To explore the aspects of cultural wealth among Syrian refugee children through their subjective perspectives about their experiences in attending a preschool intervention program and resettlement lives in Turkey.	36 refugee children	Qualitative at the end of their 9-week participation in a school-based preschool intervention program in Istanbul.	Interview	The results showed the diverse resources of assets, abilities, and knowledge that children held and used within six cultural wealth capitals: linguistic, resistive, social, familial, and aspirational capital. The rich cultural diversity that has been documented in these cities points to the agency, fortitude, and resiliency of refugee children as they navigate their educational journeys and come to terms with their new lives in settlement areas. Findings also demonstrate their grasp of social and racial justice in light of injustices including social exclusion, xenophobia, and forced relocation. Children's entire human capital and strength-based presentation act as a counterbalance to their disadvantaged narratives and current deficiency perspectives.

A11	Coba-Rodriguez, S. and Jarrett, R. L. (2022)	WOS-ERIC	To add to the rich research that examines how mothers *and* other family members support young Latino children's emergent literacy through the practices they engage in.	Low-income Latina mothers (n:17)	Qualitative	Interviews, Photo-elicitation interviewing (PEI), Participant observation/ Thematic analysis	Data paints a picture of the initiative taken by low-income Latina mothers to help their children's development by getting them involved in different reading activities. Despite having a number of demographic risk characteristics that portrayed them as lacking, mothers remained resilient. Mothers shown resourcefulness. First, moms used their resources to seek support from available family members who acted as protective factors, further fostering the development of children's literacy. Additionally resourceful, mothers sought out Head Start for both themselves and their kids.

(*Continued*)

TABLE 2.1 (Continued)

Article Code	Author, Year	Database	Purpose	Participants	Method	Data Collection Way/Data Analysis	Summary of Findings
							According to empirical studies of low-income Latino families, familismo* is a protective factor that prevents Latino children from having a difficult transition to kindergarten by allowing family responsibilities to be handled collectively (see Padilla & Villalobos, 2007). Familismo* Refers to the significance of strong family ties, intimacy, and getting along with others while supporting the welfare of the immediate family, extended family, and kinship networks.

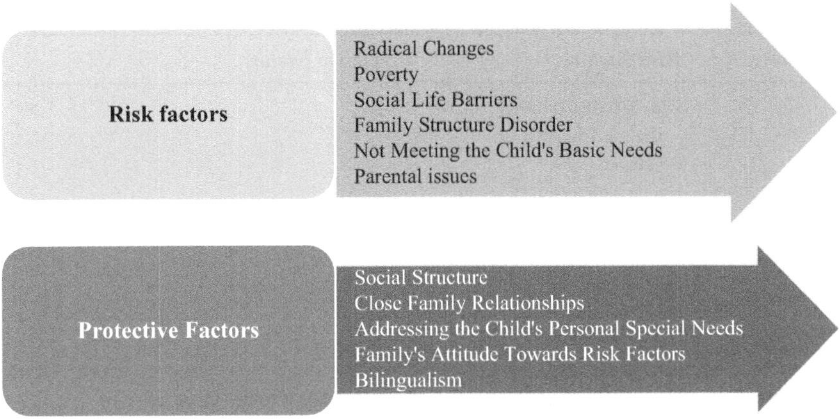

Resilience and Wellbeing in Children 27

Risk factors
- Radical Changes
- Poverty
- Social Life Barriers
- Family Structure Disorder
- Not Meeting the Child's Basic Needs
- Parental issues

Protective Factors
- Social Structure
- Close Family Relationships
- Addressing the Child's Personal Special Needs
- Family's Attitude Towards Risk Factors
- Bilingualism

FIGURE 2.2 Factors affecting children's psychological resilience and wellbeing

TABLE 2.2 Categories, themes, and sub-themes

Categories	Risk Factors	Protective Factors
Themes and sub-themes	**Radical Changes** Transition to school Relocation	**Social Structure** Media Multiple religious traditions Grandparents
	Poverty Working in low-paid jobs Fighting homelessness	**Close Family Relationships** Open communication Love Close family relationships Parenting apps Familial powers Purpose-oriented behavior development is supported To support autonomy Emphasizing competence Family as main support Adult support for durable Joint sharing of obligations in the family Strong family bond Constant talking to children
	Social Life Barriers Not knowing how to access services Having problems accessing children's health services	**Addressing the Child's Personal Special Needs** Removal of executive dysfunction by intervention Improve blocking control Strengthen independence Developing a routine

(*Continued*)

TABLE 2.2 (Continued)

Categories	Risk Factors	Protective Factors
	Fear of stigma and discrimination at school	
	Language	
	Not knowing early childhood service	
	Media,	
	Multiple religious traditions	
	Grandparents	
	Family Structure Disorder	**Family's Attitude Towards Risk Factors**
	Domestic violence	Parents see themselves as a mentor
	Lack of family support	Valuing education and opportunities
		Belief that the transition to kindergarten is critical
		The view that education is especially important for boys
		Giving importance to education, academic, and social development
		Informing the child about safety
		Mental health
		Families focus on the child's personal characteristics
	Not Meeting the Child's Basic Needs	**Bilingualism**
	Lack of Game as a need	Social, intellectual, and communicative skills acquired through multiple linguistic repertoires
	Parental issues	
	Fighting addiction	
	Mental health issues	
	Parent's negative childhood experiences	

Risk Factors for Resilience and Wellbeing

As a result of the research, risk factors affecting the psychological resilience and wellbeing of children were divided into six themes: radical changes, poverty, social life barriers, a disorder in the family structure, not meeting the basic needs of the child, and problems arising from the parents. These risk factors are:

Radical Changes: Transition to school is included in the radical changes that are determined to be a factor affecting children's psychological resilience and wellbeing. The transition to preschool is often the first major transitional step in a child's life. For this reason, children remain undecided about what they will experience and what to expect in this process (Yazici & Yüksel, 2022). For this reason, parents see the transition to school as a risk factor for their children's psychological resilience and wellbeing (A.1). However, parents also stated that a successful preschool transition would provide essential psychological resilience for the child's future transition experiences.

Poverty: There are sub-categories of working in low-paid jobs in poverty and combating homelessness, which is determined to be a factor affecting children's psychological resilience and wellbeing. The parents in this theme are those who struggle with homelessness. In this process, they work in low-paid jobs both while struggling with homelessness and to earn a living. They think that this situation has adverse effects on their children. According to the relevant literature, childhood poverty affects children's developmental areas and adult lives and is an important risk factor (Yoshikawa et al., 2012). In this meta-synthesis study, in parallel with previous studies, it was determined that parents considered poverty as a risk factor.

Social Life Barriers: Not knowing how to access services, having problems accessing children's health services, fear of stigma and discrimination at school, language, not knowing early childhood service, media, multiple religious traditions, and grandparents sub-themes. It is seen that refugees generally have problems accessing services. In a new country, a new language is seen as a significant obstacle for refugees accessing services or having information about services, thus preventing children from accessing these services. Assi et al. (2019) state that refugees' access to health services is restricted by language, financial support, and experienced professionals. An exciting finding emerges in this theme. Media and grandparents appear to be both a risk and a protective factor. When the ninth article was examined, the media had both a risk factor and a protective factor function on Timothy. In the same article, Timoth's grandparents were a protective factor for him, while Ian's grandparents were a risk factor. It was determined that Ian's grandparents appeared as a risk factor because of multiple religious traditions. As can be seen, different risk factors can affect each other as a result of meta-synthesis.

Family Structure Disorder: There are sub-themes of domestic violence and lack of family support in family structure disorder, which is determined to be one of the factors affecting children's psychological resilience and wellbeing. The sub-themes in this theme are related to being homeless, as in the poverty theme. As a result of domestic violence and lack of family support in this theme, parents and their children are struggling with homelessness and low-paid work problems in the poverty theme.

Not Meeting the Child's Basic Needs: There is a sub-theme of lack of game as a need in not meeting the basic needs of the child, which is determined to be one of the factors affecting the psychological resilience and wellbeing of children. In addition, parents identified that children would spend less time on play and more time on learning during the Kindergarten transition as a risk factor.

Parental Issues: There are sub-themes of fighting addiction, mental health issues, and parents' adverse childhood experiences in parent-related factors, which are determined to be one of the factors affecting the psychological resilience and wellbeing of children. While coping with addiction is a focus of homeless parents, mental health issues are a focus of refugees. The third article focuses on parents with awful childhood experiences and their children's intergenerational traumas. In the same study, parents also focused on protective factors for their children.

Protective Factors for Resilience and Wellbeing

As a result of the research, the protective factors affecting the psychological resilience and wellbeing of children were divided into five themes: social structure, close family relationships, addressing the child's personal special needs, family's attitude towards risk factors, and bilingualism. These protective factors are:

Social Structure: Media and grandparents' sub-themes are included in the positive social structure theme, which is determined to be a factor affecting children's psychological resilience and wellbeing. As mentioned in risk factors, media and grandparents are both protective and risk factors. Timothy's relationship with his grandparents, one of the children in the study, was seen to increase his social connectedness. In addition, Timothy's drawing of the superheroes he learned through the media created an interaction with his peers.

Close Family Relationships: Open communication, love, close family relationships, parenting practices, familial powers, supporting purpose-oriented behavior, developmental support, to promote autonomy, emphasizing competence, family as central. It includes sub-themes support, adult support for durable, joint sharing of obligations in the family, strong family bond, and constant talking to children. As mentioned in the risk factors, bad experiences in childhood can be an influential risk factor in the next generation. However, the same study identified open communication, love, and close family relationships as critical protective factors. In addition, in this theme, especially low-income parents and refugees stated that communication between family members and strong family ties benefit children.

Addressing the Child's Personal Special Needs: This theme, which was determined to be one of the factors affecting the psychological resilience and wellbeing of children, includes the sub-themes of removal of executive dysfunction by intervention, improving blocking control, strengthening independence, and developing a routine. This theme is based on the findings of a research result. A satin developed for children with Spina Bifida has looked at the differences it creates in children's daily lives. As a result, it was determined that by using this watch, they gained independence, gained routine acquisition, and interacted by showing their watches to their friends.

Family's Attitude Towards Risk Factors: Parents see themselves as a mentor, value education and opportunities, believe that the transition to kindergarten is critical, and view that education is crucial for boys. Also, there are sub-themes giving importance to education, academic, and social development, informing the child about safety, and focusing on the child's characteristics on mental health and families. In this category, parents focus on protective factors by trying to prevent risk factors to ensure their children's psychological resilience and wellbeing. For example, in the second article, parents take their children under protection and see themselves as mentors to support their children's autonomy.

Bilingualism: In this theme, which was determined to be one of the factors affecting the psychological resilience and wellbeing of children, there was a sub-theme of social, intellectual, and communicative skills acquired through multiple linguistic repertoires. As can be understood from the sub-theme, parents think that having two languages will strengthen their children in social, cognitive, and communication.

Limitations and Strengths

This meta-synthesis study has some limitations. The first of these is the small number of studies included in the review, the relatively small number of articles included in the review may affect the generalizability of the findings. Second, the context of risk factors and protective factors is discussed in the study. However, when the contexts of the studies included in the study are examined, the number of articles covering each context does not show homogeneous distribution. Finally, the inclusion criteria set may result in the loss of other different relevant information.

Despite these limitations, this study expanded the existing literature by synthesizing the experiences of zero- to eight-year-old children and their parents, creating an insight. This review may contribute to measures that will enable children to better prepare for existing risk factors, focus more on protective factors, and prevent children from being harmed mentally, emotionally, educationally, and socially.

Conclusion

By creating a meta-synthesis of the studies that focus on children's psychological resilience and wellbeing, this research aims to give a broad framework.

While the main risk factors for children's resilience and wellbeing are radical changes, poverty, social life barriers, family structure disorder, not providing for the child's basic needs, and parental issues, then protective factors include a supportive classroom environment, strong teacher–family communication, social structure, close family relationships, addressing the child's special needs, the family's attitude toward risk factors, and bilingualism. It has been concluded that some factors can be both a risk and a protective factor depending on the child's culture and context in which the child lives.

References

Assi, R., Özger-İlhan, S., & İlhan, M. N. (2019). Health needs and access to health care: The case of Syrian refugees in Turkey. *Public Health, 172,* 146–152. https://doi.org/10.1016/j.puhe.2019.05.004

*Baker, J. R., Raman, S., Kohlhoff, J., George, A., Kaplun, C., Dadich, A., Best, C. T., Arora, A., Zwi, K., Schmied, V., & Eapen, V. (2019). Optimising refugee children's health/wellbeing in preparation for primary and secondary school: A qualitative inquiry. *BMC Public Health, 19*(1), 1–11. https://doi.org/10.1186/s12889-019-7183-5

*Beers, C. (2021). Case study of a preschool transition: An example of building resilience in times of uncertainty. *Early Years, 41*(2–3), 275–290. https://doi.org/10.1080/09575146.2018.1501554

Bernard, B. (1991). *Fostering resiliency in kids: Protective factors in the family, school, and community.* Northwest Regional Educational Laboratory.

*Coba-Rodriguez, S., & Jarrett, R. L. (2022). An investigation of the perspectives of low-income Latina mothers with preschoolers transitioning to kindergarten. *Journal of Early Childhood Literacy, 22*(1), 31–65. https://doi.org/10.1177/1468798420901822

*Distefano, R., Nelson, K. M., & Masten, A. S. (2022). A qualitative analysis of autonomy-supportive parenting in families experiencing homelessness. *Family Relations, 71*(1), 147–162. https://doi.org/10.1111/fare.12626

*Erdemir, E. (2022). Uncovering community cultural wealth through an early intervention program: Syrian refugee children speaking. *Early Childhood Education Journal, 50*(2), 259–278. https://doi.org/10.1007/s10643-020-01140-7

Gizir, C. A. (2007). Psikolojik sağlamlık, risk faktörleri ve koruyucu faktörler üzerine bir derleme çalışması. *Türk Psikolojik Danışma ve Rehberlik Dergisi, 3*(28), 113–128. https://dergipark.org.tr/en/pub/tpdrd/issue/21448/229850

Hunter, A. J., & Chandler, G. E. (1999). Adolescent resilience. *Image: The Journal of Nursing Scholarship, 31*(3), 243–247.

*Jarrett, R. L., & Coba-Rodriguez, S. (2018). How African American mothers from urban, low-income backgrounds support their children's kindergarten transition: Qualitative findings. *Early Childhood Education Journal, 46*(4), 435–444. https://doi.org/10.1007/s10643-017-0868-4

*Jennings, M., Guilfoyle, A., Green, J., Cleary, Y., & Gowran, R. J. (2020). Octopus watch fosters family resilience by enhancing occupational engagement for children with Spina Bifida and/or hydrocephalus: Pilot study. *International journal of environmental research and public health, 17*(22), 8316. https://doi.org/10.3390/ijerph17228316

Keyes, C. L., Shmotkin, D., & Ryff, C. D. (2002). Optimizing well-being: The empirical encounter of two traditions. *Journal of Personality and Social Psychology, 82*(6), 1007. https://doi.org/10.1037/0022-3514.82.6.1007

*Lin, K. L. (2017). Narrative insight into the influential macrosystem elements on children's resilience development in Taiwanese public preschools. In *Narratives in early childhood education* (pp. 70–88). Routledge. https://doi.org/10.4324/9781315640549-6

Marbina, L., Mashford-Scott, A., Church, A., & Tayler, C. (2015). Assessment of wellbeing in early childhood education and care: Literature review. *Victorian Curriculum and Assessment Authority*. www.vcaa.vic.edu.au

Masten, A. S., & Coatsworth, J. D. (1998). The development of competence in favorable and unfavorable environments: Lessons from successful children. *American Psychologist, 53*, 205–220. https://doi.org/10.1037/0003-066X.53.2.205

*Miljevic-Ridicki, R., Plantak, K., & Bouillet, D. (2017). Resilience in preschool children-the perspectives of teachers, parents and children. *International Journal of Emotional Education, 9*(2), 33–43. https://www.um.edu.mt/library/oar//handle/123456789/24335

Moher, D., Liberati, A., Tetzlaff, J., Altman, D. G., & PRISMA Group*. (2009). Preferred reporting items for systematic reviews and meta-analyses: The PRISMA statement. *Annals of Internal Medicine, 151*(4), 264–269. https://doi.org/10.7326/0003-4819-151-4-200908180-00135

Newman, R. (2005). APA's resilience initiative. *Professional Psychology: Research and Practice, 36*(3), 227. https://doi.org/10.1037/0735-7028.36.3.227

Nye, E., Melendez-Torres, G. J., & Bonell, C. (2016). Origins, methods and advances in qualitative meta-synthesis. *Review of Education, 4*(1), 57–79. https://doi.org/10.1002/rev3.3065

Ozturk, Y., & Ozer, Z. (2021). Outdoor play activities and outdoor environment of early childhood education in Turkey: A qualitative meta-synthesis. *Early Child Development and Care*, 1–16. https://doi.org/10.1080/03004430.2021.1932865

Padilla, Y. C., & Villalobos, G. (2007). Cultural responses to health among Mexican American women and their families. *Family and Community Health*, 24–33.

Russell, B. (2001). *Eğitim Üzerine*. Çev. Naiz B. Say Publishing.

Rutter, M. (1987). Psychosocial resilience and protective mechanisms. *American Journal of Orthopsychiatry, 57*, 316–331. https://doi.org/10.1111/j.1939-0025.1987.tb03541.x

Ryff, C. D. (1989). Happiness is everything, or is it? Explorations on the meaning of psychological well-being. *Journal of Personality and Social Psychology, 57*(6), 1069. https://doi.org/10.1037/0022-3514.57.6.1069

Ryff, C. D., & Keyes, C. L. M. (1995). The structure of psychological well-being revisited. *Journal of Personality and Social Psychology, 69*(4), 719. https://doi.org/10.1037/0022-3514.69.4.719

Winfield, L. F. (1991). Resilience, schooling, and development in African-American youth: A conceptual framework. *Education and Urban Society, 24*(1), 5–14. https://doi.org/10.1177/001312459102400100

*Woods-Jaeger, B. A., Cho, B., Sexton, C. C., Slagel, L., & Goggin, K. (2018). Promoting resilience: Breaking the intergenerational cycle of adverse childhood experiences. *Health Education & Behavior, 45*(5), 772–780. https://doi.org/10.1177/1090198117752785

*Wright, T., Ochrach, C., Blaydes, M., & Fetter, A. (2021). Pursuing the promise of preschool: An exploratory investigation of the perceptions of parents experiencing homelessness. *Early Childhood Education Journal, 49*(6), 1021–1030. https://doi.org/10.1007/s10643-020-01109-6

Yazici, D. N., & Yüksel, N. (2022). Investigation of the reflections of the pandemic process on early childhood education by taking the opinions of teachers and parents. *International Journal of Psychology and Educational Studies, 9*, 908–921. https://dx.doi.org/10.52380/ijpes.2022.9.4.850

Yoshikawa, H., Aber, J. L., & Beardslee, W. R. (2012). The effects of poverty on the mental, emotional, and behavioral health of children and youth: Implications for prevention. *American Psychologist, 67*(4). https://doi.org/272. 10.1037/a0028015

Zolkoski, S. M., & Bullock, L. M. (2012). Resilience in children and youth: A review. *Children and Youth Services Review, 34*(12), 2295–2303. https://doi.org/10.1016/j.childyouth.2012.08.009

* *Research articles included in the meta-synthesis*

3

RISK, RIGHTS, RESPONSIBILITIES AND RESILIENCE

Considering Practical Ways of Supporting Children's Resilience

Samantha Hoyes

Introduction

This chapter explores the role of risky play, rights and responsibility in helping children to develop their resilience in early childhood. Resilience is defined as a way for individuals to 'bounce back from adversity', to manage and respond to negative situations and enable them to move forward and learn from experience (Glazzard & Bligh, 2018, p. 26). This chapter discusses how risky play, and children's rights and responsibilities with regards to risky play, can support children to manage and respond to negative situations and equip them with the skills needed to learn and move forward from experience, ultimately supporting the development of resilience. Tovey (2007) argues that it is those who work with young children who are most likely to effect change; therefore, this chapter will explore the role of the adult and the implications for practice, arguing for a curriculum which enhances 'individual competencies' of the child (Naser et al., 2020; Zins et al., 2004), creating a 'philosophy of resilience' rather than a 'philosophy of protection' (Gill, 2009).

Resilience

Resilience may be described as a phenomena, which is viewed within the context of adversity, and how 'well' individuals respond to adverse/challenging situations through a 'process of positive adaptation' (Miller-Lewis et al., 2013; Nolan et al., 2014). Subsequently, resilience is not fixed, tangible nor quantifiable. The Centre on the Developing Child (CDC) Harvard University (2022) visualises the role of resilience through a scale or see-saw. At one end of the see-saw, positive outcomes, at the other end, negative outcomes, representing the individual

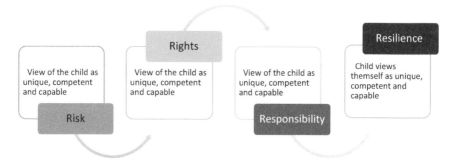

FIGURE 3.1 The 4 'R's' – risk, rights, responsibility and resilience

context and weighting of each. The fulcrum (the point at which the see-saw/ scales balance) represents the child's ability to balance/manage the weight of either outcome – the child's resilience. Noting that even when children are faced with extreme adversity, resilience can still allow the balance of positive to outweigh the negative, supporting positive life outcomes.

Key 'counterbalancing factors' include supportive adult–child relationships; 'building a sense of self-efficacy and perceived control' and 'providing opportunities to strengthen adaptive skills and self-regulatory capacities' (CDC, 2022; Miller-Lewis et al., 2013). Figure 3.1 highlights the interrelated concepts of this chapter, and the following sections will explore and consider how risky play, rights and responsibility can support the development of these key 'counterbalancing factors' underpinned by a belief in the unique, competent and capable child.

Risky Play

Defined as 'thrilling and exciting forms of physical play that involve uncertainty and a risk of physical injury' (Sandseter, 2010a), risky play can be further categorised as play involving 'great heights, high speed, dangerous tools or dangerous environments', as well as rough and tumble play and play where children can 'disappear or get lost' (Sandseter, 2007, 2010b).

The benefits of risk are widely reported (Gill, 2009; Lindon, 2011; Nikiforidou, 2017b; Sandseter & Kennair, 2011; Sandseter, 2014). These benefits are both physical and emotional. Gill (2009) presents four arguments in the promotion of risk-taking with children. These include the benefit of risk in supporting children to learn to manage risks, learning to swim for example; the role of risk in feeding children's appetite for thrill seeking; the role of risk as a risk benefit, relating to the positive side-effects of risky play, such as 'health and developmental benefits'; and the role of risk in long-term developmental benefits to the child. This includes building their 'character and personality through facing-up to adverse circumstances where they know there is the possibility of injury or loss', developing resilience and self-reliance (Gill, 2007, p. 16). Sandseter and Kennair (2011) further support these benefits, also noting the anti-phobic effects of risky play. They suggest that 'thrilling experiences' support children to overcome and master their fears caused by 'maturational and age relevant natural inhibitions', encouraging children to overcome age-appropriate experiences. They conclude that the evolution of risky play may be in part to support children's healthy development, and in particular their anxiety and ability to cope with and manage fear (Sandseter & Kennair, 2011). The aforementioned definitions of resilience and the key 'counterbalancing factors', such as 'building a sense of self-efficacy and perceived control'; and 'providing opportunities to strengthen adaptive skills and self-regulatory capacities', are furthermore highlighted, stressing the importance of risky play in the development of children's resilience.

Despite mounting evidence, recent years have seen a decline in this type of play being offered to children. With an increasing focus on adult's responsibility to keep children safe, the 'cotton wool child' (Nikiforidou, 2017b), over their responsibility to encourage developmentally appropriate challenge and risk (Children's Play Council, 2002; Gill, 2009; Nikiforidou, 2017a; Sandseter, 2012). Gill (2007, p. 61), suggests that this 'collective failure of nerve' stems from a range of avenues. These include 'wider social-cultural changes' (Gill, 2007, p. 61), overwhelming media interest in all things risk related, and societies' judgement of those risks (potentially being labelled as the irresponsible adult), alongside a culture of 'safety legislation and litigation' (Adams, 2001; Gill, 2007; Sandseter, 2012) – establishing an 'excessive fear of risk' and 'surplus safety' (Bundy et al., 2009; Wyver et al., 2010a) and creating both short- and long-term implications for children's health and wellbeing.

Nikiforidou (2017b) discusses the factors which may impact on children's desire and engagement with risk. These include individual characteristics, such as temperament and personality, as well as family and parental influences, and social situational influences, including peers. She notes how these influences interact with children's thoughts on the risk process, consisting of two processes: process 1, their cognition, which includes knowledge and dispositional elements, and process 2, how they behave and act in relation to the risk, resulting in either risk aversion or risk-taking behaviour. When it may be argued that as a society, children are presented with 'surplus safety' and safe risks, cocooned in cotton wool with all aspects of responsibility assumed by adults (Bundy et al., 2009; Wyver et al., 2010a), process 1 is largely removed. Children have limited opportunities to develop their knowledge and understanding and sense of self and capabilities; their risk literacy (Nikiforidou, 2017b, p. 18); leaving only process 2, where children act and behave. This has implications for children's understanding and ultimately their safety. Lindon (2011,

p. 46) discusses children's innate desires for thrill, excitement and challenge, and depending on individuals' dispositions, children will 'slump into inactive and unenthusiastic patterns of play' or will seek out risky behaviours without a knowledgeable other in often 'secretive' and/or 'speedy ways' potentially increasing the chance of risk. Lindon (2011) argues that children cannot 'grow up' where opportunities to develop the skills needed for adulthood, such as risk literacy, are limited by over protection.

Rights and Responsibility

Children's opportunities to take risks are heavily intertwined with children's rights – their right to protection, their right to play, and their right to participation. While this 'excessive fear of risk' comes from a variety of systems which surround the child (Bronfebrenner, 1979), it may be argued that it is society's view of childhood and the construct of the child that ultimately underpins the limiting of children's freedom with regards to play, in this instance risky play, and participation, their choice to participate in risky play. Lee (2002) offers a deeper understanding of the construct of the child through the notion of human being versus human becoming. The view of the child as human becoming relates to an individual who is, as yet, 'underdeveloped', potentially incomplete and perhaps passive in their quest to becoming a human being (McDowall-Clark, 2020, p. 123). This potential 'othering' allows adults to question children's 'competence' – a frequent concern around children's rights to risky play and participation more broadly (Gill, 2009; McDowall-Clark, 2020, p. 127), and something which impacts on children's developing resilience, as they are not viewed as unique, competent and capable.

The United Nations Conventions on the Rights of the Child (UNCRC, UNICEF, 1989), which provides a basis for the rights of the child (UNICEF, 2021), further highlights the tension of protection, play and participation. Children are viewed as both individuals with agency and rights to express themselves and have their voices heard (Articles 13 and 12, respectively), and as individuals who are in need of protection, which in many ways can view children as 'victims', potentially 'vulnerable dependent and defenceless' (Archard, 2015, p. 111). Waller (2006) highlights that the UK also has a contradictory view of childhood, enacted through curriculum frameworks. Pedagogy is usually steeped in the view of the child as unique, competent and capable (DfE, 2021), while the need to 'protect' and keep children safe positions them as ultimately vulnerable (DfE, 2021; Wyver et al., 2010b). Furthermore, Brogaard-Clausen et al. (2022) posit that children's rights and agency are positioned weakly within English curriculum frameworks when compared internationally. Society's view of children as vulnerable and in need of protection potentially promotes a 'caretaker thesis' approach (Archard, 2015; Gill,

2007, 2009). This approach, when applied rigorously, deems children unable to make autonomous decisions, and in need of a 'caretaker' to guide them (Archard, 2015, p. 71), limiting that 'handing over' of responsibility, self-efficacy, autonomy and development of competence, key skills in developing resilience.

Where children are presented with 'safe' or tokenistic risky play opportunities and/or rights through a caretaker lens, this not only limits the development of a range of skills but also impacts on children's understanding of these complex concepts. A Canadian study by Wallberg and Kahn (2011) explored children's understanding of freedom (a term they used within their rights project to support their young participant's understanding of rights). The study highlighted that children within the study had begun to understand their freedom (rights) as 'blanket permission' to get what they want and desire, even at the cost of others, as opposed to a reasonable balance 'between rights and responsibilities'. More recent research by Naser et al. (2020), demonstrated that rights were also viewed as rules, 'what they can and cannot do', highlighting an individualised view of this concept, rather than an understanding of rights and responsibilities. Handley (2005) might suggest that this is also indicative of our western culture and focus on individualism. This debate between rights and responsibilities is complex, and Howe and Covell (2010) argue that you can't have one without the other. Noting that where there is a focus on responsibility, this has the potential to lead to a 'miseducation of rights', a focus on behavioural management, and the potential to 'burden children with a sense of duty' (Howe & Covell, 2010). A focus solely on rights can create a narrow and individualised understanding of rights, with limited understanding of individual and social responsibility (Naser et al., 2020; Wallberg & Kahn, 2011). Howe and Covell (2010) suggest that 'effective education' should focus on the child's rights and allow opportunities for children to understand the link between rights and responsibility for themselves.

One of the criticisms of giving children 'responsibility' lays in these notions of a carefree childhood, freeing children from unnecessary burdens and pressures. However, McDowall-Clark (2020, p. 129) suggests that 'children who are given responsibilities, can demonstrate high levels of competence, often beyond the expectations of adults'. As children develop competence in their skills and abilities, this consequently fosters their resilience, as they learn to manage and respond to a wide variety of experiences. Cunningham (2006, p. 245) suggests that it is our changing view of childhood that has skewed our understanding of children's capabilities and our 'fixation' on providing a 'long and happy childhood that we downplay their abilities and resilience'. This chapter argues that children need opportunities to exercise their rights and take risks to develop an understanding of their responsibilities, developing a range of competencies which foster children's resilience.

The Responsible Child

Howe and Covell (2010) readily point out that responsibility for children's rights are overwhelmingly placed in the hands of the government and those who care for young children. And it is these responsible others who overrule children's rights to participation, often under the guise of protection (Handley, 2014; McDowall-Clark, 2020), in the 'best interests of the child' (UNICEF, 1989). Nikiforidou (2017b, pp. 14–15) notes that where children experience 'risk-less' situations, 'they will not experience the consequences of their actions and choices'. Without consequences, children lack an understanding of their responsibility. In essence, they are not allowed to take responsibility as their rights to make choices are restricted. Consequently, she argues that children will develop a sense of 'guilt' about their needs and may remain as 'followers' or 'risk averters'. Furthermore, if we consider the skills needed in the development of resilience, including the need for 'self-efficacy and perceived control' and 'providing opportunities to strengthen adaptive skills and self-regulatory capacities' (CDC, 2022; Miller-Lewis et al., 2013), it is clear that limited risks, rights and responsibility seek to undermine the 'unique child' and limit their emerging resilience.

There is also growing understanding in the importance of risk, rights and responsibility in understanding and developing social responsibility (Naser et al., 2020; Nikiforidou, 2017b). Naser et al. (2020) posit that 'learning and understanding child's rights as not only personal rights but also social responsibility leads to change', broadening understanding of rights as not just 'rules to live within'. This notion of developing children's responsibility does not ask children to feel unduly burdened but rather develop their understanding of the concepts of rights and responsibility, allowing them to manage and respond to situations and develop a deeper understanding of social justice: for example, Article 13, freedom of expression (UNICEF, 1989). A child has the right to express oneself and also a responsibility to listen and allow others to express themselves. Article 31, a child's right to relax and play, corresponds with a child's responsibility to allow others to relax and play (UNICEF, 1989). Children need opportunities to exercise these rights, free from over directive 'caretaking' to fully understand both individual and social responsibility. Nikiforidou (2017b, pp. 18–19) also highlights the importance of risk, rights and responsibility in our future. Discussing the importance of risk literacy, she highlights its importance in relation to supporting the UN sustainable goals (United Nations, 2015). The 17 goals, developed by the United Nations in 2015, are viewed as a 'blueprint' for a fairer more equitable world. Nikiforidou (2017b) suggests that to support sustainable development and lifestyles, both now and in the future, requires a knowledge and understanding of managing risks, weighing up positives and negatives (risk literacy), and a wider understanding of individual and social responsibility in meeting these goals. This strengthening the importance of fostering resilience both for children as individuals, but also as a wider part of society.

It is important to note here that children's rights are not dependent on children meeting 'their responsibilities'; this should never be the case; 'children's rights are primary' (Howe & Covell, 2010); however, there is a discussion to be had about how society supports children to understand their rights and how these link to children's understanding of their responsibility both to themselves and others, rather than an unnecessary burden on children's shoulders.

Considering the Role of the Adult-Risk Benefit

One way that may challenge practice is a move to a 'risk benefit' approach (Lindon, 2011). Rather than relying on media or hearsay, a proportionate approach is taken, which weighs up the potential risks against the potential benefits. Practitioners, based on the knowledge of their children, need to ask themselves, what are the genuine risks and consequences here versus the potential benefits? This requires a whole setting approach through careful reflection. Much like children, practitioners will have differing approaches to risk and rights, and risk-taking behaviour, and may also need to be supported to develop their confidence with these activities, avoiding 'anxiety-driven' assessments or tokenistic approaches to risk and rights (Lindon, 2011, p. 6). Approaches need to be a 'collective response', supported and underpinned by confident and competent practitioners (Wyver et al., 2010a). In weighing up the benefits, practitioners, and settings as a whole, need to consider the 'what' and the 'why'. What are practitioners afraid of and why would it be acceptable to limit this activity/resource/approach. This involves questioning that construct of the child and how they are viewed in the setting. Adams (2001) notes that where children learn to walk, this is indeed an incredibly risky activity, yet this is allowed and encouraged for its developmental gains. Much like the risk of learning to walk, practitioners need to consider the what and the why and truly weigh up risk benefits.

Once opportunities are offered, the practitioners' role in supporting rights and risk in play is important. Research by Sandseter (2010b) offers a deeper understanding of this process and the role of the adult, not just in providing risky play but in their interactions with the process. Sandseter identifies the concepts of paratelic and telic states in reversal theory. Paratelic state refers to an 'excitement seeking mode', while the telic state refers to an 'anxiety avoiding mode'. These states are linked to both 'personality' and 'individual difference', and 'bistability in emotions and motivation', meaning that although they are linked to personality, they are also 'dynamic states' and in some ways flexible (Apter, 1984, 2003; Sandseter, 2010b), and it is the shifting between these states that are referred to as 'reversals' (Apter, 2001; Sandseter, 2010b). Through her research, she suggests that whichever state is most dominant for a child will affect the way they experience the event. For example, those in the paratelic state will view the arousal/experience as a pleasant emotion, while those in the telic state will view the emotions as unpleasant. It is these emotions that can and will drive the decisions and the subsequent play, noting that children often experience a 'quick' reversal between these two states. What Sandseter noted was if children were in the 'telic state', 'anxiety avoidance', they ultimately withdrew from the play, limiting development opportunities, and potentially creating fear and anxiety around those types of situations, impacting resilience. Whereas when individuals were in the paratelic state, Sandseter suggests children develop a 'psychological protective frame that gives a subjective feeling of confidence' even when partaking in 'risky' activities (Sandseter, 2010b), strengthening children's resilience. Nikiforidou (2017b) previously discussed the need for the development of knowledge and understanding, and skills (process one) through education to support risk literacy and promote the protective frame. This provides a useful thinking point around the benefits of risky play and resilience, and importantly the role of the adult in this and how we might begin to support children to foster that 'psychological protective frame'. But it also highlights the importance of modelling within teams. Where the practitioners' dominant state is often that of 'telic', support and role modelling by others will also be key in supporting role reversal for practitioners so that those experiences of risk become positive ones and not ones fraught with worry and anxiety.

The example of learning to walk may also highlight elements of role reversal theory, and it also demonstrates another key approach to risk-taking, scaffolding (Kleppe, 2018). Children are not expected to be able to walk on their first attempt, nor are they encouraged to give up when they fall deeming it too dangerous, nor once mastered, are the cushions kept in place, 'just in case'. Children are given space, time, opportunity and encouragement to persevere and keep trying, key skills of resilience, not worried faces or calls to 'be careful' or watch what they are doing. Through supportive and trusting adults scaffolding, children master this skill relatively quickly, with no need for cushions in the longer term. Kleppe (2018) discusses that this involves practitioners knowing when and when not to step in, subtle lines of questioning and modelling and the ability to 'relinquish control as soon as the child can work independently'. Within his study centred on staff–child interactions in one- to three-year-olds' risky play, he identified three key aspects of the scaffolding approach: warmth and responsiveness include how practitioners 'consistently acknowledge' children's physical and emotional needs, responding with warmth and appropriately understanding their cues and signals; joint problem-solving/joint attention includes adults' ability to understand what and how the children need scaffolding and a genuine shared interest in the risk-taking activity; and promoting self-regulation, again, requires practitioners to be attuned and responsive but also understanding of when and how to step back so children remain in control, respecting children's choices. All of these aspects involved warm and responsive adults and observed not simply spoken language but also practitioners body language and gestures which were seen as important (Kleppe, 2018). These approaches, Kleppe argues, allow children to stay responsible for their risks (and rights) while supporting their wellbeing and development. This approach is also viewed as key in the development of those 'counterbalancing factors' which support resilience (CDC, 2022; Miller-Lewis et al., 2013), underpinning the interrelated nature of these concepts and the importance of the unique child at each stage as highlighted in Figure 3.1.

Attitudes, Recommendations and Implications for Practice

Risk and rights, this chapter argues, are important elements in supporting children's understanding of their responsibilities, allowing children to develop their competence, promoting resilience and solidifying a child's view of themselves as unique and capable.

Drawing back to Figure 3.1. The 4 'R's – risk, rights, responsibility and resilience – highlight the interrelated concepts of these four facets and that where either is not fully developed or provided through 'surplus safety' or 'care taking', the real opportunities to develop resilience are lessened. At each stage of the model, a view of the child as unique, competent and capable, terminology highlighted through the current Early Years Foundation Stage (EYFS) (DfE, 2021), and supported by Kleppe's (2018) research, is required to fully promote the opportunities presented and support the development of children's resilience. For this, a proportionate approach is needed where children are allowed freedom to explore and participate at their own pace through 'an atmosphere of trust'. It is through this 'atmosphere of trust' children develop their competence, confidence and resilience (Lindon, 2011, p. 4). The forest school approach offers practical guidance here, as trust is a core concept of the approach. Trust by the adults in children's capabilities and competence, and trust by children in the adults who care for them in providing an environment and opportunities that are 'as safe as is reasonably possible' (Knight, 2009). Williams-Siegfredsen (2017, p. 1) notes that generally children will not 'climb higher than they feel comfortable with', noting their general dislike of 'pain or fear' themselves. Yet often this appears forgotten in the quest to keep children safe; thus, there is mistrust that children will climb too high and hurt themselves, damaging our view and the view of themselves, as unique competent and capable. Similarly, trust is also central in considering children's rights. If we consider children's right to participation, what is it we are afraid of them choosing? Why are we unable to trust them to make choices? Without trust, both risk and rights become tokenistic and crucially limit the learning process of the experience, negating children's understanding of responsibility and limiting their opportunities to develop resilience. Therefore, practitioners must learn to 'trust' children as their first step in changing practice.

Trust in the child must also be based on our understanding of the child, and while external factors, such as 'building a sense of self-efficacy and perceived control' and 'providing opportunities to strengthen adaptive skills and self-regulatory capacities' (CDC, 2022; Miller-Lewis et al., 2013), are seen as key in developing resilience, it is also pertinent to understand that resilience is multifaceted and impacted by biological and individual attributes (Nolan et al., 2014); therefore, it is important to consider the model as a two-way process. Before considering risk, rights and responsibility, children will need some level of resilience to manage the opportunities and challenges risky play, rights and participation and responsibility offer, particularly where children may be experiencing a telic state. Consider again the example of a child learning to walk. If children are asked to walk long before they are ready, rather than build resilience, repeated failure and harm would result in deepening anxiety and fear. A deep understanding of each individual and a gradual and supported approach will need to be developed to support positive experiences and a move to the paratelic state, fostering a psychological protective frame (Sandseter, 2010b), or these experiences may only serve to lessen resilience, moving the fulcrum in the opposite direction.

In 2006, the Better Regulations Commission published 'Risk responsibility and regulation; whose risk is it anyway' (Berry et al., 2006). This document was published in response to what they felt were overly bureaucratic health and safety measures of the time in the UK. Highlighting that an 'over reliance on [the] government to manage all risks' had led to an 'erosion of personal responsibility', acknowledging society's 'disproportionate' attitude towards risk (Berry et al., 2006, p. 2).

The report highlighted four recommendations. This is no easy feat. Often through 'individualistic' approaches adults seek to remove children from danger altogether, rather than a 'collective response' which looks at society's role in supporting our children to stay safe (Wyver et al., 2010a). While Wyver et al. talk directly about parents here, it can readily be applied to practitioners and the individual roles that practitioners play. Interestingly some of the challenges here may lay in a lack of clear guidance for settings, over regulation, via channels such as Ofsted and that fear of litigation, alongside that paradox of confident and capable vulnerable children (Archard, 2015; Gill, 2007, 2009; Wyver et al., 2010b).

Conclusion

There is a vast range of evidence which stresses the importance of children's risky play and rights, and the role of responsibility in supporting children's knowledge and understanding of these complex concepts (Gill, 2007, 2009; Lindon, 2011; Naser et al., 2020; Nikiforidou, 2017a, 2017b; Sandseter, 2009, 2014; Sandseter & Kennair, 2011; Wallberg & Kahn, 2011; Wyver et al., 2010a). This chapter draws these arguments together and highlights their role in developing children's resilience and their ability to manage and respond to negative situations and enable them to move forward and learn from experience (Glazzard & Bligh, 2018, p. 26). This chapter argues that children need 'real' risk and 'real' rights, with 'real' responsibility to develop their knowledge and understanding of the consequences of their risks and rights (their actions), allowing them to manage fears, adapt, change and understand not just their individual but also their social responsibility as they develop resilience through a protective psychological frame (Sandseter, 2010b).

Gill (2009) and Tovey (2007) suggest that it is those who work with young children who are the most likely to effect change. It is intended that the model and strategies discussed within this chapter will provide practitioners with some practical ways of addressing the balance of risk, rights and responsibilities in promoting children's resilience, acknowledging that 'trust' is a central tenant of this – trust in the child's capabilities and strengths, and trust in the adults to provide an environment which is as safe as necessary, rather than as safe as possible (Knight, 2009; Lindon, 2011, p. 4).

References

Adams, J. (2001). *Risk*. Routledge.
Apter, M. J. (1984). Reversal theory and personality: A review. *Journal of Research in Personality, 18*, 265–288.
Apter, M. J. (2001). Reversal theory as a set of propositions. In M. J. Apter (Ed.), *Motivational styles in everyday life-a guide to reversal theory* (pp. 37–51). American Psychological Society.
Apter, M. J. (2003). On a certain blindness in modern psychology. *The Psychologist, 16*(9), 474–475.
Archard, D. (2015). *Children: Rights and childhood* (3rd ed.). Routledge, Taylor & Francis Group.
Berry, L., Lindsay, J., Salomon, E., & Veale, S. (2006). *Risk, responsibility and regulation – whose risk is it anyway?* Better Regulation Commission.
Brogaard-Clausen, S., Guimaraes, S., Rubiano, C., & Tang, F. (2022). International perspectives on wellbeing and democratic living in early childhood curricula. *Early Years*. https://doi.org/10.1080/09575146.2021.2010663
Bronfebrenner, U. (1979). *The ecology of human development*. Harvard University Press.
Bundy, A. C., Luckett, T., Tranter, P. J., Naughton, G. A., Wyver, S. R., Ragen, J., & Spies, G. (2009). The risk is that there is 'no risk': A simple, innovative intervention to increase children's activity levels. *International Journal of Early Years Education, 17*(1), 33–45. https://doi.org/10.1080/09669760802699878
Centre on the Developing Child at Harvard University. (2022). *Resilience*. https://developingchild.harvard.edu/science/key-concepts/resilience/
Children's Play Council. (2002). *More than swings and roundabouts: Planning for outdoor play*. National Children's Bureau.

Cunningham, H. (2006). *The invention of childhood*. BBC.
DfE. (2021). *The early years foundation stage, statutory framework*. DfE Publications.
Gill, T. (2007). *No fear. Growing up in a risk averse society*. Calouste Gulbenkian Foundation.
Gill, T. (2009). The danger of creating risk-free childhoods. *Early Years Educator, 10*(11), 38–44. https://doi.org/10.12968/eyed.2009.10.11.39790
Glazzard, J., & Bligh, C. (2018). *Meeting the mental health needs of children 4–11 years*. Critical Publishing.
Handley, G. (2005). Children's rights to participation. In T. Waller (Ed.), *An introduction to early childhood* (pp. 1–13). SAGE Publications.
Handley, G. (2014). Children's rights to participation. In T. Waller & G. Davis (Eds.), *An introduction to early childhood* (3rd ed., pp. 71–89). SAGE Publications.
Howe, R., & Covell, K. (2010). Miseducating children about their rights. *Education, Citizenship and Social Justice, 5*, 91–102. https://doi.org/10.1177/1746197910370724.
Kleppe, R. (2018). Characteristics of staff-child interaction in 1–3-year-olds' risky play in early childhood education and care. *Early Child Development and Care, 188*(10), 1487–1501. https://doi.org/10.1080/03004430.2016.1273909
Knight, S. (2009). *Forest schools and outdoor learning in the early years*. SAGE Publications.
Lee, N. (2002). *Childhood and society: Growing up in an age of uncertainty*. Open University Press.
Lindon, J. (2011). *Too safe for their own good? Helping children learn about risk and lifeskills*. National Children's Bureau.
McDowall-Clark, R. (2020). *Childhood in society for the early years* (4th ed.). Learning Matters.
Miller-Lewis, L. R., Searle, A. K., Sawyer, M. G., Baghurst, P. A., & Hedly, D. (2013). Resource factors for mental health resilience in early childhood: An analysis with multiple methodologies. *Child Adolescent Psychiatry Mental Health, 7*, 6. https://doi.org/10.1186/1753-2000-7-6
Naser, S. C., Verlenden, J., Arora, P. G., Nastasi, B., Braun, L., & Smith, R. (2020). Using child rights education to infuse a social justice framework into universal programming. *School Psychology International, 41*(1), 13–36. https://doi.org/10.1177/0143034319894363
Nikiforidou, Z. (2017a). Risk literacy: Concepts and pedagogical implications for early childhood education. *Contemporary Issues in Early Childhood, 18*(3), 322–332. https://doi.org/10.1177/1463949117731027
Nikiforidou, Z. (2017b). The cotton wool child. In A. Owen (Ed.), *Childhood today* (pp. 11–22). SAGE Publications.
Nolan, A., Taket, A., & Stagnitti, K. (2014). Supporting resilience in early years classrooms: The role of the teacher, *Teachers and Teaching, 20*(5), 595–608. https://doi.org/10.1080/13540602.2014.937955
Sandseter, E. B. H. (2007). Categorizing risky play: How can we identify risk-taking in children's play? *European Early Childhood Education Research Journal, 15*, 237–252.
Sandseter, E. B. H. (2009). Characteristics of risky play. *Journal of Adventure Education & Outdoor Learning, 9*(1), 3–21. https://doi.org/10.1080/14729670802702762
Sandseter, E. B. H. (2010a). *Scaryfunny. A qualitative study of risky play among preschool children* [Doctoral thesis, Norwegian University of Science and Technology].
Sandseter, E. B. H. (2010b). 'It tickles in my tummy!' – understanding children's risk-taking in play through reversal theory. *Journal of Early Childhood Research, 8*, 67–88. https://doi.org/10.1177/1476718X09345393.
Sandseter, E. B. H. (2012). Restrictive safety or unsafe freedom? Norwegian ECEC practitioners' perceptions and practices concerning children's risky play. *Childcare in Practice, 18*(1), 83–101.

Sandseter, E. B. H. (2014). Early childhood education and care practitioners' perceptions of children's risky play; examining the influence of personality and gender. *Early Child Development and Care, 184*(3), 434–449. https://doi.org/10.1080/03004430.2013.794797

Sandseter, E. B. H., & Kennair, L. E. O. (2011). Children's risky play from an evolutionary perspective: The anti-phobic effects of thrilling experiences. *Evolutionary Psychology, 9*(2), 257–284.

Tovey, H. (2007). *Playing outdoors: Spaces and places, risk and challenge.* Open University Press.

United Nations. (2015). *UN sustainable development goals.* https://sdgs.un.org/goals

United Nations Children's Emergency Fund (UNICEF). (1989). *The United Nations convention on the rights of the child.* https://downloads.unicef.org.uk/wp-content/uploads/2010/05/UNCRC_PRESS200910web.pdf?_ga=2.78590034.795419542.1582474737-1972578648.1582474737

United Nations Children's Emergency Fund (UNICEF). (2021). *The United Nations convention on the rights of the child.* https://www.unicef.org.uk/what-we-do/un-convention-child-rights/.

Wallberg, P., & Kahn, M. (2011). The rights project: How rights education transformed a classroom. *Canadian Children, 36*(1), 31–35.

Waller, T. (2006). "Don't come too close to my octopus tree": Recording and evaluating young children's perspectives on outdoor learning. *Children, Youth and Environments, 16*(2), 75–104.

Williams-Siegfredsen, J. (2017). *Understanding the Danish forest school approach: Early years education in practice* (2nd ed.). Routledge.

Wyver, S., Bundy, A., Naughton, G., Tranter, P., Sandseter, E. B. H., & Ragen, J. (2010b). Safe outdoor play for young children: Paradoxes and consequences [Conference session]. AARE Annual Conference, Melbourne, Australia. 2071WyverBundyNaughtonTranterSandseterRagen.pdf aare.edu.au

Wyver, S., Tranter, P., Naughton, G., Little, H., Sandseter, E. B. H., & Bundy, A. (2010a). Ten ways to restrict children's freedom to play: The problem of surplus safety. *Contemporary Issues in Early Childhood, 11*(3), 263–277. https://doi.org/10.2304/ciec.2010.11.3.263

Zins, J. E., Weissberg, R. P., Wang, M. C., & Walberg, H. J. (Eds.). (2004). *Building academic success on social and emotional learning: What does the research say?* Teachers College Press.

PART 2
Theoretical and Practical Perspectives

4

"THE CHILDREN ARE GRAND!"

Educators' Perspectives on Educator and Child Wellbeing During the COVID-19 Pandemic

Maja Haals Brosnan, Rhona Stallard and Natasha O'Donnell

Introduction

With the arrival of the COVID-19 pandemic in early 2020, every Early Childhood Education and Care (ECEC) provider in Ireland closed for three-and-a-half months. When ECEC providers resumed operations, the context of their pedagogical work had been altered significantly (Early Childhood Ireland [ECI], 2020). The research on which this chapter is based seeks to understand the general impact of COVID-19 on ECEC practice but here we focus specifically on aspects of the research that showed interesting trends relating to educators' perspectives on wellbeing both in children and themselves.

The closure of ECEC settings produced distinct challenges and stressors for children, families and educators (Henderson et al., 2022). Children experienced a drastic change in their routines and isolation from their friends, family and communities. Parents grappled with the responsibility of providing learning experiences for young children in isolation, alongside a myriad of other responsibilities (Darmody et al., 2020). The most vulnerable children experienced the impact of such changes with the most intensity (Darmody et al., 2020). Educators were faced with a broad range of guidelines issued from the government in order to reopen their services during COVID-19 (ECI, 2020) and expressed concerns about children's wellbeing and participation based on challenges arising from COVID-19-related service closures, such as resettling children into the setting, establishing health and safety measures and rebuilding relationships with parents (ECI, 2020). There is much to consider in order to better understand the impact of COVID-19 on ECEC, such as awareness of, and support for, educator wellbeing, and the impact on children's wellbeing, due to COVID-19-related changes to ECEC practice. Exploration and

DOI: 10.4324/9781003345664-6

analysis of the fundamental challenges arising during the COVID-19 pandemic have the potential to contribute further to our understandings of the sophisticated nature of ECEC provision.

In this chapter, we specifically address the question of educators' (intersubjective) understanding of COVID-19's impact on young children's wellbeing. This includes considering how educators believe that young children are being impacted by COVID-19, including what understandings educators hold of children's wellbeing. A key finding in the data is a strong sense of educators operating with an image of the child as naturally adaptable and resilient in the response to COVID-19. This was evidenced, according to educators, in children's smooth transition back into ECEC settings where the majority of children settled back into daily life in their settings with ease and confidence. Educators formulated a sense of themselves as being negatively impacted by COVID-19. While some educators experienced anxiety and worry related to contracting the virus, all educators experienced stress, frustration and anxiety in relation to the increased responsibility associated with implementing safety measures aimed at reducing the spread of COVID-19. This was seen to negatively impact their wellbeing. According to Cumming et al. (2021, p. 50), "A child's right to high quality education not only relies on a competent and skilled workforce, but one in which educators are well." Here, we explore the erosion of educators' wellbeing and strategies employed to support the wellbeing of both educators and children in the setting. We suggest that multiplicity of factors, including the strain placed on educators' wellbeing, may have influenced the educators' image of the child.

A social constructivist qualitative research design was employed. A small number of early childhood educators and owner–managers of ECEC settings in Ireland were interviewed about their views on the impact of COVID-19 restrictions on children's wellbeing, on curriculum, on pedagogical practices and educators' own professional identity and wellbeing. Ten participants completed three waves of interviews each, at three-month intervals. This method of data collection allowed for the collection of rich, detailed data giving insight into how participants' experiences unfolded over time. This method also allowed for clarification and elaboration of understandings developed in the previous wave of data collection. It provided a strong sense of how the individual and collective experience of COVID-19 was recontextualised over time. In addition to obtaining informed consent, seeking voluntary participation and ensuring confidentiality, ethical considerations included being sympathetic to the stressful and difficult circumstances faced by ECEC educators. The research received ethical approval from the participating institutions' Ethical Review Boards.

COVID-19 and Young Children's Wellbeing

Society is attuned to the impact and legacy of COVID-19, and educators are aware of the potential detrimental implications for children in ECEC

(Toros & Falch-Eriksen, 2022). During initial social restriction measures, young children experienced unprecedented constraints to their civil liberties, which have been reported to have had a negative impact on their daily lives (Egan et al., 2021).

A child's wellbeing is the foundation for their overall development, and in particular for their social and emotional development (Laevers & Declercq, 2018), a key to their overall learning (Kostelnik et al., 2015). Children's wellbeing is considered as elementary in their right to health, play and affection (Bradford, 2012), thus fulfilling their potential (Laevers, 2005). Children thrive when with peers, conferring benefits to their wellbeing, which highlights the social benefit of ECEC. Yet children experienced a high degree of isolation during the lockdowns of 2020 (Fegert et al., 2020; Howes et al., 2020; Pascal et al., 2020; Singh et al., 2020). The implications of recurring lockdowns and social restrictions present a significant and potentially long-lasting risk to children's wellbeing (Benner & Mistry, 2020; Gromada et al., 2020). Education is recognised as an important protective factor, playing a significant role in the wellbeing of young children (Hamad et al., 2018). Jalong (2021) cautioned that following the return to in-situ ECEC, there was a need to provide young children with appropriate emotional support, addressing the isolation, anxiety and potential trauma experienced (Barnett et al., 2021), mindful of the potential long-term implications of the pandemic (Jandrić, 2020), the understanding of which are limited.

COVID-19 disrupted the education of 1.6 billion children globally (UNICEF, 2021). While wellbeing remained a priority of educators who endeavoured to utilise remote, online engagement (Alan, 2021), such as meeting via the conferencing tool Zoom for circle time or storytelling and provision of recorded videos, educators and families experienced significant challenges in continuing to connect with each other in the online space. Many children lacked access to technology (Dias et al., 2020; Jeffrey, 2020), and for children of such a young age, navigating engagement with educators and peers via technology alone was not deemed a suitable pedagogical approach, given the value of learning through play (Plowman, 2011).

Aistear, the Irish National Curriculum Framework (National Council for Curriculum and Assessment (NCCA), 2009), highlights the significance of the interactions between children and the learning environment supporting and shaping all domains of learning, including that of wellbeing and belonging, one of *Aistear's* four key themes (National Council for Curriculum and Assessment (NCCA), 2009). The reopening of ECEC settings, in the context of COVID-19, saw changes in the physical and social environments (Witt et al., 2020). ECEC settings were advised to rotate the use of play equipment in order to sterilise toys and to implement a "play pod" model of grouping educators and children, a model designed to limit social interactions and support infection control. Such changes had the potential to influence children's wellbeing within settings.

"The Children Are Grand" – Educators' Perspectives on Children's Adaptation to COVID-19 Restrictions

"The children are grand" was a turn-of-phrase that emerged regularly in the data and signifies a position educators assumed in relation to their understandings of young children's wellbeing when ECEC services reopened after COVID-19 lockdowns. As one participant explained:

> So yeah, it's been, it's been grand, like the kids are just amazing, hasn't affected them at all. They're absolutely fantastic. They all come back great, maybe the odd one or two, but like, genuinely fantastic.

Similar sentiments were evident across the data, with other educators suggesting:

> [T]hey're so much more adaptable to things than us, really they are. They, just you know, they will take that as the normal now and they're happy enough. And yes, it's great, they're great.

The interview data indicated that while children have been impacted by COVID-19 in one way or another, the majority of children seem to be "absolutely fine" because "children are so adaptable" and "they just adjust." COVID-19-related public health measures implemented in settings, according to the educators, became "normal" for the children, the parents and the educators very quickly. Educators believed that children to be resilient, feeling that young children are flexible to circumstances changing and have the ability to cope readily with such changes.

> I just think they just adapted to it very quickly. It wasn't a huge change. Like the pods, that would have been the biggest one and they adapted to that so quickly.

Educators recognised that children found particular aspects of lockdowns difficult, such as being isolated from their extended family, peers and community. However, the majority of educators interviewed felt that such difficulties would not impact children in the long term as children were able to re-establish relationships and playful lives very quickly when ECEC settings reopened. They recognised that the pedagogical experiences they were offering to children following the return to the ECEC setting after lockdown had the potential to support children in challenges to their wellbeing, as a result of COVID-19. Thus, educators were intentional in their engagement with an emergent curriculum, creating opportunities to support children's wellbeing. ECEC has a long tradition of focusing on the psychosocial dimensions of young children's development; the findings of this research identified that participants were attuned to the key role of ECEC pedagogies in supporting and developing children's wellbeing (French et al., 2022). However, cursory reflection was given to the position and perspective of young children's wellbeing in the wake of spells of social isolation. While an ability to adapt is a fundamental trait of resilience, inherent vulnerability exposed by the pandemic received less attention. As one participant described:

> There's a process for them to do and they understand that and they absorb that. They didn't fight against us, it was just as if you were saying to them, okay take off your coat, they just do all the other processes as well. Children are very adaptable, I think. A lot of people are worried about how children are, where they're going to be after this. We see our children very well adapted; we would have vulnerable children in our service as well and like everybody else, they just thrive on routine and understanding the processes of keeping safe.

Despite claims to children being adaptable and naturally resilient, many educators identified ways in which children may have been impacted by COVID-19 lockdowns. Some participants emphasised that children appear to be more cautious or anxious upon their return to the setting. One educator felt that children from more disadvantaged backgrounds had their physical and social development adversely impacted due to increased screen time and less access to movement opportunities outdoors. Moreover, several educators argued that increased screen time had negatively impacted children's language development and gross motor skills.

"Children Need To Be Children" – Strategies Supporting Children's Wellbeing and Resilience

Children have experienced significant disruption to their lives (Barlett et al., 2020; OECD, 2020), which we do not yet fully understand. We know from past events, such as natural disasters, the impact may be lifelong (Kar, 2009; Le Brocque et al., 2017), particularly for young children, some of whom may find it cognitively and verbally challenging to process such events (Durbin, 2010). Strengthening children's resilience has been understood as an appropriate way to respond to such disruption. Aistear (National Council for Curriculum and Assessment (NCCA), 2009) highlights the importance of children becoming resilient and resourceful. Johnson et al. (as cited in Kaplan, 1999) described resilience as fluid, a constant negotiation. Other research indicating early childhood resilience is a dynamic, ecological and culturally situated process, involving both children and adults (Millican & Middleton, 2020). Educators are attuned to resilience and recognise it as individual to children

(Sameroff & Rosenblum, 2006), while understanding that it is also dependent on the broader context: peers, siblings, parents and educators. To support resilience in children, it requires resilient communities (OECD, 2019).

Behind the positive narrative expressed by educators of children as easily adaptable, and the implicit casting of children as naturally resilient, it was evident in the data that educators employed a diverse range of strategies to build children's resilience by focusing, whether consciously or unconsciously, on children's wellbeing and relationships. As ECEC settings reopened, the educators who participated in the research emphasised the focus on providing children with as "normal" an experience as possible by "leaving COVID at the door" and making it fun and relaxed for children as a deliberate strategy to restore children's wellbeing.

As a participant expressed:

> When our children came back . . . we decided the most important thing we wanted for those children was, we want them to have fun. . . . They had been stuck in their homes for a long, long time. We had reports from parents that children were having nightmares, children were worrying. So, we made it our mission, the biggest thing last summer was FUN in capital letters: we had paddling pools, we had slides into paddling pools, we had water balloons, barbecues, festival days, just fun, fun, fun, fun. And children really grew from that, they grew, became more confident. They got their sense of themselves back from that. Most or lots of the parents would have emailed . . . within two weeks of being back their children were like their former selves. The anxiousness had disappeared, the concern, the worry, like all of those things, because, you know, children, they need to be children.

The educators in this setting focused on the importance of children experiencing joy in their daily lives. There was a recognition of the importance of a connection with others as a key endeavour of ECEC. Implicit in such a pedagogical focus is the notion that joy is an essential and normal feature of ECEC practice and that educators were vigilant to restore such normality. There was a sense that there was a need to counteract potential adverse impacts of COVID-19, as suggested by the comment that the anxiety children experienced at home is alleviated with the return to ECEC. Another educator also expressed the thought that everyday community experiences could restore wellbeing and counteract adverse effects:

> [T]they've adapted and accepted that as well. Because there are still some fun things that they can do. Especially now around Christmas because they're still going on the little trains, they're doing all these Santa experiences. I think that's very special for them. They're seeing grandparents

and they're all kind of doing their own bubble-type things. So, I think for the majority, their well-being would be good. Like certain times they'd be down but it wouldn't be . . . they were like adapted and they're kind of not focused on what they can't do anymore.

Other participants emphasised the sense that there was value in everyday, "normal" experiences, and this was seen to be a potential protective factor to the likely adverse impact COVID-19 could have on children. Thus, an educator expressed:

Whatever about this pandemic, having lasting effects on people's psyches. I think that something like trying to create physical distance for children of that age, having such absorbing kind of brains could have lasting effects for them. It's the idea that they can't just approach something as much as they'd like to. That could stick with them. So, I would have been very keen on keeping things as normal as possible with regards to that.

While participants tended to articulate that children are "fine" and that they are "adaptable," the participants simultaneously demonstrated an increased concern, sometimes implicitly, for children's wellbeing. There was a sense that normal, everyday, quality pedagogical practice creates unique opportunities for young children to express themselves and to process their experiences. The strategies that are inherent in everyday quality early childhood pedagogical practices were implied as fostering wellbeing and therefore as an important mitigating factor to the stress children had experienced during the restrictions of the pandemic. There was a strong sense in the data that there was an increased focus on children's joy and involvement, and curriculum decisions were described as being developed with a sensitive recognition that came from knowing children individually. From such strategies emerges a particular understanding of resilience that is in turn built upon a particular image of the child as inhabiting a lifeworld that is distinct from the adult and thus needing to construct their own understandings of their own biographical experiences and that this needs to be heard and valued (James, 2009).

I feel that children are extremely intuitive. And they know whether you have time for them or not. And I did find at one point in the room, it was just like a chorus of [participant name, participant name, participant name]. And that was kind of alarm bells for me. So, I had to kind of pull everyone together as a team and just say, you know, who are you interacting with during the day. I made a post-it note system where we were writing one post-it, per child, per day. The feedback goes back to the parents just to put some more parental involvement and we got to know the friends and things like that.

The emphasis on being a part of an everyday community, whose environment affords normality for children, was viewed as a protective factor and was thought to contribute to building resilience, by restoring wellbeing through intentional, relational pedagogy and affording children opportunities to re-establish familiar patterns and experiences. There were significant features of practice that were altered dramatically, becoming key strategies in supporting children's wellbeing and resilience. These changes were due in no small part to the influence of the pandemic. Some of these features of practice were noted in the first wave of interviews, and their influence persisted across each of the three waves of interviews. It was notable that perspectives and practices related to outdoor play were altered; all participants said that while spending time outdoors had always been important, they were now spending the majority of their time outdoors. Furthermore, three of the participants were making significant improvements to the outdoor space, so that it would lend itself to being used most of the time. This was reported as a positive influence of COVID-19. The analysis of the data emphasised a slowing down in pace and giving much more space for children and educators to simply be present and enjoy play time together. Participants reported less rushing, less overloading of equipment and materials, less focus on getting through lots of activities, instead to focus on children's joy, on their creativity and independence, on exploring the outdoors. This is consistent with an idea of a slow pedagogy, referring to listening to and being in-tempo with young children (Clark, 2020).

> We go out them first thing [when the children arrive in the morning], and we realized that made such a difference. . . . And so, we started being outside more from then, but what COVID has done is it made us put a cover [a simple outdoor shelter]. And that has meant that then on rainy days we were straight out into the rain, and we just stand under the cover. And we're watching the rain and have pots and pans, to catch the rain. And it's great craic and puddles and stuff like that. So, the cover has meant that we are outside more, and my goodness, we are out everyday.

However, the pedagogical strategies that educators employed seemed to contrast with the rhetoric they engaged. On the one hand, participants in the research tended to ascribe a rhetoric of innocence to the children, in particular, saying that the age of the child related to a lack of recognition and understanding of the intensity and gravity of the pandemic, as a participant expressed:

> The ECCE age group, I do find . . . they're very easy with regards to new things because everything's really new for them. So COVID comes along and it's just another new thing. We're stuck in our ways, we're older, we're grown up. Kids don't see the world the same way we do from that point

of view. So, when they talk about COVID, it's almost quite flippant and casual, they're like, Oh, yeah, COVID, we have to wash our hands. There's a virus. And that's all it is. From that point of view, I don't see that they feel the negative aspects of it that much, really, maybe slightly older kids, but I haven't seen much negative expression of it.

Such views of younger children speak to former ideas of the "innocent child" (Sorin, 2005), an image of the young child as just accepting changes unquestioningly. It implies a view of the preschool child as not fully understanding COVID-19, thus not being impacted by the pandemic. In consideration of Sorin's (2005) constructions of childhood, there was once a view of the child as innocent and passive; we now recognise the child as agentic, co-constructing learning and sharing power. Ideas of the agentic child influences "normal" practice in non-crisis times. However, at the same time, the descriptions the educators gave of the pedagogical decisions they made inferred a deep consideration of the agency and position of the young child; furthermore, there was an inherent recognition of the value of the psychosocial emphasis of the ECEC curriculum following from service closures, social restrictions relating to the pandemic and a sensitivity to other pandemic related influence. Thus, there appears to be a contrast between the rhetoric of educators in relation to children's wellbeing and the pedagogical practices employed.

Masten and Gewirtz (2006) argue that quality care and learning opportunities are essential to developing resilience in early childhood, yet this was something many participants felt they struggled to provide under COVID-19, in particular in the first wave of interviews. This research reported negative and limiting implications of COVID-19 on pedagogical practice, raising the question of whether a focus on wellbeing as addressed through normality alone is sufficient. Many expressed the sentiments voiced by one educator that care took priority over learning:

> I think initially, planning and curriculum fell by the wayside a little bit. Because everybody was in crisis mode a little bit. It was like, look, the kids just need to be here, the parents need to work at home, let's just give them a safe space where they feel like they can express themselves and be happy. It got very simplified. I mean, I can't speak for everyone, but I felt like, the vibe in my setting anyway. . . . [I]t didn't matter so much if we weren't hitting the markers with regards to emergent learning and assessment. As long as the kids were happy, they were being looked after, that was the main objective. . . . It's been tough for people to have education and care. In fact, they mostly just switched to being all about care.

Other participants identified that educators in their setting, including themselves, had low morale and seemed to be operating in a state of crisis, reducing their ability to incorporate an intentional pedagogy into the care of children. There was a perspective among participants that curriculum became difficult to focus on as "survival" took centre stage – simply getting through the day, managing the cleaning, maintaining play pods, physical distancing from other adults, in particular restoring children's wellbeing through the provision of a safe space, took focus away from curriculum.

Interconnections: The Role and Importance of Educator Wellbeing

Participants shared their perceptions of their own wellbeing. Participants identified difficulties in focusing on children's learning and curricular provision and expressed that this was due to educators' own eroding wellbeing. Given that resilience is a process involving adults and children (Millican & Middleton, 2020), it is essential to recognise and understand how educators' experiences, and resilience, impact their focus on supporting children's resilience and wellbeing. One educator suggested: "the children's well-being, really, is based on how happy the staff are." Another participant expressed a similar view:

> The children have been wonderful, absolutely wonderful, and children that we're really supporting and helping, with lots of different strategies, it's all come good for them. . . . For my staff, it's been different; I've had to support them a lot. They've struggled, and it hasn't been easy for them. But I suppose everybody is trying to cope with things as best they can.

Educators also spoke of feeling overwhelmed by the responsibility of keeping children and their families safe while also being expected to provide high-quality care and education for children. They spoke of feeling forgotten by the government and having to navigate unchartered territory in isolation, without support or guidance.

According to the United Nations (UN) (2020), educators around the world were unprepared for the unprecedented position in which they found themselves, navigating numerous difficulties in sustaining education and adapting pedagogical methods. The situation was exacerbated for educators in ECEC who found themselves profoundly affected (Friendly et al., 2021) the world over. In fact, the impact was such, Canada introduced significant changes to policies pertaining to early education (Friendly et al., 2021), enhancing both the recognition and working conditions of early educators. Using a demands-resources model (Bakker & Demerouti, 2007), Sokal et al. (2020) identified educator burnout, due to professional demand exceeding resources, the requirements of the role far surpassing educators' capacity. Educators are often lauded for their own resilience (Beltman et al., 2019; Irvine et al., 2016; Liu et al., 2018), yet they acknowledge feeling overlooked and undervalued (Doocy et al., 2021) as they navigated COVID-19 restrictions. There is a volume of research which recognises the challenging working conditions of educators, and an understanding that these may lead to high levels of work-related stress, emotional exhaustion and staff turnover (Blackburne & Oke, 2022; McMullen et al., 2020; Irvine et al., 2016; Jena-Crottet, 2017; Jones et al., 2017; OECD, 2019; Thorpe et al., 2020; Totenhagen et al., 2016). Even prior to the pandemic, research into the wellbeing of educators emerged (Irvine et al., 2016; Phillips et al., 2016; Totenhagen et al., 2016) with COVID-19 both intensifying pre-existing stressors and introducing new challenges. Further amplifying the challenges faced, many services that support and mentor ECEC settings also found themselves operating in a predominantly remote capacity (Crawford et al., 2021), unable to provide much-needed in-person mentoring.

Some of the research concerning the wellbeing of educators (Ylitapio-Mäntylä et al., 2012; Hall-Kenyon et al., 2014) indicates that educators often compromise their wellbeing (Cumming, 2016), which is reported as particularly relevant to educators of young children experiencing traumatic life events (Kwon et al., 2021), not necessarily recognising the negative impact this has on children (McMullen et al., 2020). Educators experiencing stress are often less able, or available, to meet the emotional needs of children (Zinsser et al., 2013). Educators regularly indicate a level of commitment to children which negatively impacts their own emotional wellbeing. Research conducted by Shirley et al. (2020) indicated that educators working in positive environments, able to control their role and engage in professional collaboration, are best positioned to meet the needs of children. This workplace description appears far removed from that experienced under COVID-19 government measures pertaining to ECEC. COVID-19 greatly increased the demands on educators, negatively impacting their wellbeing. In a recent study (Eadie et al., 2021), 86% of educators reported COVID-19 as having a negative impact on their wellbeing. While this may not be surprising, it is intriguing that 37% of educators reported it as having a negative impact on their relationships with children (ibid.).

For a concept that is currently the focus of much attention and discourse, defining educator wellbeing is a rather complex task. While we tend to think of wellbeing as a positive emotional state, it is essential for educator wellbeing to consider such components as stress and burnout. Research highlights the importance of this consideration, as it shows that staff turnover has adverse implications for the social-emotional outcomes of children (King et al., 2016). The more we explore the topic of educator wellbeing, the clearer the inextricable link between educator wellbeing and quality provisions for children (Blackburne & Oke, 2022; Corr et al., 2015). In 2019, the OECD reported educator–child interactions to have the single greatest impact on the quality of ECEC programmes, yet the ability to sustain these interactions is directly connected to the wellbeing of educators (Roberts et al., 2016; Kim & Choi, 2018).

With this in mind, let us revisit educators' perceptions of their own wellbeing compared to that of the children in their care. Several educators appeared to imply, or directly state, that they felt the need to "leave COVID at the door" and restore normality in the ECEC setting. They expressed that this need not only for the children but also for themselves. Thus, one participant stated:

> And when we're all together in the classroom, you actually forget about COVID, even though you're wearing a mask, it's only if somebody asks you to blow some bubbles that you kind of go, oh, that's one thing I can't do but other than that it's been wonderful. And it's actually been wonderful for me as an early years' educator to be able to escape from reality.

Other educators stated a similar personal need to escape anxiety and worry of being at home, thinking about COVID-19 and not working, and expressed a sense of relief as ECEC settings were allowed to reopen. The time spent with children, and focusing on keeping children happy and safe, took their minds off their own anxiety. The need to keep things "as normal as possible" for children may thus perhaps also offer educators the comfort of pre-pandemic times. As another participant confided:

> I tried not to worry about it once. I know we know that COVID is here everyday and we do our best. I think they (children) needed routine. We left COVID at the door, and everyone was happy for a few hours.

Image of the Child and Educator Wellbeing

Returning to the idea of the image of the child as central to views on children's wellbeing, there is the possibility that educators are falling back on an adult-centric view. Lightfoot (1978) coined the word "childism" to address the assumption that children, unlike adults, can readily recover from adversity, as their emotions do not run as deep as adults. It may be such "childism" that accounts for the perceptions hold educators regarding children's ability to adjust and thus cope with the disruptions brought on by COVID-19. It may be that an emphasis on a need to feel normal and be happy, for educators and children alike, facilitated a narrative of children as easily adaptable once "normal" routine and play opportunities were facilitated through appropriate pedagogy. This narrative appeared to cast children's play, and thus adaptation, as "normal" and mostly unimpacted by COVID-19.

The emotionally intense environment in which educators work sees an expectation and normalisation of emotional relationships, often resulting in the nurturing work of educators going unacknowledged. Educators' efforts are simply viewed as an irrefutable part of their role (Osgood, 2010). Hochschild's work (1983) on emotional labour identified a need to suppress personal feelings in order to maintain a focus on the positive emotional states of those in our care. Keeping children happy is often identified as a priority for educators, even when it requires disregarding personal feelings (Cefai & Cooper, 2017) or "deep acting" (Hochschild, 2012, pp. 185–198). The pandemic gave us all cause for concern, and it is possible that educators' perceptions of children's resilience may be influenced by invisible expectations and a desire to ensure everything felt "normal" for children. The narrative of easy adaptation may indeed arise from not recognising how educators themselves engaged in levels of emotional acting (Horner et al., 2020), diminishing their own experiences and emotional state, all the while providing support for children, to ensure their happiness. Children may well have shown an incredible ability to adapt upon their return to ECEC, yet they returned to a carefully prepared environment, planned by educators, and designed to ensure a positive experience awaited children. Children may have demonstrated great resilience, but educators observed this resilience through engagement, through activities designed to support children and through play which offered opportunities for children to process and make sense of their experiences. In casting ECEC as counteracting potentially negative impacts of COVID-19 on children, educators did not recognise their own crucial role in children's wellbeing and resilience. Yet this very role seemed to impact negatively on educators' own wellbeing, thus juxtaposed to that of children. Feeling drained, educators expressed difficulties in focusing on curriculum and children's learning and thus seizing those crucial moments for more directly and actively focusing on resilience-building within ECEC.

Concluding Remarks

Besides the economy and health care, education is considered the third fundamental component of a pandemic-resilient society (Fay et al., 2020). For educators in ECEC, education is finely balanced with care, an integral part of their role (Hayes, 2007). Given the suggestion that this care component often results in silencing and marginalisation (Aldridge et al., 2010), it is interesting to note that society has rediscovered the value of caring professions (Cameron & Moss, 2020). While it is acknowledged that educators are not counsellors or therapists (Kahuroa et al., 2021), it is also recognised that they have the potential to support both young children and their families, thus enhancing the post COVID-19 global recovery process (Murray, 2020). However, when the demands placed on the workforce are too high, this is likely to have a negative impact on mental health (Bakker & Demerouti, 2014; Dicke et al., 2017; Skaalvik & Skaalvik, 2018). Given the newly acquired responsibilities, added to the ever-increasing demands of their role, the wellbeing of educators has been brought into sharp focus (Eadie et al., 2021).

ECEC settings are unique as a workplace. They are designed as an environment in which children may grow and thrive. Yet, recognising the interdependence of children and educators, the environment must also provide educators with opportunities to thrive (Corr et al., 2015; Zinsser et al., 2013). When young children feel overwhelmed, they often require the support of a caring adult, someone they trust, to engage in co-regulation (Barnardos, 2021). This ensures that children feel cared for and safe, which has a long-term impact on their ability to develop and maintain relationships.

As we conclude this chapter, we return to the statement that "*Children need to be children.*" As a society, we not only began to accept COVID-19 measures but such was also the desire for normality; many of us started referring to these extreme, albeit necessary, measures as "the new normal." This very act of legitimising our shared experience also served to diminish the value of our response. Our very language belied our efforts, "the new normal" becoming the rug under which to sweep our fears and isolation, or a cloak with which to hide the cracks in our own resilience. Perhaps the narrative of children as grand or fine, easily adaptable, emerges from this greater societal narrative of "the new normal," perhaps in an attempt by educators to reassure themselves that the children were fine, that they were resilient. The truth of the matter is that COVID-19 provoked anxiety in all of us, children (Lades et al., 2020; Orgiles et al., 2020) and adults alike, and educators were thrust onto the front line, providing emotional support for children. However, in their efforts to view children as protected from the detrimental impacts of the pandemic, educators risk not recognising the opportunities they were providing, the ways in which they supported children, to give them the time and space to process their experiences, in other words to actively build children's resilience. This raises the important question of the role of curriculum and pedagogy, respectively, in supporting young children's wellbeing and resilience, in particular in relation to educators' role in play moments denoting experiences such as those relating to COVID-19 in order to seize these as teachable moments in which wellbeing and resilience can be further supported.

References

Alan, U. (2021). Distance education during the COVID-19 pandemic in Turkey: Identifying the needs of early childhood educators. *Early Childhood Education Journal*, *49*(1). https://doi.org/10.1007/s10643-021-01197-y

Aldridge, J., Kilgo, J., & Emfinger, K. (2010). The marginalization of women educators: A consequence of no child left behind. *Childhood Education*, *87*(1), 41–47.

Bakker, A. B., & Demerouti, E. (2007). The job demands-resources model: State of the art. *Journal of Managerial Psychology*, *22*, 309–328. https://doi.org/10.1108/02683940710733115

Bakker, A. B., & Demerouti, E. (2014). Job demands-resources theory. In P. Y. Chen & C. L. Cooper (Eds.), *Work and wellbeing* (pp. 37–64). Wiley Blackwell. https://doi.org/10.1002/9781118539415.wbwell019

Barlett, J. D., Griffin, J., & Thomson, D. (2020). Resources for supporting children's emotional well-being during the COVID-19 pandemic. *Child Trends*. https://www.childtrends.org/publications/resources-for-supporting-childrens-emotional-well-being-duringthe-COVID-19-pandemic

Barnardos. (2021). *A "new normal": Snapshot report on the needs of children and young people since full-time return to education in August 2021*. Department for Education and Skills.

Barnett, M. D., Maciel, I. V., Johnson, D. M., & Ciepluch, I. (2021). Social anxiety and perceived social support: Gender differences and the mediating role of communication styles. *Psychological Reports*, *124*(1), 70–87. https://doi.org/10.1177/0033294119900975

Beltman, S., Dobson, M. R., Mansfeld, C. F., & Jay, J. (2019). The thing that keeps me going: Educator resilience in early learning settings. *International Journal of Early Years Education*, *28*(4), 303–318. https://doi.org/10.1080/09669760.2019.1605885

Benner, A. D., & Mistry, R. S. (2020). Child development during the COVID-19 pandemic through a life course theory lens. *Child Development Perspectives*. https://doi.org/10.1111/cdep.12387

Blackburne, C., & Oke, M. (2022). Orientation quality: Exploring the role of early childhood educators from a capabilities approach-how can we tell the dancer from the dance? *National Early Years Research Day Proceedings*, *3*, 14–25.

Bradford, H. (2012). *The well-being of children under three*. Taylor and Francis Routledge Publications.

Cameron, C., & Moss, P. (2020). *Transforming early childhood in England: Towards a democratic education*. University College London Press.

Cefai, C., & Cooper, P. (2017). Mental health promotion in schools. *Cross Cultural Narratives and Perspectives*. Sense Publishers. https://doi.org/10.1007/978-94-6351-053-0

Clark, A. (2020). Towards a listening ECEC system. In C. Cameron & P. Moss (Eds.), *Transforming early childhood in England: Towards a democratic education*. UCL Press.

Corr, L., Cook, K., LaMontagne, A., Waters, E., & Davis, E. (2015). Associations between Australian early childhood educators' mental health and working conditions: A cross-sectional study. *Australasian Journal Early Childhood*, *40*(3), 69–78. https://doi.org/10.1177/183693911504000310

Crawford, A., Vaughn, K. A., Guttentag, K. L., Varghese, C., Oh, Y., & Zucker, T. A. (2021). "Doing what I can, but I got no magic wand:" A snapshot of early childhood educator experiences and efforts to ensure quality during the COVID-19 pandemic. *Early Childhood Education Journal*, *49*, 829–840. https://doi.org/10.1007/s10643-021-01215-z

Cumming, T. (2016). Early childhood educators' well-being: An updated review of literature. *Early Childhood Education Journal*, *45*, 583–593. https://doi.org/10.1007/s10643-016-08186

Cumming, T., Wong, S., & Logan, H. (2021). Early childhood educators' well-being, work environments and 'quality': Possibilities for changing policy and practice. *Australian Journal of Early Childhood*, *46*(1), 50–65. https://doi.org/10.1177/1836939120979064

Darmody, M., Smyth, E., &d Russell, H. (2020). *The implications of the COVID-19 pandemic for policy in relation to children and young people: A research review*. ESRI survey and statistical report series 94. ESRI. https://doi.org/10.26504/sustat94

Dias, M. J. A., Almodóvar, M., Atiles, J. T., Vargas, A. C., & León, I. M. Z. (2020). Rising to the challenge: Innovative early childhood teachers adapt to the COVID-19 era. *Childhood Education, 96*(6), 38–45. https://doi.org/10.1080/00094056.2020.1846385

Dicke, T., Stebner, F., Linninger, C., Kunter, M., & Leutner, D. (2017). A longitudinal study of teachers' occupational well-being: Applying the job demands-resources model. *Journal of Occupational Health Psychology, 23*(2), 262–277. https://doi.org/10.1037/ocp0000070

Doocy, S., Kim, Y., Montoya, E., & Chávez, R. (2021). *The consequences of invisibility: COVID-19 and the human toll on California early educators.* Centre for the Study of Child Care Employment, University of California, Berkeley.

Durbin, C. E. (2010). Validity of young children's self-reports of their emotion in response to structured laboratory tasks. *Emotion, 10*(4), 519–535. https://psycnet.apa.org/doi/10.1037/a0019008

Eadie, P., Levickis, P., Murray, L., Page, J., Elek, C., & Church, A. (2021). Early childhood educators' well-being during the COVID-19 pandemic. *Early Childhood Education Journal, 49*, 903–913. https://doi.org/10.1007/s10643-021-01203-3

Early Childhood Ireland. (2020). Plan for reopening. *Early Times*, Issue 25.

Egan, S. M., Pope, J., Moloney, M., Hoyne, C., & Beatty, C. (2021). Missing early education and care during the pandemic: The socio-emotional impact of the COVID-19 crisis on young children. *Early Childhood Education Journal, 49*, 925–934. https://doi.org/10.1007/s10643-021-01193-2

Fay, J., Levinson, M., Stevens, A., Brighouse, H., Geron, T., & Fellow, P. (2020). *Schools during the COVID-19 pandemic: Sites and sources of community resilience. (COVID-19 rapid response impact initiative white paper 20).* Edmond J. Safra Center for Ethics at Harvard University. https://ethics.harvard.edu/fles/center-forethics/files/20schoolsduringpandemic2.pdf?m=15922 32939

Fegert, J. M., Vitello, B., Plener, P. L., & Clemens, V. (2020). Challenges and burden of Coronavirus (COVID-19) pandemic for child and adolescent mental health: A narrative review to highlight clinical and research needs in the acute phase and the long return to normality. *Child Adolescence Psychiatry Mental Health, 14*(1), 1–11.

French, G., Mckenna, G., Giblin, F., Concannon-Gibney, T., Farrell, T., Gillic, C., Halligan, C., Lake, G., Ní Dhiorbháin, A., Ní Láimhín, M., & O'Neill, S. (2022). *Literature review to support the updating of Aistear, the early childhood curriculum framework.* https://ncca.ie/en/resources/literature-review-to-support-the-updating-of-aistear-the-ear-childhood-curriculum-framework/

Friendly, M., Forer, B., Vickerson, R., & Mohamed, S. S. (2021). COVID-19 and childcare in Canada: A tale of ten provinces and three territories. *Journal of Childhood Studies, 46*(3), 42–52.

Gromada, A., Richardson, D., & Rees, G. (2020). *Childcare in a global crisis: The impact of COVID-19 on work and family life.* United Nations. https://doi.org/10.18356/16d757a1-en

Hall-Kenyon, K. M., Bullough, R. V., MacKay, K. L., & Marshall, E. E. (2014). Preschool teacher well-being: A review of the literature. *Early Childhood Education Journal, 42*(3), 153–162. https://doi.org/10.1007/s10643-013-0595-4

Hamad, R., Elser, H., Tran, D. C., Rehkopf, D. H., & Goodman, S. N. (2018). How and why studies disagree about the effects of education on health: A systematic review and meta-analysis of studies of compulsory schooling laws. *Social Science & Medicine, 212*, 168–178. https://doi.org/10.1016/j.socscimed.2018.07.016

Hayes, N. (2007). *Perspectives on the relationship between education and care in early childhood: A research paper.* National Council for Curriculum and Assessment (NCCA).

Henderson, L., Bussey, K., & Ebrahim, H. B. (Eds.). (2022). *Early childhood education and care in a global pandemic: How the sector responded, spoke back and generated knowledge* (1st ed.). Routledge. https://doi.org/10.4324/9781003257684

Hochschild, A. R. (1983). *The managed heart: The commercialization of human feeling.* University of California Press.

Hochschild, A. R. (2012). *The managed heart. Commercialisation of human feeling* (3rd ed.). University of California Press.

Horner, C. G., Brown, E. L., Mehta, S., & Scanlon, C. L. (2020). Feeling and acting like a teacher: Reconceptualizing teachers' emotional labor. *Teachers College Record, 122*(5), 1–36. https://doi.org/10.1177/016146812012200502

Howes, S., Monk-Winstanley, R., Sefton, T., & Woudhuysen, A. (2020). *Poverty in the pandemic: The impact of coronavirus on low income families and children.* Child Poverty Action Group.

Irvine, S., Thorpe, K., McDonald, P., Lunn, J., & Sumsion, J. (2016). *Money, love and identity: Initial findings from the national ECEC workforce study.* QUT: Summary Report from the National ECEC Workforce Development Policy Workshop.

Jalong, M. R. (2021). The effects of COVID-19 on early childhood education and care: Research and resources for children, families, teachers, and teacher educators. *Early Childhood Education Journal, 49*, 763–774. https://doi.org/10.1007/s10643-021-01208-

James, A. (2009). Agency. In J. Qvortrup, W. Corsaro, & M.-S. Hoing (Eds.), *The Palgrave handbook of childhood studies* (1st ed.). Palgrave MacMillan.

Jandrić, P. (2020). Editorial: Post-digital research in the time of COVID-19. *Postdigital Science and Education, 2*, 233–238. https://doi.org/10.1007/s42438-020-00113-8

Jeffrey, S. H. (2020). Supporting Head Start employee well-being during the COVID-19 pandemic. *JAACP Connect, 7*(4).

Jena-Crottet, A. (2017). Early childhood teachers' emotional labour. *New Zealand International Research in Early Childhood Education, 20*(2), 19–33. https://doi.org/10.3316/informit.675313221536539

Jones, C., Hadley, F., & Johnstone, M. (2017). Retaining early childhood teachers: What factors contribute to high job satisfaction in early childhood settings in Australia? *New Zealand International Research in Early Childhood Education, 20*(2), 1–18. https://doi.org/10.3316/informit.675331854507798

Kahuroa, R., Mitchell, L., Ng, O., & Johns, T. (2021). Children's working theories about COVID-19 in Aotearoa New Zealand. *European Early Childhood Education Research Journal, 29*(1), 6–20. https://doi.org/10.1080/1350293X.2021.1872672

Kaplan, H. B. (1999). Toward an understanding of resilience: A critical review of definitions and models. In M. D. Glantz & J. L. Johnson (Eds.), *Resilience and development: Positive life adaptations* (pp. 17–83). Kluwer Academic Publishers.

Kar, N. (2009). Psychological impact of disasters on children. Review of assessment and interventions. *World Journal of Pediatrics, 5*(1), 5–11. https://doi.org/10.1007/s12519-009-0001-x

Kim, J., & Choi, M.-K. (2018). Effect of burnout of preschool teachers on teacher-child interaction: The mediating role of psychological well-being. *Korean Journal of Child Studies, 39*(3), 127–139. https://doi.org/10.5723/kjcs.2018.39.3.127

King, E. K., Johnson, A. V., Cassidy, D. J., Wang, Y. C., Lower, J. K., & Kintner-Dufy, V. L. (2016). Preschool teachers' financial well-being and work time supports: Associations with children's emotional expressions and behaviours in classrooms. *Early Childhood Education Journal, 44*(6), 545–553. https://doi.org/10.1007/s10643-015-0744-z

Kostelnik, M. J., Soderman, A. K., Whiren, A. P., Rupiper, M. L., & Gregory, K. M. (2015). *Guiding children's social development and learning: Theory and skills* (8th ed.). Cengage.

Kwon, K., Horm, D. M., & Amirault, C. (2021). Early childhood teachers' well-being: What we know and why we should care. *Zero to Three Journal, 41*(3), 35–44.

Lades, L. K., Laffan, K., Daly, M., & Delaney, L. (2020). Daily emotional well-being during the COVID-19 pandemic. *British Journal of Health Psychology.* https://doi.org/10.1111/bjhp.12450

Laevers, F. (2005). *Well-being and involvement in care settings. A process-oriented self-evaluation Instrument (SIC's)*. Kind en gezin; Research Centre for Experiential Education.

Laevers, F., & Declercq, B. (2018). How well-being and involvement fit into the commitment to children's rights. *European Journal of Education, 53*(3), 325–355. https://doi.org/10.1111/ejed.12286

Le Brocque, R., De Young, A., Montague, G., Pocock, S., March, S., Triggell, N., Rabaa, C., & Kenardy, J. (2017). Schools and natural disaster recovery: The unique and vital role that teachers and education professionals play in ensuring the mental health of students following natural disasters. *Journal of Psychologists and Counsellors in Schools, 27*(1), 1–23. https://doi.org/10.1017/jgc.2016.17

Lightfoot, S. L. (1978). *Worlds apart: Relationships between families and schools*. Basic Books.

Liu, L. B., Song, H., & Miao, P. (2018). Navigating individual and collective notions of teacher well-being as a complex phenomenon shaped by national context. *Compare A Journal of Comparative and International Education, 48*(1), 128–146. https://doi.org/10.1080/03057925.2017.1283979

Masten, A. S., & Gewirtz, A. H. (2006). *Resilience in development: The importance of early childhood*. Encyclopaedia of Early Childhood Development, University of Minnesota.

McMullen, M. B., Lee, M. S. C., McCormick, K. I., & Choi, J. (2020). Early childhood professional well-being as a predictor of the risk of turnover in childcare: A matter of quality. *Journal of Research in Childhood Education, 34*(3), 331–345. https://doi.org/10.1080/02568543.2019.1705446

Millican, R., & Middleton, T. (2020). A need for resilience. In A. T. Ahmed Shafi, R. Middleton, & S. Millican (Eds.), *Reconsidering resilience in education* (pp. 3–16). Templeton Springer International Publishing.

Murray, J. (2020). In a time of COVID-19 and beyond, word needs early childhood educators. *International Journal of Early Years Education, 28*(4), 299–302. https://doi.org/10.1080/09669760.2020.1839830

National Council for Curriculum and Assessment (NCCA). (2009). *Aistear: The early childhood curriculum framework: Background paper*. NCCA.

OECD. (2019). *Changing the odds for vulnerable children: Building opportunities and resilience*. OECD Publishing. https://doi.org/10.1787/a2e8796c-en

OECD. (2020). *Policy responses to Coronavirus: Combatting Covid-19's effect on children*. OECD Publishing. https://read.oecd-ilibrary.org/view/?ref=132_132643-m91j2scsyh&title=Combatting-COVID-s-19-effect-on-children

Orgiles, M., Morales, A., Delveccio, E., Mazzeschi, C., & Espada, P. J. (2020, April 24). Immediate psychological effects of COVID-19 quarantine in youth from Italy and Spain. *PsyArXiv*. https://doi.org/10.31234/osf.io/5bpfz

Osgood, J. (2010). Reconstructing professionalism in ECEC: The case for the critically reflective emotional professional. *Early Years, 30*(2), 119–133.

Pascal, C., Bertram, T., Cullinane, C., & Holt-White, E. (2020). *COVID-19 and social mobility impact: Early years (issue brief no. 4)*. The Sutton Trust. https://www.suttontrust.com/ourresearch/coronavirus-impacts-early-years/

Phillips, D., Austin, L. J. E., & Whitebook, M. (2016). The early care and education workforce. *Future of Children, 26*(2), 139–158. Retrieved January 9, 2020, from http://www.jstor.org/stable/43940585

Plowman, L., Stevenson, O., McPake, J., Stephen, C., & Adey, C. (2011). Parents, preschoolers and learning with technology at home: Some implications for policy. *Journal of Computer Assisted Learning, 27*, 361–371.

Roberts, A., LoCasale-Crouch, J., Hamre, B., & DeCoster, J. (2016). Exploring teachers' depressive symptoms, interaction quality, and children's social-emotional development in Head Start. *Early Education and Development, 27*(5), 642–654. https://doi.org/10.1080/10409289.2016.1127088

Sameroff, A. J., & Rosenblum, C. (2006, December). Psychosocial constraints on the development of resilience. *Annals of the New York Academy of Sciences, 1094*, 116–124. https://doi.org/10.1196/annals.1376.010

Shirley, D., Hargreaves, A., & Washington-Wangia, S. (2020). The sustainability and unsustainability of teachers' and leaders' well-being. *Teaching and Teacher Education, 92*, 1–12.

Singh, S., Roy, D. K., Parveen, S., Sharma, G., & Joshi, G. (2020). Impact of COVID-19 and lockdown on mental health of children and adolescents: A narrative review with recommendations. *Psychiatry Research, 293*, 113429. https://doi.org/10.1016/j.psychres.2020.113429

Skaalvik, E. M., & Skaalvik, S. (2018). Job demands and job resources as predictors of teacher motivation and well-being. *Social Psychology of Education, 21*(5), 1251–1275. https://doi.org/10.1007/s11218-018-9464-8

Sokal, L. J., Trudel, L. G. E., & Babb, J. C. (2020). Supporting teachers in times of change: The job demands-resources model and teacher burnout during the COVID-19 pandemic. *International Journal of Contemporary Education, 3*(2), 67–74. https://doi.org/10.11114/ijce.v3i2.4931

Sorin, R. (2005). Images of childhood: Perception and practice in early childhood education. *Canadian Children-Journal of the Canadian Association for Young Children, 30*(2), 4–8.

Thorpe, K., Jansen, E., Sullivan, V., Irvine, S., & McDonald, P. (2020). Identifying predictors of retention and professional well-being of the early childhood education workforce in a time of change. *Journal of Educational Change, 21*, 623–647. https://doi.org/10.1007/s10833020-09382-3

Toros, K., & Falch-Eriksen, A. (2022). The voices of parents in child protective services: A qualitative analysis of families' struggles with COVID-19. *Developmental Child Welfare, 4*, 97–113.

Totenhagen, C. J., Hawkins, S. A., Casper, D. M., Bosch, L. A., Hawkey, K. R., & Borden, L. M. (2016). Retaining early childhood education workers: A review of the empirical literature. *Journal of Research in Childhood Education, 30*(4), 585–599. https://doi.org/10.1080/02568543.2016.1214652

United Nations. (2020). *Policy brief: Education during COVID-19 and beyond.* https://www.un.org/sites/un2.un.org/fles/sg_ policy_brief_COVID-19_and_education_august_2020.pdf

United Nations International Children's Emergency Fund UNICEF. (2021). *At least one-third COVID-19: At least a third of the world's schoolchildren unable to access remote learning during school closures, new report says.* https://www.unicef.org/pressreleases/COVID-19-least-third-worlds-schoolchildren-unableaccess-remote-learning-

Witt, A., Ordóñez, A., Martin, A., Vitiello, B., & Fegert, J. M. (2020). *Child and adolescent mental health service provision and research during the COVID-19 pandemic: Challenges, opportunities, and a call for submissions.* Child and Adolescent Psychiatry and Mental Health. https://doi.org/10.1186/s1303 4–020–00324–8

Ylitapio-Mäntylä, O., Uusianutti, S., & Määttä, K. (2012). Critical viewpoint to early childhood education teachers' well-being at work. *International Journal of Human Sciences*, *9*(1), 458–483.

Zinsser, K. M., Bailey, C. S., Curby, T. W., Denham, S. A., & Bassett, H. H. (2013). Exploring the predictable classroom: Preschool teacher stress, emotional supportiveness, and students social-emotional behaviour in private and Head Start classrooms. *Dialog*, *16*(2), 90–108.

5

HOW TO CREATE A MORE OPEN-LISTENING CLIMATE IN EARLY YEARS SETTINGS

A Multi-Professional Perspective When Supporting Children's Wellbeing

Alison Moore

The data informing this chapter reveals a rich picture of children's and parents' lives at home before and after attending the setting and are presented using Portraiture to 'listen for a story' (Lawrence-Lightfoot & Hoffmann Davis, 1997). The practitioners' perspectives and understanding of their practice in relation to child voice were explored through focus groups, and semi-structured interviews with senior managers. The data evidenced areas of good practice with examples of a listening culture that had positive outcomes for children's and parents' wellbeing.

The findings also revealed a disconnect within the multi-professional context and defined roles of early years and family support, resulting, at times, in a misdirection of focus away from the children's wellbeing and placing more emphasis on parental support. The findings suggest re-defining the multi-professional roles by applying a rights-based lens to support practitioners in creating a more open-listening climate, focusing on the child's voice, when considering how best to support children's wellbeing and that of the parents in early years settings.

Introduction: Setting the Scene

The theory of child wellbeing has been extensively researched over several decades, and evidence suggests that the concept of child wellbeing in early years is complex (Pollard & Lee, 2003; Elfer & Dearnley, 2007; Roberts, 2007, 2010; Morrow & Mayall, 2009; Page, 2011). The research suggests the need to develop a greater understanding and clearer definition of wellbeing and what

DOI: 10.4324/9781003345664-7

influences and impacts on a child's and a family's wellbeing. In their systematic review of the child wellbeing literature, Pollard and Lee (2003, p. 59) found:

> '[W]ell-being is a commonly used but is an inconsistently defined term in the study of child development . . . [acknowledging] the study of wellbeing as a significant emerging frontier . . .'. Their findings suggest there has been a focus on 'studying children's disorders, deficits and disabilities', [rather than] 'examining children's strengthens and abilities . . . [to] discover the core elements of wellbeing that enable children to flourish and thrive.'

Subsequent research exploring child's mental health and wellbeing has been rapidly expanding, with an increased focus on the youngest children in early years settings (Abbott & Langston, 2005; Mayr & Ulich, 2009; Waters, 2009; Bradford, 2012a; Mashford-Scott et al., 2012; Casey, 2012; Manning-Morton, 2014). There appears to be a growing consensus across the research substantiating the need to develop '*a shared language for understanding the concept of wellbeing*' (Sunderland, 2019). Findings from research shows explicit links between the quality of children's earliest lived experiences, both at home and in an early years setting that then determine if children develop poor or good levels of wellbeing (Marmot, 2010; Field, 2010; Allen, 2011). Field (2010, p. 5) evidenced the importance of the quality of a child's earliest experiences, reporting the damaging impact of growing up in challenging home circumstances and parents not able to meet the basic needs of their children.

There is overwhelming evidence corroborating the need to develop a greater understanding of the negative impact that adverse childhood experiences (ACEs) have on children's wellbeing and that of the parents (Burke, 2018; Dermody et al., 2018). There is ample support for the assertion that the most critical period of a child's life, where these adverse childhood experiences have the greatest detrimental impact, is the period between conception and the age of two years old (Field, 2010; The WAVE Trust, 2014; Garvey, 2017; Conkbayir, 2017, 2023; Zeeedyk, 2020). The research on ACEs and being aware, informed and responsive when providing support to children and parents is beyond the scope of this chapter. However, there has been growing support for the need to apply a holistic approach when considering children's and families' wellbeing (Bradford, 2012; Manning-Morton, 2014; Lumsden, 2020; Toros et al., 2021), and this chapter reports on the aspect of considering children's wellbeing through a child-rights-based lens when considering early years practice.

When applying a holistic and child-rights-based lens in practice, practitioners who are supporting children and parents need to have a good understanding of the need for early intervention that promotes resilience. Luthar and Cicchetti (2000, p. 858) refer to resilience as '*a dynamic process wherein individuals display positive adaptation despite experience of significant adversity or trauma*'. The findings in my research would suggest that interventions such as those identified in the parent portraits and practitioner narratives provide a range of '*protective factors*' that foster and strengthen resilience, to reduce the impact of adversities on children. Masten (2011) refers to protective factors that are especially important for children and that relate to experiencing emotion-based interactions from sensitive caring adults.

Contextualising the Case Study

Although the doctoral research took place in children's centres (DCSF, 2007), the approach and methodology are transferable to all those agencies providing services to children and families. As reflected in this chapter, the focus of the research was to listen to the perspectives of parents of children under five years of age and practitioners' delivering appropriate support services.

The rationale for conducting the doctoral research grew from my earliest experiences of working within a multi-professional context in the early 1980s in a family centre (previously Day Nurseries) (Thane, 2011). Family centres provided early years day-care services for both working parents [on a fee-paying basis] and allocating places for children who were receiving support from the local authority and, at the time, subject to court orders (pre-Children Act, 1989), that is, Child in Need. By definition, the child/children and family would be supported by Social Services and a Social Worker, who would work alongside the early years practitioners, providing a Family Support model.

I reflected on my earliest experience supporting young mothers (14–15 years of age) who had been made a Ward of Court and were therefore living within the care system with their baby. At times, it appeared that the young mothers, who were children themselves and their babies, were invisible in practice. This is a concept I will return to later in the chapter. The Local Authority and support services were put in place to 'protect' both the mother and baby, by applying a Supervision Order (Children Act, 1989 [section 31]) following concerns that the child may be '*suffering, or is likely to suffer, significant harm*' (Part IV). This would be of concern should the child, (the mother) and their baby remain living in their family home.

The practice and policies within the family centre appeared on the surface, to be an empowering model, yet judgements about the parenting capacity of the young mothers were being passed by the foster carers, early years practitioners and social care. Therefore, decisions were being made that would have a long-term impact on the future of the mother and baby. A 'done to' and not 'working with' approach to family support appeared to be in evidence. Upon reflection, I was left asking, where was the voice of both mother (still legally defined as a child) and their baby, in this process? (Moore, 2021).

Over the last decade, there has been a succession of cases of child deaths, as a result of neglect and child abuse. These have consequently been subject to Serious Case Reviews (SCRs) in several local authorities in the UK, including a number in the local authority where the doctoral research took place (Laming, 2003, 2009; Haringey Local Safeguarding Board, 2009; Radford, 2010; Lock, 2013; Lundberg, 2013). The subsequent findings and 'lessons learnt', reported in these SCRs, have consistently acknowledged a series of missed opportunities to intervene and act, by the agencies who had sight of the children and their families. The authors all refer to the lack of sharing information, poor communication and missed opportunities to intervene early in the children's lives, as key contributing factors, leading up to the tragic deaths. It seems the children, in many of the cases, could be considered to be '*invisible* . . .' (Ferguson, 2017; Lumsden, 2020). Evidence from research suggests that in cases where Social Workers were undertaking home visits, '*social workers were* (on some occasions *not child-focused*' (Ferguson, 2017, p. 1007). In the case of the tragic death of Daniel Pelka, Lumsden (2020, p. 108) considered that '*his* (Daniel's) *short life is a profound example of how infants and young children can be "invisible" even when they are "visible" to health and education professionals, social services and the police*'.

Creating a More Open-Listening Climate

My research explored how an open-listening climate in early years setting can facilitate child voice, and it provided a space to reflect on practice, from a multi-professional context of early years and family support. Lumsden (2020, p. 116) highlights the need for practitioners providing support services to:

> 'understand their role in supporting young children and their parents . . .' and 'Parents and caregivers need to be enabled . . . to enhance their parenting skills [with support] from practitioners and professionals'.

The importance of listening to children has been the subject of multiple studies (Clark & Moss, 2001, 2005; Lancaster & Broadbent, 2003; Clark et al., 2005; Dahlberg & Moss, 2007) while Bath (2013) suggests the concept of listening to children needs to be continually theorised by applying an alternative lens through which to consider the concept. Lyndon et al. (2019, p. 1) acknowledge '*there is yet to be a uniform definition of children's voices or listening practices*', however they go on to affirm the widely acknowledged understanding that '*listening is multi-modal, including non-verbal cues and requires interaction and response*'. In her article, Bath (2013) draws attention to the need to apply an ethical and rights-based perspective, when considering how children are listened to and how this may be achieved in early years practice, using reflection. Bath (2013) suggests considering a praxeological approach, as supported by Pascal and Bertram (2016) and others (Olivera-Formosinho & Formosinho, 2012; Lyndon et al., 2019; Gaywood et al., 2020) to develop our understanding of listening cultures or climates and to create early years education settings as democratic spaces where '*listening to and observing young children and parents is an integral part of understanding what they are feeling and experiencing, and what it is they need from their early education experience*' (Pascal & Bertram, 2016, p. 74). Henderson (2018, p. 24) reminds us:

> [I]t [listening to children's voices] is not a simple linear practice . . . there are indeed many ways to listen (as is attested by extensive research in the field) but it's left to the practitioners to take responsibility for how they listen as there is no 'A to Z' of listening.

Research conducted by Cath Arnold and the Pen Green Centre Team (2010) made the explicit link between emotional wellbeing and resilience, when reflecting on their early years services provided for families. They acknowledged the importance of '*dialogue . . . [and] hearing, acknowledging and respecting the views and experiences of parents*' (Whalley et al., 2013).

The focus of this chapter will be an illustration of how practitioners can develop a greater understanding of children and families' wellbeing through listening to their stories. Creating a more open-listening climate that places the child at the heart of their practice.

Theoretical Lenses

The concept of children's wellbeing was considered by weaving together two theoretical frameworks within the research. Bronfenbrenner's ecological model of development (Bronfenbrenner, 1979) reflects the emphasis on biological influences (Tudge et al., 2009) and the interrelatedness of the child's environment both at home and the early years setting, acknowledging the importance of connecting with significant adults in a child's life and applying a holistic lens to view the child's world. The Lundy Model of Child Participation (Lundy, 2007) was adopted and adapted and applied with adults participating in the research. This provided a child-rights lens through which to view the lived experience of children and their parents as well as exploring practice. Anning and Ball (2008, p. 11) reflect that Bronfenbrenner's ecological model was the '*underpinning theoretical model for the development of the Sure Start initiative* [later reformed into children's centres] *having been heavily influenced by the Head Start Programme*'. The model acknowledges the interrelatedness of a child's environment, relationships and their impact on a child's development and ultimately wellbeing. It illustrates the intrinsic connection between the quality of provision and practice (in this case early years services), childhood experiences and the overlap from wider influences that impact on the life of the child and family. My conceptualisation of the theoretical lenses in my study resonates with research conducted by others (Bronfenbrenner, 1979; Lundy,

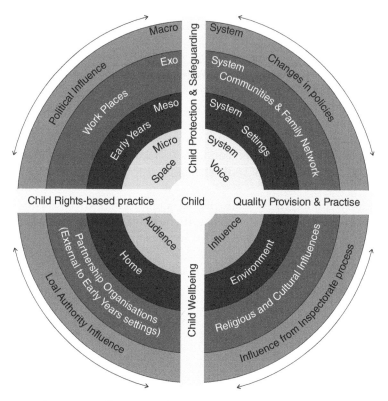

FIGURE 5.1 A conceptualisation of the theoretical lenses

Source: Adapted from Bronfenbrenner (1979), Lundy (2007) and Lansdown (2018)

2007; Lansdown, 2018) (Figure 5.1), and I applied a child-rights lens (Lundy, 2007), seen here in the micro-system, to 'wrap around' the child to ensure the child remained the focus of early years practice.

The Overarching Research Study

The aim of the overall study was to consider how an open-listening climate in early years settings can facilitate child voice. Through capturing the perspectives of the parents' lived experiences and those of their children, the study aimed to increase understanding about their lives before and after accessing support services. The aim of capturing the practitioners' perspectives of their practice, as considered through an early years and child-rights lenses, facilitated the exploration from multiple perspectives. This holistic approach helped to fuse together the relationship between the setting, including both early years and family support services and the parents. The aim was to influence practice by considering what changes may need to happen in order to create a more collaborative, open-listening climate in a multi-professional context. When applying a holistic approach from which to consider the concepts of child voice (Manning-Morton, 2014), I applied the four distinct lenses of:

- Child protection and safeguarding
- Quality provision and practice
- Child wellbeing and
- Child rights, which crossed through all layers of influence (Figure 5.1)

Participants and Context of the Study

Five parents (all mothers), 19 practitioners from early years and family support and four senior managers took part in the study. This chapter and the findings presented will focus on child wellbeing as illustrated through the portrait of one parent and their child and the perspectives captured from practitioners and senior managers that can be linked to the concept of a child's wellbeing and that of the parent.

The Lundy Model and accompanying participation check list (DCYA, 2015) were used during data collection and data analysis, and a further level of thematic analysis was applied, as informed by Braun and Clarke (2006, 2013). I adopted portraiture as a methodological approach to listening to parents' stories and as a method within research that I believe has the potential to ensure that children and families are 'made visible' in our services (Lumsden, 19 June 2020). The use of portraiture as considered by Cope et al. (2015, p. 6) '*enables the illustration of real people in real settings through the 'painting of their stories.*' I consider this methodological approach to 'sit comfortable' within a praxeological paradigm and one that assures that those telling their stories '*feel seen, fully attended to, recognised, appreciated and respected*' (Cope et al., p. 8). I used an artist's interpretation to further illustrate the parent's story, to capture the image portrayed before and after support.

General Findings

In this section on general findings, I will share the portrait of one parent and child, Paula and her son Ben (pseudonyms were used throughout the thesis) having applied the Lundy Model (2007) to analyse the parent's narrative of their lived experience. The remainder of the findings, in this section, reflect some of the practitioners' and senior managers' perspectives, from the focus groups and semi-structured interviews conducted. These illustrate the specific area of child and family wellbeing as this is the focus of this chapter.

78 Alison Moore

Paula and Ben's Portrait

Family Tree

Paula, aged 33, is a single mom with one son. She has one sister and her mom in her extended family who do not live in the City. Paula describes their contact as '*limited*'.

Paula starts her story describing her own challenged childhood, growing up with her own mother suffering from mental health and cancer, resulting in both Paula and her sister going in and out of care during their early childhood.

These early childhood experiences had a '*destructive*' impact on Paula, and as a teenager, she found herself involved with drugs, crime and in negative relationships that resulted in pregnancy. Paula ended up being given a custodial sentence while pregnant, and as a result, she had her son in a women's prison. She was eventually moved to a Mother & Baby Unit and then onto an open prison, which Paula describes this as '*having more*

FIGURE 5.2 Starting life behind bars

freedom' with her son to shop once a week and start to rehabilitate into the community

Key Challenges

Paula's son was two years old when she was released, and as her relationship with her own mom had broken down having had no contact with her for the previous six years, she was on her own with her son. Paula tried to rebuild their relationship but found it '*mentally draining . . . hard because of the past*', and she had to make the decision to start again somewhere new away from the past experiences to limit the chance of reoffending and going back to her old ways. Paula and her son were placed in a Mother & Baby hostel until being re-housed in her current property, knowing no one. Paula felt that she was alone with her son and referred to the challenges her son faced at this point; having been born in prison, he had very little awareness of danger of the roads, and she feared that he would get hurt. She described herself as '*depressed and lonely at this time, having had her own very destructive background*' [having] *gone in prison and come out with her son 'attached to her hip'*. While out in the local park one day, she met another mom with a young child who told her about the children's centre and offered to take her along.

Services and Support

Paula felt that she had a '*great deal going on*' that she wasn't playing enough with her son. So, the family support worker came into the home and modelled play with her son. So, the family support worker came into the home to address this. Paula had begun to drink again as she was '*lonely . . . and scared of history repeating itself*. The family support worker gave Paula support to seek additional help from an agency to support with her alcohol dependency. Paula described having a '*rapport*' with her family support worker. '*She supported me no matter what my background . . . she started to encourage me as I wanted to do social work and support others*'.

Paula was supported to go to college for an access course and eventually successfully achieved her degree. She was very proud of her achievement 'my *family support worker came to my graduation . . . she is a pretty amazing women . . . my inspiration and the only one who listened to me*'. Paula said that the consistency of one family support worker was the key, and although she knows she can ask for help if she isn't there, this constant in her life was important.

Feelings of Support and Services

Paula praised the children's centre services and family support worker, and although her son is now older and past the age of support from the centre, Paula knows she is still able to pick up the phone for advice. She still uses the centre to access a computer, when she was studying especially. Her son benefitted from the play in the home sessions as Paula needed to learn how to play with him. The services and support got her out of the house and address the loneliness Paula felt and connect her to other families in similar circumstances. Paula described her son as having challenging behaviour (especially about the roads), and the centre helped with this.

He attended the crèche when Paula attended courses which helped him play with other children. She has also been on trips to the seaside. Paula was able to get debt advice *'unfortunately this support stopped because of the cuts'* but Paula described, when she looked back at what she had received as having *'done a lot of work'*.

Impact

Paula referred to being *'reassured'* by the family support worker when times became difficult. The centre supported her son's social skills, and he eventually went to the nursery. Paula said, *'without the centre (she) probably would have been lost'*. She says she owes her *'morals, values and parenting'* to the Family Support Worker. Paula was helped to become a volunteer with Home Start, and this gave her the experience as an *'ex-offender when no one else would give her a chance'* and she then had the experience for her degree and to look for work.

Aspirations

Paula described herself as *'feeling like Britain in bloom . . . it gave me the reassurance that I needed to go on and put it all back . . . give it back by using my experiences'*. Paula says she is the *'first one to break the cycle'*. Paula has achieved her degree and gained a job as a Family Support Worker in another agency supporting vulnerable clients. Paula hopes to continue onto complete a Master's in education, but the finances are a barrier to higher education.

She spoke of the cuts at the centre over the last few years that meant she couldn't use the phone there if she needed it *'it's a joke really . . . the computer being restricted'* but always felt and still feels supported.

How to Create a More Open-Listening Climate **81**

Applying a Child-Rights Lens (Lundy, 2007; DCYA, 2015)

Paula and Ben's Portrait – Narrative of Space

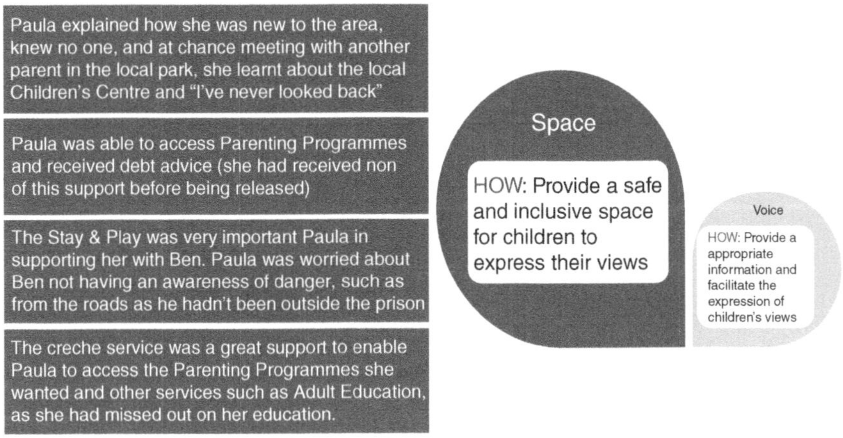

Paula explained how she was new to the area, knew no one, and at chance meeting with another parent in the local park, she learnt about the local Children's Centre and "I've never looked back"

Paula was able to access Parenting Programmes and received debt advice (she had received non of this support before being released)

The Stay & Play was very important Paula in supporting her with Ben. Paula was worried about Ben not having an awareness of danger, such as from the roads as he hadn't been outside the prison

The creche service was a great support to enable Paula to access the Parenting Programmes she wanted and other services such as Adult Education, as she had missed out on her education.

Space
HOW: Provide a safe and inclusive space for children to express their views

Voice
HOW: Provide a appropriate information and facilitate the expression of children's views

FIGURE 5.3 Narrative of space

Narrative of Voice

Paula and Ben's Portrait – Narrative of Voice

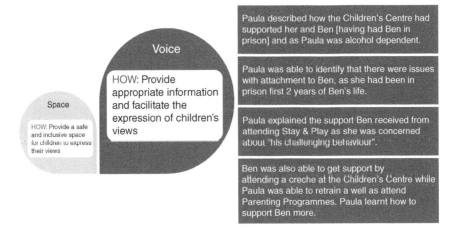

Voice
HOW: Provide appropriate information and facilitate the expression of children's views

Space
HOW: Provide a safe and inclusive space for children to express their views

Paula described how the Children's Centre had supported her and Ben [having had Ben in prison] and as Paula was alcohol dependent.

Paula was able to identify that there were issues with attachment to Ben, as she had been in prison first 2 years of Ben's life.

Paula explained the support Ben received from attending Stay & Play as she was concerned about "his challenging behaviour".

Ben was also able to get support by attending a creche at the Children's Centre while Paula was able to retrain a well as attend Parenting Programmes. Paula learnt how to support Ben more.

FIGURE 5.4 Narrative of voice

82 Alison Moore

Narrative of Audience

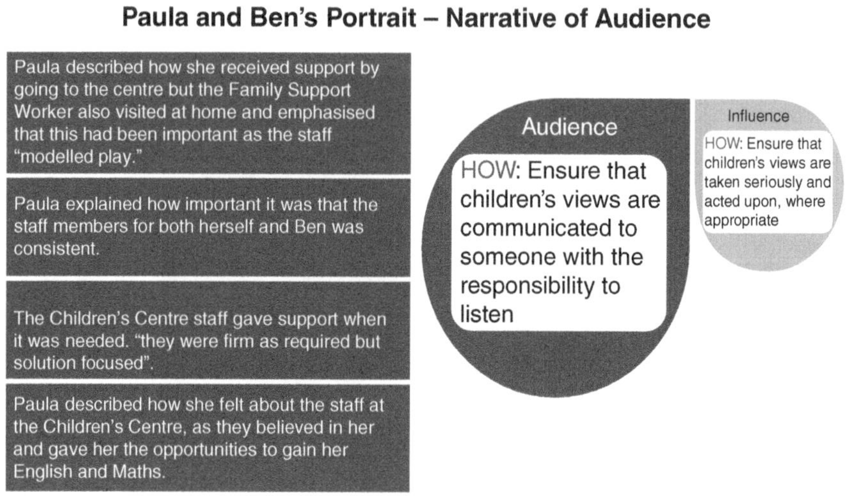

Paula and Ben's Portrait – Narrative of Audience

Paula described how she received support by going to the centre but the Family Support Worker also visited at home and emphasised that this had been important as the staff "modelled play."

Paula explained how important it was that the staff members for both herself and Ben was consistent.

The Children's Centre staff gave support when it was needed. "they were firm as required but solution focused".

Paula described how she felt about the staff at the Children's Centre, as they believed in her and gave her the opportunities to gain her English and Maths.

Audience
HOW: Ensure that children's views are communicated to someone with the responsibility to listen

Influence
HOW: Ensure that children's views are taken seriously and acted upon, where appropriate

FIGURE 5.5 Narrative of audience

Narrative of Influence

Paula and Ben's Portrait – Influence

Audience
HOW: Ensure that children's views are communicated to someone with the responsibility to listen

Influence
HOW: Ensure that children's views are taken seriously and acted upon, where appropriate

Paula was able to become a volunteer at a local Charity with the support of the Children's Centre and accessing further training.

By attending the Children's Centre Ben gained confidence and independence and he was able to socialise with other children.

Paula acknowledged their lives would have been very different without the Children's Centre.

Through being able to volunteer and then go on an acces course, Paula graduated with a degree and was able to secure a job as a Family Support Worker in an organisation supporting other vulnerable families.

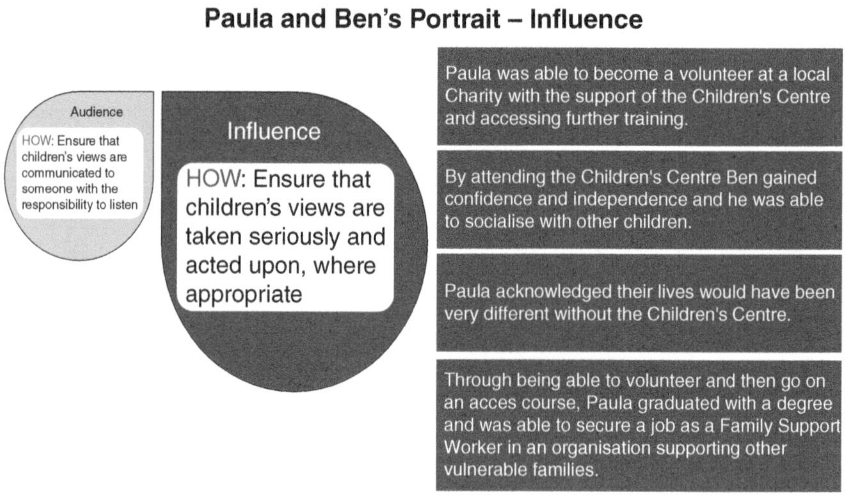

FIGURE 5.6 Narrative of influence

How to Create a More Open-Listening Climate 83

Paula and Ben's Portrait

FIGURE 5.7 Aspirations – a sense of pride

Practitioners' and Senior Managers' Perspectives

The narratives presented in this section of this chapter were drawn from data collected from the focus groups with early years and family support practitioners and senior managers, who took part in semi-structured interviews, across both Children's Centres. Applying the Lundy Model (2007), the Child Participation Checklist (DCYA, 2015) overlaid with Thematic Analysis (Braun & Clarke, 2006, 2013) provided a deeper level of analysis that can be considered as 'thick description' (Geertz, 1973). The themes highlighted, that were developed within the research study, will reflect on child wellbeing as a focus for this chapter. Coding is used throughout to ensure confidentiality, that is, Early Years Practitioners (EYP), Family Support Practitioner (FSP) and Senior Managers (SM).

Summary Discussion – Space

Creating a space for parents and children to be able to engage positively with the early years setting is clearly important and has been emphasised in both the parent and child's portrait and the practitioners' reflections on their practice.

Reflecting on child wellbeing: Key themes that developed – SPACE

1. Support Services
2. Home Visits and New Birth Visits
3. Making Children 'Visible'
   Subtheme: Observations and Recording
4. Relationships
   Subtheme: Communication

FIGURE 5.8 Presentation of themes – SPACE

Reflecting on child wellbeing: Key themes that developed – VOICE

1. Play
2. Multi-professional approach and assessment
3. Parent Partnership

FIGURE 5.9 Presentation of themes – VOICE

The need to develop trusting relationships with the parents and the children is evident, and as the findings show, '*the first encounter had been important in establishing relationships, a rapport and trust*' (Moore, 2020, p. 452). Listening to the 'lived experience' of Paula and Ben helps illustrate the complexities and critical periods in their lives and elicit meaning and the parent's and child's 'interpretation' of how they attribute these experiences. It also helps practitioners in developing an understanding of the potential impact these experiences may have had on their wellbeing.

Clark et al. (2005, p. 182) asked us to consider the '... *ethics of an encounter* ...' making the explicit link between the need to construct '...*a culture of listening* ...' and practitioners listening and developing relationships to support children's and adults' emotional wellbeing. The concept of creating a more open-listening climate in an early years setting was a core aspect examined in the main study. The practitioners' and senior managers' perspectives on their practice, in relation to space, provide some examples of how they consider they have created a 'listening culture', and they reflect on specific aspects of their work to emphasise the importance. Evans (2022, p. 12) considers that '*the starting point for creating spaces for the voices of young children to be heard begins with the ethos of the setting*', and the findings clearly show

How to Create a More Open-Listening Climate   85

how the environments and spaces can be created and why this is so important. Providing services, such as Baby Massage, Stay & Play and Creche support, were highlighted as significant spaces where relationships could be developed with parents and children. Paula identified with specific services that were provided for both herself and Ben to meet their needs at a specific moment in time and the difference this made to their emotional as well as physical wellbeing. The 'timing' of these encounters should not be underestimated, and in the case of Paula and Ben's story, it is evident that accessing the Children's Centre services came at a critical point in their lives and a pivotal emotional turning point.

While there was evidence of good practice models in relation to a 'listening climate' at both study sites, as the findings show, the research revealed *'a disconnect within the multi-professional context . . . resulting at times, in a*

EYP4	"[Creche,Stay & Play]...Have things planned and [just] provided with no expected outcome... let children feel able to do what they want... comfortable in the environment"
SM2	"I need to make sure the child is the focus again, we do get lost with all the paperwork, they [staff] are making an impact on children's lives"
FSP1	"Focus on the child on a home visit...Is there an opportunity for joint visits with Early Years or SENCO?" "we can make referrals to early years services...creche, holiday schemes"
FSP4	"Concentrate on the 'Red Book' [Personal Child Health Record] and make note of child's needs...complete a PreCaf"
EYP3	"Can ask them [parents] what they [child] are like at home..." "[Creche]...when a mom was worried their child wasn't speaking [Arabic or English] I was able to reassure mom when I went on a Book Start visit at home and heard the child speak Arabic"

FIGURE 5.10   A cluster selection of participants' reflections on child wellbeing

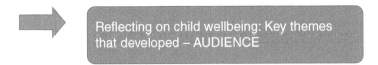

1. Support Services
   Subtheme: Working across teams
2. Parenting Programmes
3. Training

FIGURE 5.11   Presentation of themes – AUDIENCE

misdirection of focus away from the child's wellbeing and placing more emphasis on parental support' (Moore, 2021, p. iv). A key recommendation from the research was that

> organisations working with children in the context of early years, as well as within multi-professional teams, should [consider] adopting a child rights-based lens to facilitate child voice and efficacy by placing the child as the focus of the work.
>
> *(Moore, 2021, p. 238)*

Summary Discussion – Voice

Lundy (2007, p. 933) suggests, '*There is significant overlap between Space and Voice*', and the findings reflect how the two are interrelated, in practice. The critical incidents and adversities experienced by Paula, throughout her life, had in her own words '*a destructive impact* [growing up]' (Moore, 2021, p. 138). This had a detrimental effect on Paula's wellbeing, leading to alcohol and drug dependency and eventually a custodial sentence. It is important that Paula's voice was 'heard', and the right support services identified. Paula was acutely aware of the ongoing issues she faced in respect of depression,

SM1	"Who will support them [children], us everyone, I think we've all got the' power'... like when they say it takes a village to raise a child"
SM3	"Staff are continually discussing with one another what they have heard or seen and then acting upon this... this is evidenced by how the nursery environment is created... the child centred approach and the chanes we make"
EYP4	"[need to] share experiences... [early years] go on home visits and [family support] attend early years' services... there should not be a barrier"
FSP6	"Encouraging the families to come out of the home environment... doesn't matter how busy we are... help the family, help the child"
FS12	"[Home Visit] focus on the child... give support and encouragement to parent... [Targeted Parenting Programme] help parents to understand the impact of a challenging environment has on the child... support them to get out of the environment"
FSP11	"[It's a] Learning curve... we have the 'power' [as the audience] it's whether we recognise that... need to share information"
EYP2	"Always room for improvement... Staff need to communicate with each other [especially] when they have concerns... you can read a report [on the electronic recording system] but there needs to be communication [between teams]"

FIGURE 5.12 A cluster selection of participants' reflections on child wellbeing

Reflecting on child wellbeing: Key themes that developed – INFLUENCE

1. Safeguarding
   Subtheme: Record Keeping
   Safe Environment
2. Partnership Working

FIGURE 5.13 Presentation of themes – INFLUENCE

isolation and the effects of poor attachment, due to the circumstances of Ben's birth, affecting her ability to bond with Ben. What was essential is that Ben's voice, in the broadest sense, was 'heard' (UN, 1989; Clark & Moss, 2001; Clark et al., 2005; Lundy, 2007; Wall et al., 2019). The themes developed from the perspectives of practitioners and senior managers reflect that a range of strategies and opportunities were created to identify Ben's needs. Providing early years support through play experiences for Ben gave some assurance that Ben was '*visible*' in the service [(Lumsden, 2020, p. 108). Some examples were given of a multi-professional approach, at both study sites; however, the findings suggest aspects of practice could be improved. It was acknowledged that early years practitioners were able to provide greater opportunities to engage with children and parents together and such as using observation and play environments, to 'listen to' and respond effectively. A further recommendation was to

> adopt the Lundy Model of Child Participation . . . [as a theoretical framework] to bridge the gap between multi-professional teams. . . . Explore every opportunity for collaboration across the teams, through professional dialogue and integration of daily practice.
>
> *(Moore, 2021, p. 238)*

Summary Discussion – Audience

A recurring theme across the findings was the interconnectedness of Centre Provision and the Home Environment and both were considered of equal importance, with the need to consider the explicit links between '*the early learning environment, both the home and early years setting*' (Hayes et al., 2017, p. 3). The main premise of Bronfenbrenner's ecological model (1979), and his later research (Bronfenbrenner and Morris, 1998, 2006), was the need for a child to be the focus of our practice, while acknowledging the interconnectedness of the relationships between other aspects of the child's lived experiences, including the family and early years setting. In respect of 'who are the audience?', the findings from the portrait and practitioners' and senior manager's perspectives on their practice acknowledge *'the multi-perspectives and the bi-directional influences . . . the child and parent's immediate life circumstances and the environment'* (Moore, 2021, p. 26).

Paula found it invaluable to have the centre accessible for herself and Ben, while also seeing the importance of home visits and the staff being able to *'model play'*. The need for *'firm yet supportive staff . . .* [and] *consistent key worker/s'* was important, to support the wellbeing of them both.

The research shows how important it is for *'parents and children to have an appropriate and effective audience . . . when* [creating] *an open listening climate'* (Moore, 2020, p. 453) and developing responsive services to meet the needs. Paula was aware of the impact of the lived experiences and home environment, on Ben's wellbeing, and this was considered very important. A key aspect of the research was parents identifying themselves as the audience for listening to their children.

While the findings reflect examples of good practice within both early years and family support services, supported by the senior managers, it was less evident how a multi-professional and holistic approach, to supporting children and parents' wellbeing, was achieved. The research suggests *'developing collaborative practices to provide a seamless and coherent approach to facilitate a more open listening climate to facilitate child voice'* (Moore, 2021, p. 238).

FSP6	"Never 'lose' the family... doesn't matter how busy we are... importance of safeguarding"
FSP4	"Safe environment... children's safety... checking health and safety on home visits and making sure the home is a safe environment"
FSP8	["Team Around the Child Meetings]... well-structed and lead by the Children's Centres and focused on the child... other agencies 'shy' away from taking the lead, it always comes back to the Children's Centre"
SM1	"I definitely want more joint working with early years and family support... so changing the way we have always worked [separate]... it is crucial for the children and parents"
EYP6	"Need to work closely with nurseries and schools–link to the whole family and older children"
EYP4	"[need to improve] collaboration between departments and have joint team meetings"

FIGURE 5.14 A cluster selection of participant s' reflections on child wellbeing

Summary Discussion – Influence

It is evident from the findings, shared in this chapter on child wellbeing, that the support that Paula and Ben received made a great difference to their lives and life chances, influenced by the study sites, specific services and by Paula and Ben themselves. The portrait reflects the achievements that Paula made, graduating with her degree, despite the adversities and challenges of her own childhood. Paula was clear on her aspirations and what she wanted for the wellbeing of Ben and with the support from the services, as well as reaching out to other partner agencies, Paula reached her initial 'goals'. Early years practitioners were able to clearly articulate the aspects of their roles and specific service provision where they felt they were able to influence children's development and meet the needs of children and Family Support practitioners identified key aspects of their role, that is, creating a *'Team around the child'*, and delivering targeted support services alongside home visiting, to support parents. Strategically, senior managers acknowledged the role they had to play in managing and leading good practice and were evidently committed to improving collaborative work practices while acknowledging this would need to be operationally from within and across the services as well as strategically with the support of management boards, partners and the local authority.

The research suggests that a solution to supporting these developments would be:

> To undertake training and continual professional development that underpins previous recommendations . . . developing a greater understanding of child rights and the UNCRC and implantation in practice . . . [and] . . . how child voice can best be facilitated through creating a more open listening climate.
>
> *(Moore, 2021, p. 239)*

Conclusion

In the doctoral research, which inspired me to write this chapter on perspectives of child wellbeing in early years, I advocate applying an early years and child rights-based approach when considering how to create a more open-listening climate in early years settings and in a multi-professional context. Adopting the Lundy Model of Child Participation (2007) in my research with adults, in this case the parents' and practitioners, has been acknowledged as being '*a powerful new area of research*' (Swadener, 2020, p. 393). My innovative way of listening to parents' and children's lived experience before and after accessing support services was inspired using Portraiture to tell their stories (Lawrence-Lightfoot, 1983). The use of portraiture, as introduced earlier in this chapter has, I believe, given 'voice' to both parents and their children, reflecting an empowering and praxeological approach in research. Applying portraiture in my research assured that I was *'engaged in a discourse between two mutually informative aspects of the methodology . . . the act of collecting and making sense of the data'* (Lawrence-Lightfoot & Hoffmann Davis, 1997, p. 60).

It is evident that there are examples of good practice models in place in relation to supporting children's and parent's wellbeing which supports the view that *'early years settings, using a multi-disciplinary approach with other services, have an important role in supporting families and parents'* (Manning-Morton, 2014, p. 144). It has also been acknowledged that more can be done to ensure that a holistic approach is applied when working within a multi-professional context to ensure that the wellbeing of children remain the priority while also recognising the need to support parent's wellbeing.

When reflecting on how children and adults build resilience, research conducted by the Centre of the Developing Child suggests that there are protective factors that

> help children achieve positive outcomes in the face of significant adversity . . . and [when] families strengthen these factors, they optimize resilience across multiple contexts. . . . Adults who strengthen skills in themselves can model positive behaviors for their children, thereby improving the resilience of the next generation.
>
> *(Centre on the Developing Child, n.b.)*

The findings in this chapter illustrate several of the protective factors considered to be of importance in supporting children and adults to develop resilience over time. Of key importance is the need to develop supportive relationships with responsive adults by accessing a range of high-quality and positive early experiences. Important policy and procedural recommendations, at both a strategic and operational level, may be extracted from the main findings, as illustrated by the parent and child's portrait and practitioners' and senior managers' perspectives of their practice.

References

Abbott, L., & Langston, A. (2005). *Parents matter supporting the birth to three matters framework*. Open University Press.

Allen, G. (2011, January). *Early intervention: The next steps (404489/0111)* [Online]. Cabinet Office. Retrieved April 10, 2012, from http://www.dwp.gov.uk/docs/early-intervetionnextsteps

Anning, A., & Ball, M. (2008). *Improving services for young children: From sure start to children's centres*. SAGE Publications.

Arnold, C., & The Pen Green Centre Team. (2010). *Understanding schemas and emotion in early childhood*. Sage.

Bath, C. (2013). Conceptualising listening to young children as an ethic of care in early childhood education and care. *Children & Society, 27*, 361–371.

Bradford, H. (2012). *Appropriate environments for children under three*. Routledge.

Braun, V., & Clarke, V. (2006). Using thematic analysis in psychology. *Qualitative Research in Psychology*, *3*(2), 77–101. https://www.tandfonline.com/doi/abs/10.1191/1478088706qp063oa

Braun, V., & Clarke, V. (2013). *Successful qualitative research. A practical guide for beginners*. SAGE Publications.

Bronfenbrenner, U. (1979). *The ecology of human development*. Harvard University Press.

Bronfenbrenner, U., & Morris, P. (1998). The ecology of developmental processes. In W. Damon & R. M. Lerner (Eds.), *Handbook of child psychology: Vol. 1. Theoretical models of human development* (pp. 993–1028). Wiley and Son.

Bronfenbrenner, U., & Morris, P. (2006). The bioecological model of human development. In R. M. Lerner & W. E. Damon (Eds.), *Handbook of child psychology: Vol. 1. Theoretical models of human development* (6th ed., pp. 793–828). John Wiley and Sons.

Burke, H. (2018). The deepest well: Healing the long-term effects of childhood adversity. Bluebird.

Casey, B. (2012). Children's well-being: Priorities and considerations. *Journal of Child Health Care*, *16*(2), 107–108. https://journals.sagepub.com/doi/pdf/10.1177/1367493512451061

Centre on the Developing Child. (n.b.). *In brief: The science of resilience*. https://developingchild.harvard.edu/resources/inbrief-resilience-series

Clark, A., Kjørholt, A, T., & Moss, P. (2005). *Beyond listening children's perspectives on early childhood services*. The Policy Press.

Clark, A., & Moss, P. (2001). *Listening to young children: The Mosaic approach*. National Children's Bureau.

Clarke, A., & Moss, P. (2005). *Spaces to play: More listening to children using the Mosaic approach*. National Children's Bureau.

Conkbayir, M. (2017). *Early childhood and neuroscience: Theory, research and implications for practice*. Bloomsbury.

Conkbayir, M. (2023). *The neuroscience of the developing child. Self-Regulation for wellbeing and a sustainable future*. Routledge.

Cope, V., Jones, B., & Hendricks, J. (2015). Portraiture: A methodology through which success and positively can be explored and reflected. *Nurse Researcher*, *22*(3), 6–12.

Dahlberg, G., & Moss, P. (2007, January). *Beyond quality in early childhood education and care – languages of evaluation*. CESifo DICE Report. https://doi.org/10.4324/9780203966150

Department for Children, Schools and Families (DCSF). (2007). *Sure start children's centres: Phase 3 planning and delivery* [Online]. Ref: 00665–2007BKT-EN. Retrieved October 2, 2017, from http://webarchive.nationalarchives.gov.uk/20100609115022/http://www.dcsf.gov.uk/everychildmatters/publications/documents/laesurestartchildrenscentresphase3planningdelivery/

Department of Children and Youth Affairs [DCYA]. (2015, June 17). *National strategy on children and young people's participation in decision making 2015–2020*. Retrieved April 1, 2017, from http://dcya.gov.ie/documents/palyandrec/20150617NatStatParticipationReportpdf

Dermody, A., Gardner, C., Davis, S., Lambert, S., Dermody, J., & Fein, M. (2018). Resilience in the face of trauma: Implications for service delivery. *Irish Probation Journal*, *15*, 161–177. Research Gate.

Elfer, P., & Dearnley, K. (2007). Nurseries and emotional wellbeing: Evaluating an emotionally containing model of professional development. *Early Years*, *27*(3), 267–279. https://doi.org/10.1080/09575140701594418

Evans, E. (2022). Under threes as active meaning-makers in England. In L. Arnott & K. Wall (Eds.), *The theory and practice of voice in early childhood*. An international exploration (pp. 11–19). Routledge.

Ferguson, H. (2017). How children become invisible in child protection work: Findings from research into day-to-day social work practice. *British Journal of Social Work, 47*, 1007–1023.

Field, F. (2010). *The foundation years: Preventing poor children becoming poor adults. The report of the independent review of poverty and life chances.* HM Government. Retrieved May 12, 2011, from http://www.frankfield.co.uk

Garvey, D. (2017). *Nurturing personal, social and emotional development in early childhood: A practical guide to understanding brain development and young children's behaviour.* Jessica Kingsley Publications.

Gaywood, D., Bertram, T., & Pascal, C. (2020). Involving refugee children in research: Emerging ethical and positioning issues. *European Early Childhood Research Journal, 28*(1), 149–162. Special edition children and families with migrant/refugee background in ECEC services Chiara Bove and Nima Sharmahd (guest Eds). http://doi.org/10.1080/1350293x.2020.1707369

Geertz, C. (1973). *The interpretations of cultures.* Basic Books.

Haringey Local Safeguarding Board. (2009). *Serious case review: Baby Peter.* https://www.basw.co.uk/system/files/resources/basw_111257-10_0.pdf

Hayes, N., O'Toole, L., & Halpenny, A. M. (2017). *Introducing Bronfenbrenner a guide for practitioners and students in early years education.* Routledge.

Henderson, E. (2018). *Autoethnography in early years childhood education and care. Narrating the heart of practice.* Routledge.

Laming, L. (2003). *The Victora Climbiè inquiry report of an inquiry by Lord Laming.* HMSO.

Laming, L. (2009). *The protection of children in England: A progress report by Lord Laming.* HMSO.

Lancaster, Y. P., & Broadbent, V. (2003). *Listening to young children.* Open University Press.

Lansdown, G. (2018). *Conceptual framework for measuring outcomes of adolescent participation.* UNICEF.

Lawrence-Lightfoot, S. (1983). *The good high school: Portraits of character and culture.* Basic Books.

Lawrence-Lightfoot, S., & Hoffmann Davis, J. (1997). *The art and science of portraiture.* Jossey-Bass.

Lock, R. (2013). *Serious case review Re: Daniel Pelka.* Coventry Safeguarding Children Board.

Lumsden, E. (2020). The (IN) visibility of infants and young children. In J. Murray, B. B. Swadener, & K. Smith (Eds.), *The Routledge international handbook of young children's rights* (pp. 107–119). Routledge.

Lundberg, B. (2013). *Serious case review in respect of the death of Keanu Williams.* Birmingham Children's Safeguarding Board.

Lundy, L. (2007). 'Voice' is not enough: Conceptualising article 12 of the United Nations convention of the rights of the child. *British Educational Research Journal, 33*(6), 927–942.

Luthar, S., & Cicchetti, D. (2007). The construct of resilience: Implications for interventions and social policies. *Development and Psychopathology, 12*(4), 857–885. https://doi.org/10.1017/s0954579400004156 (Original work published 2000)

Lyndon, H., Bertram, T., Brown, Z., & Pascal, C. (2019). Pedagogically mediated listening practices: The development of pedagogy through the development of trust. *European Early Education Research Journal, 27*(3), 360–370. http://doi.org/10.1080/1350293x.2019.1600806

Manning-Morton, J. (2014). *Exploring well-being in the early years.* The Open University Press.

Marmot, M. (2010). *Fair society, healthy lives the Marmot review* [Online]. Retrieved April 20, 2012, from http://www.instituteofhealthequity.org/resources-reports/

fair-society-healthy-lives-themarmotreview/fair-society-healthy-lives-full-report-pdf.pdf

Mashford-Scott, A., Church, A., & Tayler, C. (2012, November 7). *Seeking children's perspectives on their wellbeing in early childhood settings*. Springer Science+Business Media.

Masten, A. (2011). Resilience in children threatened by extreme adversity: Frameworks for research, practice, and translational synergy. *Development and Psychopathology, 23*(2), 493–506. https://doi.org/10.1017/S095457411000198

Mayr, T., & Ulich, M. (2009). Social-emotional well-being and resilience of children in early childhood settings – PERIK: An empirically based observation scale for practitioners. *Early Years Journal of International Research & Development, 29*(1), 45–57.

Moore, A. (2020). How to create an open listening climate. Using the Lundy model of child participation with adults. In J. Murray, B. B. Swadener, & K. Smith (Eds.), *The Routledge international handbook of young children's rights* (pp. 447–459). Routledge.

Moore, A. (2021). *Parents' and practitioners' perspectives on how an open listening climate in early years settings can facilitate child voice* [PhD thesis, Birmingham City University in Collaboration with the Centre for Research in Early Childhood (CREC)].

Morrow, V., & Mayall, B. (2009). What is wrong with children's well-being in the UK? Questions of meaning and measurement. *Journal of Social Welfare and Family Law, 31*(3), 217–229.

Olivera-Formosinho, J., & Formosinho, J. (2012). Praxeological research in early childhood: A contribution to a social science of the social. *European Early Childhood Education Research Journal, 20*(4), 471–476.

Oliveria-Formosinho, J., and Formosinho, J. (2016). Pedagogy-in-participation the search for a holistic praxis. In J. Formoshino & C. Pascal (Eds.), *Assessment and evaluation for transformation in early childhood* (pp. 26–55). Routledge.

Page, J. (2011). Do mothers want professional careers to love their babies? *Journal of Early Childhood Research, 9*(3), 310–323. https://journals.sagepub.com/doi/epdf/10.1177/1476718X11407980

Pascal, C., & Bertram, T. (2016). The nature and purpose of assessment and evaluation within participatory pedagogy. In J. Formosinho & C. Pascal (Eds.), *Assessment and evaluation for transformation in early childhood* (pp. 59–92). Routledge.

Pollard, E. L., & Lee, P. D. (2003). Child well-being: A systematic review of the literature. *Social Indicators Research, 61*(1), 59–78.

Radford, J. (2010). *Serious case review under chapter VIII 'Working together to safeguard children': In respect of the death of a child: Case number 14*. Birmingham Safeguarding Children Board.

Roberts, R. (2007). *Companionable learning: The development of resilient wellbeing from birth to three* [Online] [PhD thesis, University of Worcester in Association with Coventry University]. Retrieved May 10, 2014, from https://eprints.worc.ac.uk/511/1/Rosie_Roberts_complete_thesis.pdf

Roberts, R. (2010). *Wellbeing from Birth*. SAGE Publications.

Sunderland, H. (2019). Supporting toddlers' wellbeing: Reflections on the impact of the toddler wellbeing (ToWE) project. *TACTYC Reflections: 2019 Reflections*. http://www.tactyc.org.uk/reflections/

Swadener, B. B. (Ed.). (2020). Introduction young children's participation rights. In J. Murray, B. B. Swadener, & K. Smith (Eds.), *The Routledge international handbook of young children's rights* (pp. 389–394). Routledge.

Thane, P. (2011, October 6). *The history of early years childcare based on a presentation at the department of education*. http://www.historyandpolicy.org/seminars/seminar/department-for-education-series-1-2011-12

Toros, K., Tart, K., & Falch-Eriksen, A. (2021). Collaboration of child protective services and early childhood educators: Enhancing the well-being of children in need. *Early Childhood Education Journal*, 995–1006. https://doi.org/10.1007/s10643-020-01149-y

Tudge, J. R. H., Mokrava, I., Hatfield, B. E., & Karnik, R. B. (2009). Uses and misuses of Bronfenbrenner's bioecological theory of human development. *Journal of Family Theory and Review*, *1*(4), 198–210. https://onlinelibrary.wiley.com/doi/abs/10.1111/j.1756-2589.2009.00026.x

UN. (1989). *Convention on the rights of the child*. Retrieved April 2013, from https://www.unicef.org.uk/rights-respectingschools/wpcontent/uploads/sites/4/2017/01/Summary-of-the-UNCRC.pdf

Wall, K., Cassidy, C., Robinson, C., Hall, E., Beaton, M., Kanyal, M., & Mitra, D. (2019). Look who's talking: Factors for considering the facilitation of very young children's voices. *Journal of Early Childhood Research*, *17*(4), 263–278. https://journals.sagepub.com/doi/10.1177/1476718X19875767

Waters, J. (2009). Wellbeing. In T. Walker (Ed.), *An introduction to early childhood* (2nd ed.). SAGE Publications.

The WAVE Trust. (2014). *1001 critical days: The importance of the conception to age two period June 2014 a cross party manifesto: Andrea Leadsom MP, Frank Field MP, Paul Burstow MP, Caroline Lucas MP*. http://www.wavetrust.org/1001-criticaldays-the-importance-of-the-conception-to-age-two-period

Whalley, M., Arnold, C., Orr, R., & The Pen Green Team. (2013). *Working with families in children's centres and early years settings*. Hodder Education.

Zeeedyk, S. (2020). *Sabre tooth tigers and teddy bears: The connected baby guide to attachment*. Connected Baby Ltd.

6
RESILIENCE AND CHILDREN WITH DISABILITIES

The Role of Positive Relationships and Friendships

Kyriakos Demetriou

Introduction

The ability to cope with adverse situations is directly related to resilience since individuals with resilience are those who are able to resist and recover from challenges. As children develop resilience, they become more capable of accepting challenges, coping with frustration and overcoming failure. Several adaptation strategies improve the child's circumstances under adverse conditions and, therefore, allow the child to cope better. Two examples that are considered adaptive coping strategies are problem-solving skills and asking for help from others (Folostina et al., 2015).

However, children's ability to respond to challenges and adverse circumstances varies. In the case of children with disabilities, many argue that the possession of such coping skills is minimal or non-existent. They often interpret this because of the disability per se. However, Reivich and Shatte (2002) stress that there is no dichotomy between resilient and non-resilient people. It is rather a matter of having coping skills in varying degrees that differ from individual to individual. Thus, children with disabilities, as every child, are born with an innate capacity for resilience (Zolkoski & Bullock, 2012). This capacity for resilience depends on a variety of environmental factors that may enable or disable its development (Alvord & Grados, 2005). These environmental factors involve several resources that the individual will utilise in order to overcome and manage risks. These resources come from their families, friendship circles, communities, as well as the larger society (Murray & Doren, 2013).

This chapter aims to explore resilience in children with disabilities, with emphasis on positive relationships and the formation of friendships between children with and without disabilities, as important elements in building resilience in such populations. The importance of friendships in the lives of children with disabilities and the challenges of this are explored through the literature and lead to discussions about the role of early years provision. The practice of enhancing resilience and wellbeing through enabling positive relationships with peers, boosting acceptance and promoting friendships between children with and without disabilities in inclusive settings is explored.

Resilience in the Case of Children With Disabilities

Resilience as a psychological term remains a contested concept when it comes to the lives of children with disabilities. Runswick-Cole and Goodley (2013) argue that the traditional approaches to understanding resilience contributes to the discrimination and marginalisation that children with disabilities often face. This is mainly due to the misconception that those who are disabled are 'vulnerable' and 'passive', thus they are seen as less or even not 'resilient'. Yet children with disabilities who manage to do things that are usually expected of children with disabilities are automatically considered to be 'resilient'.

This erroneous impression that resilience is absent in the lives of most people with disabilities is confirmed by several studies (e.g. Dunn & Dougherty, 2005; Prilletenksy, 2009). Children with disabilities are often included on the list of children who are at-risk along with those who experience hardships such as poverty, abuse, violence and illness. Such adverse events are seen as potential hazards and are considered as risk factors that increase the possibility of negative early life experiences (Ofiesh & Mather, 2013). It is apparent that children with disabilities are often exposed to negative experiences within the school environment, as well as experiencing challenges in several aspects of their development (Montague et al., 2008). These challenges most likely affect their academic competence and self-confidence (Nalavany et al., 2011), something that may put them at risk of being negatively stigmatised.

On the contrary, there are studies supporting the view that individuals who manage to succeed despite the hardships, suffering and exposure to adversity and challenges – including those with disabilities – are considered resilient (Goldstein & Rider, 2013). Masten (2001) believes that resilience-related skills can be possessed by every child either with a disability or not, provided that a child's basic adaptational systems are not compromised in any way. Fee and Hinton (2011) found that the vast majority of children diagnosed with a progressive and eventually fatal chronic neuromuscular disorder who participated in their study appeared to be resilient despite the adversity that they experienced. In addition, there are longitudinal studies that explored the factors that contribute to resilience of individuals with disabilities. Zolkoski and Bullock (2012) found that resilience is an attribute that can be found in such individuals and that resilient disabled youth look for personal control over their lives, are willing to seek out and accept support, set their own goals, possess a strong will to succeed and demonstrate high levels of persistence. This confirms Werner's (1989) finding that many 'high-risk' children developed into 'healthy' adults despite the environmental disadvantages they were exposed to during their childhood. Her findings have been applied to the case of individuals with chronic illness who are characterised as 'resilient' if they manage to adapt and adjust despite the difficulties.

Studies in the 2000s began applying the risk and resilience framework – which categorises several factors into risk factors and protective factors – to the social domain of learning disabilities (Wong, 2003). Among protective factors, Cosden et al. (2002) include non-academic strengths of a children with disabilities such as positive temperament, physical attractiveness, social behaviour, athletic skills, supportive and effective parents and teachers, and self-understanding. Other studies highlight a number of 'success attributes' that operate as protective factors and contribute to children's resilience (McNamara & Willoughby, 2010). An example of a success attribute is the ability of children with disabilities to maintain a positive self-concept despite their learning difficulties. Ofiesh and Mather (2013) interpret this as self-acknowledgement of the academic nature of their difficulties, a perception that somehow protects their self-concept and self-worth.

The presence of a learning disability was considered as a risk factor that, on the one hand, may increase the possibility of producing negative outcomes but, on the other hand, a learning disability on its own cannot be a predictor of future behaviour (Cosden et al., 2002). It is apparent that a combination of other aspects linked to the social environment of the child (i.e. personal, familial and social aspects) may determine future behaviours and social, academic and vocational outcomes. This is because the interpretation of risk differs cross-culturally, as it depends on interwoven individual and environmental factors. In other words, how risk is perceived and defined is of great importance when it comes to 'being risky' children with disabilities. For instance, children and their families are at risk of isolation when they are excluded from groups and activities. Therefore, the opportunities to take risks as part of playful activities (i.e. climb a tree) become fewer. However, there is a contradiction here as individuals with disabilities experience discrimination, exclusion and even violence in their communities, encounters that can be considered as exposure to high levels of risk (Goodley & Runswick-Cole, 2011). Of course, people who have power and control over their lives are far more likely to take risks. Nonetheless, the amount of power and control that individuals with disabilities have differs cross-culturally. Therefore, it is critical to understand risk in terms of how society and culture respond to disabilities, rather than as something dependent on the presence of an impairment in an individual.

Disability Studies and Resilience

Several negative assumptions and deficit-focused models about children growing up in adversity – including children with disabilities – have been underlined in traditional research on resilience in development (Masten, 2001). Bearing this argument in mind, further research is of significance to our exploration. Understanding of resilience descends from the field of medicine. In the 1970s, the first research studies on resilience in the behavioural sciences made their appearance (Zolkoski & Bullock, 2012). Although, contemporary research on resilience focuses on children's wellbeing and the promotion of resilience through prevention, intervention and policy change, there is a long history of research connecting resilience with attempts to understand and prevent the development of psychopathology, as well as research focusing on treatment of mental health problems which were seen as major threats to development (Masten, 2007). It is worth mentioning here that viewing disability through the lens of medicalisation implies that disability is a personal tragedy without paying any attention to the obstacles that society places in the way of people with disabilities. These views perpetuate a generally negative attitude and stigma towards disability resulting in the unfair treatment of people with disabilities in every aspect of their life, including the educational system (Demetriou, 2022).

As mentioned earlier, the notion of risk has been associated with resilience. In essence, Masten (2001) argues that exposure to risks and adverse conditions is a prerequisite to the level of resilience of an individual. Characteristically, she states that 'individuals are not considered resilient if there has never been a significant threat to their development, there must be current or past hazards judged to have the potential to derail normative development' (p. 228). This implies that in order to characterise an individual child – from a background that is considered 'at risk'– as 'resilient', the child must somehow succeed in his/her life despite all the challenges (Runswick-Cole & Goodley, 2013). Although Masten's work and ecological approaches to resilience have been influential in the field, they received some criticism, especially when it comes to the applications of the predictable and causal relationships between 'risk' and 'protective' factors in the case of people with disabilities and the relationships between the individual and their environment. One of the criticisms that such approaches receive has to do with their failure in interpreting the constructions and connotations of the terms: 'vulnerability' and 'risk'. Therefore, resilience as a concept becomes problematic when referring to individuals with disabilities because such individuals are often considered not to develop 'normally' due to an impairment that makes them dependent on medical, other professionals and other individuals without disabilities. As a result, their dependency prevents them from exposure to risk but also from acquiring coping skills that would otherwise include them in the category of 'resilient' (Runswick-Cole & Goodley, 2013).

In the field of disability studies, resilience is seen as a politically recognised notion that is associated with self-advocacy (Goodley, 2005). However, self-advocacy implies the right of self-determination of individuals who are considered as having a disability. This right is often not attributed to them as individuals but as members of a group of fellows. Thus, this right recognises the capacity of those groups to be independent from service providers and professionals when it comes to decision-making, but not the capacity of individuals with disabilities when it comes to their self-determination. Goodley points out that '*resilience often exists in spite of disablement*, outside self-advocacy groups and in response to a disabling community. Consequently, the term "self-advocate" may emphasise "otherness" by giving the impression that people with learning difficulties only exhibit self-advocacy in self-advocacy groups' (pp. 333–334).

Having said this, we understand that there is an impression that people with disabilities are the weak ones who are given power by the self-claimed powerful ones (Goodley, 2005) and that they are not resilient enough when they act independently. Thus, when several stakeholders intend to 'empower' people with disabilities, there is a risk of maintaining the victim status that they are often attributed (Goodley & Moore, 2000). Bearing this in mind, we can see that a focus on resilience in the lives of people with disabilities runs the risk of transferring blame and responsibility to those people who lack the individual characteristics that lead to resilience. Our emphasis should be rather placed on the negative societal attitudes and systems that maintain oppressive environments for people with disabilities (Young et al., 2008).

The Role of Environmental Factors and Sources of Resilience

Resilience research has shown that a child's ability to deal with adverse situations varies over time depending on biological, psychological and environmental influences as well as the exchanges between them. The role of various individual and environmental factors has been studied and conceptualised through models such as Bronfenbrenner's (1979) social-ecological systems theory and Garmezy's (1985) model of risk and resilience. These models can be applied in our attempts to interpret the impact of the several environmental factors (family, peers, etc.) on the children's holistic development.

Regarding these factors, a child's temperament, predisposition to stress and level of anxiety are among the biological factors. Children's ability to think positively in adverse conditions is affected by psychological factors, including ideas about their own personal value and competence, as well as expectations regarding social support and beliefs about the world in which they live. A child's environment can have a significant effect on his or her development by satisfying the child's needs such as love, acceptance, protection, safety, shelter and food (Folostina et al., 2015).

Ungar (2007) suggests deconstructing resilience and reconstructing it again in a way that is enabling for individuals with disabilities by considering the resources that reinforce resilience. He adopts a constructivist approach to resilience and defines it as 'the outcome from negotiations between individuals and their environments for the resources to define themselves as healthy amidst conditions collectively viewed as adverse' (Ungar, 2004, p. 242). In other words, the resources that are available to individuals will determine how they, and whether they are able to, express resilience. Such resources have to do with access to material resources, relationships, identity, power and control, cultural adherence, social justice and cohesion.

Focusing on the accessibility that children with disabilities have in the aforementioned resources is of great importance. Apparently, in order to reinforce resilience in the lives of children with disabilities, efforts should be made not only at individual and family levels but also to counterbalance the misbalances caused societal barriers (i.e. attitudinal and structural barriers) that maintain oppression in the lives of people with disabilities (Young et al., 2008). King et al. (2003) introduce a conceptual model of the factors affecting the recreation and leisure participation of children with disabilities, as a key step towards counterbalancing the misbalances due to barriers that maintain oppression in the lives of people with disabilities. One of the factors of their model refers to the importance of the presence of supportive relationships for the child. The more positive and supportive the relationships of a child with disabilities, the better the child's emotional, behavioural and social function, and therefore, child participation in daily activities is achieved.

Positive Relationships and Friendships as Sources of Resilience

The fact that many children with disabilities manage to improve their academic and social status in adulthood is an indication that people with disabilities can succeed in life and highlights the key role that environmental protective factors play in order for them to have such positive adult outcomes (Wong, 2003).

For each child to have the best possible quality of life, it is valuable to understand what may contribute to resilience. One of the attributes of resilient children is being socially competent. Social competence includes empathy, care, communication skills and a sense of humour (Zolkoski & Bullock, 2012). These are attributes that allow competent children to form positive relationships and social bonds with adults and peers in their environment. In fact, healthy interactions between the individual and family, peers and community reinforce the relevant protective factors that lead to the escalation of resilience (Fergus & Zimmerman, 2005).

A protective early social environment has impact on the life span, and social attachments, including friendship, can boost resilience to stress and adversity and diminish both genetic and environmental vulnerabilities (Abraham et al., 2021). Feldman (2020) argues that the 'affiliative brain' supports resilience in several ways. For instance, this network at its optimal operation enables individuals to create and sustain social bonds throughout life. The impact of experiencing affect synchrony, during the early years of one's life, on social competencies appear from the preschool years. At this stage, children begin to have 'best friends' and enter social institutions built by the culture. Culture-specific ways of experiencing affect synchrony shape children's social competencies with other children. Synchrony seems to operate as a protective factor that fosters resilience, since it triggers children's ability to function more adequately in the social world, form friendships and engage in peer activity.

Special emphasis is placed on the role of friendships as a quality source of resilience. Meaningful friendships that are established in the early years of children's development provide opportunities to acquire and practice substantial skills relevant to the development of personal, social, emotional, cognitive and communicative skills (Guralnick et al., 2007; Theobald et al., 2017). There is evidence showing that the formation and maintenance of close peer friendships, especially by children who are considered as being at high risk, are characteristics that predict high levels of competence in several domains such as academic and personal life, despite the challenges that they have experienced in their lives (Doll et al., 2003). In fact, having good quality friendships, peer relations, social support and opportunities to participate in group activities with peers operate as protective factors (Fee & Hinton, 2011).

There are only a few studies focusing on the nature of the relationships between children with and without disabilities in inclusive settings. Morrison and Burgman (2009) explored the friendship experiences of children with disabilities in mainstream Australian schools. Participants described sharing interests and being caring, helpful and kind as important attributes that a friend should have. From participants' descriptions, friendships between children with disabilities and peers without disabilities may not be always fully reciprocal. That is to say, some children with disabilities may be the recipients of help or assistance that they often do not return back to their friends in full. Despite the limited reciprocity of such friendships, they can still be meaningful, as they are still beneficial for one or both children. Even a partially reciprocal friendship provides greater emotional and practical benefits, enhancing health and wellbeing for all children.

Children benefit from friendships because they foster social development and emotional stability, which helps them to become resilient. Ofiesh and Mather (2013) consider support that an individual receives from the social environment as a protective factor that reduces stress and promotes physical and psychological health and overall wellbeing. Expanding upon this, positive peer relationships and friendships support children with disabilities or those with chronic illness to cope with major stressors. It seems that emotional support, guidance and positive feedback that children receive are key in positive adjustments and decreased behavioural problems. For example, Fee and Hinton (2011) found that in the case of boys with a chronic neuromuscular disorder, the presence of friendship and positive peer relationships reduced the risk of them exhibiting behavioural problems. On the contrary, children with limited social support were considered as being 'at risk' for significant behaviour problems.

Children with disabilities are now more likely to attend mainstream schools. However, this does not necessarily imply that they are socially included, since several barriers continue to exist along with the societal attitudes and norms towards people with disabilities (Morrison & Burgman, 2009). These norms and stereotypes are fuelled by the society but also by the schooling system: the hidden curriculum and the school's ethos, which are both influenced by the principles and customs of the educational system and the beliefs and values of educators, parents and children themselves. For Runswick-Cole and Goodley (2013), the cultural aspects of disability and impairment and the way people with disabilities experience their lives are formed within an individual's relationship with others in the community. Developmental cultural psychology suggests that interactions with important others shape individuals' beliefs and understandings around disability, its cultural meanings and stigmatisation (Kayama et al., 2019). The way people with disabilities experience disability and stigma can vary even within a cultural group due to several sociocultural issues, like socio-economic status, parents' education level and access to other people with disabilities (Darling, 2013), as well as gender roles and expectations (Dawn, 2014). The way they experience disability and stigma also depends on the features of the individual, characteristics of personality, the quality of interactions with others and thus their access to resilience resources. The presence of resilience resources, such as support from family and friends (Conder et al., 2015), can help individuals cope with stigmatisation. Therefore, it may be the case that people experience disability differently, depending on their personalities, but also on the resources they have access to.

Peer acceptance and support, as well as peer social comparisons, are identified as risk factors by Cosden et al. (2002). This implies that a child with a disability who is rejected by his peers is more likely to be at risk. The disability itself must not be considered as the only risk factor, not only because of the heterogeneity of such a population but also because there are no risk factors that exclusively apply to individuals with disabilities but not to others (Wong, 2003). Reduced acceptance of children with disabilities by their peers may be due to a unwelcoming school environment (Demetriou, 2021) but also due to factors within the children with disabilities, such as lack of interpersonal understanding both in the classroom and on the playground and a lower level of social functioning (Ofiesh & Mather, 2013). However, regardless of their possible lower level of social functioning, children with disabilities tend to have positive attitudes towards their peers. This may be a result of the disability per se (Palombo, 2001), or it may be a coping mechanism (Robertson et al., 1998) that protects them from the consequences of peer rejection and exclusion.

In general, barriers to friendship formation and maintenance will most likely cause detrimental consequences for children with disabilities. It will lead to a limited support network which is necessary for coping with challenges in life (Ofiesh & Mather, 2013). For example, studies with children with limb deficiencies showed that depression symptoms and maladjustment are significantly correlated with a lack of social support (Fee & Hinton, 2011). Another example is when children with disabilities experience failed attempts at school which have a negative impact on their self-worth, especially when they are associated with negative feedback from teachers and peers. Even in cases where teachers provide positive feedback and are supportive, the negative stance of their peers who may humiliate children with learning difficulties due to reduced academic competence may cause irreparable damage to their self-concept (Salza, 2003).

Promoting Relationships and Friendships

The development of resilience is achieved through interventions to the social environment of children, especially the school environment. Connecting with peers is considered an essential internal asset for the development of personal coping skills and resources and thus for the enhancement of resilience. For this reason, a number of school-level interventions with the involvement of children, educators and parents focus on the development of social support networks and the enhancement of interpersonal relationships with others.

Positive relationships with teachers and supportive peers seem to enhance resilience. An inclusive whole-school environment that is reflected in the school's policies and practices will ensure that all children feel a sense of belonging and community. A diverse and inclusive learning environment promotes social acceptance, engagement and friendship (Odom et al., 2011). In such settings, both children with and without disabilities take part in activities together. According to Guralnick and colleagues (2007), children with disabilities who interacted with children without disabilities over a two-year period became more socially responsive, developed more positive interactions with their peers and engaged in fewer unoccupied or independent play activities. By collectively participating in such activities, children will master a variety of skills and social competences through social interactions and the formation of friendships (Diamond & Hong, 2010). In turn, this will lead to high subjective wellbeing (Anderson et al., 2012), good mental and physical health, self-identity development, promotion of creativity and expression (King et al., 2003), and resilience.

Harris (2015) argues that resilience is not a fixed attribute; thus, it is something that can be taught by enhancing a set of protective mechanisms that will modify a child's response to risk. Children, especially those with a disability, must be taught essential copying skills in order for them to be able to deal with the challenges they will face and thus succeed in a complex society. In this aspect, resilience is approached as a spiritual skill that allows a child to prevent, minimise, overtake and overcome the detrimental effects of any kind of adversity. In this perspective, resilience is seen as an attribute that must be enhanced through the promotion of a positive and spiritual framework in inclusive educational settings. Particularly, educators should enhance dispositions in children with disabilities that focus on social and executive function skills and relational attributes such as kindness, friendship and empathy. These attributes can be enhanced by building healthy peer relationships between children with and without disabilities though the participation of children with disabilities in daily class activities and play with peers without disabilities. Opportunities to participate in such activities will be beneficial for both parties, especially when children face challenging situations collaboratively (Harris, 2015). However, several environmental and attitudinal barriers incommode seamless participation in everyday cultural activities for children with disabilities. Therefore, an effective way to promote positive relationship and consequently resilience is though providing an increased number of opportunities for children with disabilities to participate in activities in schools and extracurricular activities.

Participation in this kind of activities, such as sports, music and drama, provide opportunities for children to participate in prosocial groups where their efforts and contributions are recognised and valued. In Morrison and Burgman's (2009) study, participants reported that opportunities to participate in extracurricular activities, such as visiting friends' houses, participating in sports and participating in other activities, enrich friendships outside of school. For this reason, children should be encouraged to participate in and contribute to daily activities that allow them to feel that they are contributing to the world. Specifically, an activity of contributing to the world is when children are given opportunities to assist other children (Alvord & Grados, 2005).

Participation opportunities will in turn enhance socialisation and friendship formation. Friendships are deepened because of shared experiences and feelings of acceptance and belongingness. Doll (1996) stresses that since the majority of students' opportunities for socialisation occur within school settings, educators can intervene to promote meaningful friendships. Having a supportive social environment that sustains students' academic success is important for students with learning disabilities (Elbaum & Vaughn, 2001). This supportive environment, where children with disabilities have opportunities to form quality friendships, develop social skills and enjoy social acceptance, is better achieved in inclusive school settings. Wiener and Tardif (2004) concluded that the selection of the most appropriate placement is crucial and that, for optimal social and emotional adjustment, the inclusive classroom must be preferred.

Developmental cultural psychology suggests that interactions with important others, including parents, peers and educators, shape individuals' beliefs and understandings around disability, its cultural meanings and stigmatisation (Varenne & McDermott, 1998). In smaller and traditional societies, where inclusion is a relatively novel approach, some erroneous understandings about disability may be recorded, as many children without disabilities may view their peers with disabilities as being at a disadvantage: as subjects of others' sympathy and pitifulness; being lonely and totally dependent on others (Demetriou, 2021). Therefore, it is evident that children without disabilities should be prepared to accept children with disabilities in their school settings; this action will adjust possible erroneous understandings about disability. In practice, the ambiance of acceptance must be promoted through the implementation of appropriate interventional programmes that enhance children's personal experiences through experiential learning and the correction of misconceptions. The organisation of joint events with other schools that have students with disabilities should be promoted, when possible, to foster social interaction between children with and without disabilities. In such collaborative activities, children should be encouraged to initiate activities (King et al., 2003) and to engage in playful interactions in safe playful contexts. Active participation rather than mere physical proximity will raise awareness of disability and encourage the development of social and functional competence in children, primarily through their interactions (Demetriou, 2022).

Programmes such as these should be carefully designed in order to raise awareness and promote critical empathy and understanding but not give the wrong impression that an individual needs one-way support. The acceptance of differences should not be interpreted to mean that children with disabilities are less equal or that they only require assistance from the children without disabilities. This misunderstanding could lead to unbalanced peer relationships and perceptions of children with disabilities as unequal. As a result, interventional programmes should emphasise that within reciprocal and mutual partnerships, both children with and children without disabilities have something to contribute. Furthermore, the voices of children with disabilities should be heard in establishing practices that fit their needs and promote interaction with their peers for such programmes to be successful.

Conclusion

In this chapter, we have explored the impact of disabilities on the wellbeing of children, highlighting the crucial role of friendships in fostering happiness and resilience. For a visual overview of the key concepts discussed throughout this chapter, please refer to Figure 6.1.

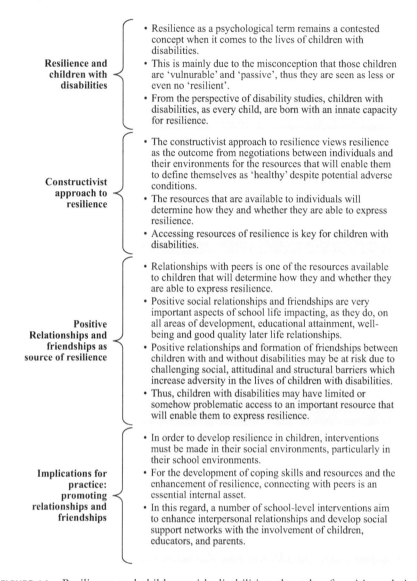

FIGURE 6.1   Resilience and children with disabilities: the role of positive relationships and friendships

Individuals with disabilities may have poorer outcomes in terms of well-being in comparison with their peers without disabilities. Both children with disabilities (Foley et al., 2012) and children without disabilities (Fattore et al., 2009) refer to the importance of having close friends for them to be happy with their lives, among other factors. Among the reasons given for friendships' importance are that they provide a sense of belonging and acceptance, assistance with personal matters, support on important decisions, and sources of information.

However, the positive relationships and formation of friendships between children with and without disabilities may be at risk due to challenging social, attitudinal and structural barriers which increase adversity in the lives of children with disabilities. This means that children with disabilities may have limited or problematic access to an important resource that will enable them to express resilience. Therefore, the promotion of acceptance of diversity and the correction of erroneous understanding about disability – that derives from societal stereotypes about disability that still mark societies – must be enhanced through opportunities to engage in activities that include sharing things with each other and engaging in play together, both elements that help children acquire coping strategies that are attached to resilience. This also highlights the importance of reconsidering teachers' training. Effective training should emphasise not only general information about inclusion and special educational needs but also the knowledge, skills and techniques to create enabling environments where children will thrive through positive relationships and peer interactions. Thus, this venture comprises a major challenge because it requires a major reformation of school policies and practices for them to align with the principles of inclusion, so that all children have the opportunity to thrive in an environment of acceptance and respect based on positive social relationships. To succeed, however, the co-operation of all stakeholders involved is required so that all children – including those with disabilities – are not deprived of access to this important source of resilience in a protective early learning and social environment.

References

Abraham, E., Letkiewicz, A. M., Wickramaratne, P. J., Bunyan, M., van Dijk, M. T., Gameroff, M. J., Posner, J., Talati, A., & Weissman, M. M. (2021). Major depression, temperament, and social support as psychosocial mechanisms of the intergenerational transmission of parenting styles. *Development and Psychopathology*, 1–15.

Alvord, M. K., & Grados, J. J. (2005). Enhancing resilience in children: A proactive approach. *Professional Psychology: Research and Practice*, 36(3), 238.

Anderson, C., Kraus, M. W., Galinsky, A. D., & Keltner, D. (2012). The local-ladder effect: Social status and subjective well-being. *Psychological Science*, 23(7), 764–771.

Bronfenbrenner, V. (1979). *The ecology of human development*. Harvard University Press.

Conder, J. A., Mirfin-Veitch, B. F., & Gates, S. (2015). Risk and resilience factors in the mental health and well-being of women with intellectual disability. *Journal of Applied Research in Intellectual Disabilities*, 28(6), 572–583.

Cosden, M., Brown, C., & Elliott, K. (2002). Development of selfunderstanding and self-esteem in children and adults with learning disabilities. In B. Y. L. Wong & M. Donahue (Eds.), *Social dimensions of learning disabilities* (pp. 33–51). Erlbaum.

Darling, R. B. (2013). *Disability and Identity: Negotiating self in a changing society*. Lynn Rienner Publishers.

Dawn, R. (2014) "Our lives, our identity": Women with disabilities in India. *Disability and Rehabilitation, 36*(21), 1768–1773.

Demetriou, K. (2021). Intentions of children without disabilities to form friendship with peers with physical disability: A small-scale study. *Early Child Development and Care, 191*(13), 2141–2157.

Demetriou, K. (2022). Do you want to play with me? Acceptance and preference dilemmas in choosing playmates with physical disability. *Early Child Development and Care, 192*(6), 947–963.

Diamond, K. E., & Hong, S. Y. (2010). Young children's decisions to include peers with physical disabilities in play. *Journal of Early Intervention, 32*(3), 163–177.

Doll, B. (1996). Children without friends: Implications for practice and policy. *School Psychology Review, 25*(2), 165–183.

Doll, B., Murphy, P., & Song, S. Y. (2003). The relationship between children's self-reported recess problems, and peer acceptance and friendships. *Journal of School Psychology, 41*(2), 113–130.

Dunn, D. S., & Dougherty, S. B. (2005). Prospects for a positive psychology of rehabilitation. *Rehabilitation Psychology, 50*(3), 305–311.

Elbaum, B., & Vaughn, S. (2001). School-based interventions to enhance the self-concept of students with learning disabilities: A meta-analysis. *The Elementary School Journal, 101*, 303–329.

Fattore, T., Mason, J., & Watson, E. (2009). When children are asked about their well-being: Towards a framework for guiding policy. *Child Indicators Research, 2*, 57–77.

Fee, R. J., & Hinton, V. J. (2011). Resilience in children diagnosed with a chronic neuromuscular disorder. *Journal of Developmental and Behavioral Pediatrics: JDBP, 32*(9), 644.

Feldman, R. (2020). What is resilience: An affiliative neuroscience approach. *World Psychiatry, 19*(2), 132–150.

Fergus, S., & Zimmerman, M. A. (2005). Adolescent resilience: A framework for understanding healthy development in the face of risk. *Annual Review of Public Health, 26*, 399–419.

Foley, K. R., Blackmore, A. M., Girdler, S., O'Donnell, M., Glauert, R., Llewellyn, G., & Leonard, H. (2012). To feel belonged: The voices of children and youth with disabilities on the meaning of wellbeing. *Child Indicators Research, 5*(2), 375–391.

Folostina, R., Tudorache, L., Michel, T., Erzsebet, B., Agheana, V., & Hocaoglu, H. (2015). Using play and drama in developing resilience in children at risk. *Procedia-Social and Behavioral Sciences, 197*, 2362–2368.

Garmezy, N. (1985). Stress-resistant children: The search for protective factors. In J. E. Stevenson (Ed.), *Recent research in developmental psychopathology. Journal of child psychology and psychiatry book* (Suppl. 4, pp. 213–233). Pergamon Press.

Goldstein, S., & Rider, R. (2013). Resilience and the disruptive disorders of childhood. In *Handbook of resilience in children* (pp. 183–200). Springer.

Goodley, D. (2005). Empowerment, self-advocacy and resilience. *Journal of Intellectual Disabilities, 9*(4), 333–343.

Goodley, D., & Moore, M. (2000). Doing disability research: Activist lives and the academy. *Disability & Society, 15*(6), 861–882.

Goodley, D., & Runswick-Cole, K. (2011). The violence of disablism. *Journal of Sociology of Health and Illness, 33*, 602–617.

Guralnick, M. J., Neville, B., Hammond, M. A., & Connor, R. T. (2007). The friendships of young children with developmental delays: A longitudinal analysis. *Journal of Applied Developmental Psychology, 28*(1), 64–79.

Harris, K. I. (2015). Children's spirituality and inclusion: Strengthening a child's spirit with community, resilience and joy. *International Journal of Children's Spirituality*, *20*(3–4), 161–177.

Kayama, M., Johnstone, C., & Limaye, S. (2019). The experiences of disability in sociocultural contexts of India: Stigmatization and resilience. *International Social Work*. https://doi.org/10.1177/0020872819828781

King, G., Lawm, M., King, S., Rosenbaum, P., Kertoy, M. K., & Young, N. L. (2003). A conceptual model of the factors affecting the recreation and leisure participation of children with disabilities. *Physical & occupational therapy in pediatrics*, *23*(1), 63–90.

Masten, A. S. (2001). Ordinary magic: Resilience processes in development. *American Psychologist*, *56*, 227–238.

Masten, A. S. (2007). Resilience in developing systems: Progress and promise as the fourth wave rises. *Development and psychopathology*, *19*(3), 921–930.

McNamara, J. K., & Willoughby, T. (2010). A longitudinal study of risk-taking behavior in adolescents with learning disabilities. *Learning Disabilities Research & Practice*, *25*(1), 11–24.

Montague, M., Enders, C., Dietz, S., Dixon, J., & Cavendish, W. M. (2008). A longitudinal study of depressive symptomology and self-concept in adolescents. *The Journal of Special Education*, *42*(2), 67–78.

Morrison, R., & Burgman, I. (2009). Friendship experiences among children with disabilities who attend mainstream Australian schools. *Canadian Journal of Occupational Therapy*, *76*(3), 145–152.

Murray, C., & Doren, B. (2013). Resilience and disability: Concepts, examples, cautions, and prospects. In M. L. Wehmeyer (Ed.), *The Oxford handbook of positive psychology and disability* (pp. 182–97). Oxford University Press.

Nalavany, B. A., Carawan, L. W., & Rennick, R. A. (2011). Psychosocial experiences associated with confirmed and self-identified dyslexia: A participant-driven concept map of adult perspectives. *Journal of learning disabilities*, *44*(1), 63–79.

Odom, S. L., Buysse, V., & Soukakou, E. (2011). Inclusion for young children with disabilities: A quarter century of research perspectives. *Journal of Early Intervention*, *33*(4), 344–356.

Ofiesh, N., & Mather, N. (2013). Resilience and the child with learning disabilities. In S. Goldstein & R. Brooks (Eds.), *Handbook of resilience in children* (pp. 349–370). Springer.

Palombo, J. (2001). *Learning disorders and disorders of the self*. Norton.

Prilletensky, O. (2009). Critical psychology and disability studies: Critiquing the mainstream, critiquing the critique. In D. Fox, I. Prilletensky, & S. Austin (Eds.), *Critical psychology: An introduction* (2nd ed., pp. 250–266). SAGE Publications.

Reivich, K., & Shatte, A. (2002). *The resilience factor: 7 keys to finding your inner strength and overcoming life's hurdles*. Broadway Books.

Robertson, L. M., Harding, M. S., & Morrison, G. M. (1998). A comparison of risk and resilience indicators among Latino/a students. Differences between students identified as at-risk, learning disabled, speech impaired and not at-risk. *Education and Treatment of Children*, 333–353.

Runswick-Cole, K., & Goodley, D. (2013). Resilience: A disability studies and community psychology approach. *Social and Personality Psychology Compass*, *7*(2), 67–78.

Salza, L. (2003). Struggling to learn in school: Confessions of a lunch-pail school head. *Perspectives: The International Dyslexia Association*, *29*(2), 26–27.

Theobald, M. A., Danby, S. J., Thompson, C., & Thorpe, K. (2017). Friendships. In S. Garvis & D. Pendergast (Eds.), *Health & wellbeing in childhood* (2nd ed., pp. 141–160). Cambridge University Press.

Ungar, M. (2007). Contextual and cultural aspects of resilience in child welfare settings. In I. Brown, F. Chaze, D. Fuchs, J. Lafrance, S. McKay, & S. Thomas Prokop

(Eds.), *Putting a Human Face on Child Welfare* (pp. 1–24). Centre of Excellence for Child Welfare.

Ungar, M. A. (2004). Constructionist discourse on resilience: Multiple contexts, multiple realities among at-risk children and youth. *Youth & Society, 35*, 341–365.

Varenne, H., & McDermott, R. (1998). *Successful failure: The school America builds*. Westview Press.

Werner, E. E. (1989). High-risk children in young adulthood: A longitudinal study from birth to 32 years. *American Journal of Orthopsychiatry, 59*, 72–81.

Wiener, J., & Tardif, C. Y. (2004). Social and emotional functioning of children with learning disabilities: Does special education placement make a difference? *Learning Disabilities Research & Practice, 19*(1), 20–32.

Wong, B. Y. (2003). General and specific issues for researchers' consideration in applying the risk and resilience framework to the social domain of learning disabilities. *Learning Disabilities Research & Practice, 18*(2), 68–76.

Young, A., Green, E., & Rogers, K. (2008). Resilience and deaf children: A literature review. *Deafness Education International, 10*, 40–55.

Zolkoski, S. M., & Bullock, L. M. (2012). Resilience in children and youth: A review. *Children and Youth Services Review, 34*(12), 2295–2303.

PART 3

Applied Practices and Initiatives With Young Children

7
THE COMPASSION–RESILIENCE CONNECTION

Their Place in Early Childhood Education in a Global Arena

Harriet Broadfoot

Introduction

In the context of an increasingly complex globalised world and the challenges it presents, there is a need for an alternative narrative in early education (Moss & Robert-Holmes, 2021): one that focuses on the broader educational goals of individual and collective wellbeing. In face of which resiliency and compassion, core global competencies for sustainability (Giangrande et al., 2019; Lambrechts, 2020; United Nations Educational, Scientific and Cultural Organization [UNESCO], 2020, 2019) are foundational capacities and important embodied modes of being essential for thriving, connectedness and wellbeing, while supporting that of others (human and nonhuman) (Broadfoot & Pascal, 2020; Engdahl & Furu, 2022; Ives et al., 2019). Drawing on empirical studies, this chapter argues for the importance of positioning compassion as a catalyst for supporting and sustaining emotional resilience, which in turn protects a sense of 'being-well' and vice versa. In other words while a precursor for both, through experiencing compassion a form of feedback loop emerges between resilience and wellbeing.

With an interest in early childhood education (ECE), global citizenship and sustainability, this chapter's focus is emotional resilience at the individual level but in a collective compassionate context. It explores the interconnected threads of compassion, resilience and wellbeing, and the need for them to be fostered in ECE in a global arena, through which I reflect upon their place in the early education of children as global citizens with needs, rights and capabilities in light of global sustainability agenda and ECE policy in England. Considering ECE settings as sites that produce and reproduce cultural practices (Hayashi & Tobin, 2015) within an ethic of care (Taggart, 2016),

DOI: 10.4324/9781003345664-10

I adopt a sociocultural lens which highlights the important role of positive relationships (Drake et al., 2019; Nah et al., 2020; Nolan et al., 2014; Werner, 2013) and environment (Shonkoff & Phillips, 2000; Bronfenbrenner & Morris, 1998). As key principles of England's Early Years Foundation Stage (EYFS: DfE, 2021), this further links with contemporary debate about quality and professionalism within the field.

Chapter Structure

After a brief background situating resilience and compassion as important embodied modes of being in context of holistic wellbeing, that is, sustainability, I present three sections focusing on resilience, wellbeing and compassion. These follow a line of questioning unpicking conceptualisations of the aforementioned concepts as well as their importance and relevance to each other and ECE as shown here:

Resilience

> What is resilience and why does it matter?
> Why is emotional resilience important within ECE?

Wellbeing

> What is wellbeing?
> Why is wellbeing important in ECE?

Compassion

> What is compassion?
> Compassion's connection with wellbeing and resilience
> Why is compassion important in ECE?

The elements of this chapter are then drawn together in a final section that reflects upon implications for daily practice regarding fostering young children's emotional resilience while enhancing wellbeing of all in an ECE community; that is, through **living, playing and learning as a community of compassion.**

Background

Educating children in a complex turbulent world with an unforecastable future problematises the question of what 'skills' and knowledge might be of educational focus. To support and enable young children to lead a flourishing life despite challenges and adversities, and lay foundations for empowering them as global citizens to attend to and have caring concern for the welfare of human and nonhuman others, brings me to a focus on compassion, wellbeing and resilience. Further to this, they are situated as core components within both the behavioural and socio-emotional learning dimensions of education for global citizenship and sustainability (Asah & Singh, 2019; United Nations Educational, Scientific and Cultural Organization [UNESCO], 2020). As Ives et al. (2019, p. 208) point out, 'people's "inner worlds" – their emotions, thoughts, identities and beliefs . . . lie at the heart of actions for sustainability' while also being an aspect of sustainability itself. These notions are encapsulated in the United Nations Sustainable Development Goals numbers 3 'Good Health and Well-being' and 4.7 'Education for sustainability' (United Nations Educational, Scientific and Cultural Organization [UNESCO], 2017). It is important to note that when it comes to compassion and resilience while there are biological factors at play, we live and exist in an interconnected, interdependent web of relations (Holt-Lunstad et al., 2010; Spikins, 2017). A key thought running through this chapter therefore and one which I invite readers to reflect upon is expressed in United Nations Educational, Scientific and Cultural Organization [UNESCO's] (2019, p. 51) Reimagining Our Futures Together report which stipulates 'our inner lives influence our environments, and at the same time are deeply affected by them'. With this in mind, environments in which children are treated with compassion and provided with opportunities to develop their innate capacity for it should permeate ECE (Broadfoot, 2019), contributing to their wellbeing, developing resilience (Engdahl & Furu, 2022) and compassionate relations with themselves as well as human and nonhuman others.

These interwoven phenomena are essential for enabling children to 'engage more fully with their whole lives' (Weare, 2022, p. viii) in, for and with the world, while having the foundations to live well and positively respond to what the future may hold. In this respect, I suggest that resilience and compassion are important embodied modes of being for the holistic wellbeing of the children themselves and the wider world.

Resilience

What Is Resilience and Why Does It Matter?

Resilience is most often positioned as a complex, dynamic process (Nolan et al., 2014; Masten & Barnes, 2018) influenced by personal attributes and environmental factors (Ungar, 2013) that manifests as the capacity to cope with internal and external stressors (Werner, 1996) in a positive, flexible way (Masten & Barnes, 2018). In this manner emotional resilience is connected with an individual's wellbeing, with low levels of resilience contributing to a lower sense of wellbeing and a higher degree of resilience promoting wellbeing (discussed further later). As opposed to a fixed character trait, which was the focus of much early research on resilience, this fluid, context-dependent view of resilience suggests that experience of it will vary across the life course (Windle, 2011), making it important to focus on how it can be nurtured in both adults and children.

Emotional Resilience

Elaborating on the aforementioned conceptualisation of resilience, emotional resilience can be understood not as a trait but as a capacity to flexibly meet negative and stressful experiences and challenges rather than trying to avoid or eliminate them. This involves a process of positive adaptations (Masten, 2001; Masten & Barnes, 2018) that draw upon resources such as positive emotions to sustain wellbeing (Ong et al., 2010; Tugade & Fredrickson, 2004). Let's take bamboo as an illustrative example. In a storm, bamboo adapts to and endures the adverse conditions by bending with strong winds, thereby enabling it to avoid stress fractures and continue to thrive. Much like bamboo, despite adverse circumstances, emotional resiliency enhances our capacity to thrive, enabling us to positively adapt to and live through stressful situations while retaining a sense of dignity and self-worth – in other words it helps us navigate the storm and protects a state of 'being-well'. However, as Masten and Barnes point out (2018, p. 2):

> "One of the most important implications of this definition is the idea that the resilience of a developing person is not circumscribed within the body and mind of that individual. The capacity of an individual to adapt to challenges depends on their connections to other people and systems external to the individual through relationships and other processes".

Collective Context

As inherently social creatures living and necessarily existing within social relationships (Holt-Lunstad et al., 2010; Spikins, 2017), the sociocultural context in which we are situated cannot be ignored. Rather, an individual's capacity to adapt to challenges is in part contingent on the external environment in the shape of connections with people and process within the systems in which they are embedded (Masten & Barnes, 2018). In particular, research with children continues to highlight the important role of positive relationships and connections (Einarsdottir et al., 2022; Pascal & Bertram, 2021; Brogaard-Clausen & Robson, 2019). For Masten (2001) young children need experiences that nurture the aforementioned adaptive systems that contribute to an individual's resilience. In this manner, viewing resilience as a capacity that can be strengthened through opportunities and experiences (Masten, 2001) in one's environment and relationships, or conversely suppressed by them (Ungar, 2013), leads to a consideration of the sociocultural contexts and conditions in which young children live (Rogoff et al., 2018). Therefore, while a psychological perceptive on emotional resilience places resilience within the wellbeing discourse, with emotional resilience promoting a sense of wellbeing, considering this through a sociocultural lens points towards the interaction of relationships, practices and conditions of ECE communities; factors that promote and protect emotional resilience (Masten & Barnes, 2018; Nolan et al., 2014), thereby situating an individual's **emotional resilience within a collective context**. This is echoed in Rutter's (2012) conceptualisation of resilience which recognises it as a **process influenced by social supports**, again suggesting that resilience can be nurtured within social contexts – such as, I suggest, the early years setting.

Why Is Emotional Resilience Important Within ECE?

The early years of life are considered an especially important time for nurturing resilience (Masten, 2001) with experiences in early childhood environments providing a foundation for lifelong learning and wellbeing (Masten & Barnes, 2018; Shonkoff & Phillips, 2000; United Nations Educational, Scientific and Cultural Organization [UNESCO], 2019). With adaptations to cope with stressors, setbacks, risks and challenges contributing to sense of wellbeing (Masten & Barnes, 2018), resilience in turn impacts children's capacity to learn and develop healthily (Conkbayir, 2017) and engage with family, community (Banerjee et al., 2016) and the wider world (as noted in p. 115).

Children in Early Education

Research into resilience highlights that a salient feature in promoting and protecting children's emotional resilience are caring, responsive relationships that promote positive emotions which in turn contributes to their sense of wellbeing (Kim-Cohen et al., 2004; Masten & Barnes, 2018; Werner, 1996). For example, Werner and Smith's (1992) longitudinal study following 700 children from birth to adulthood found that a stand-out aspect within the children's community was the positive relationships provided by a caring teacher who acted as both role model and source of emotional support. This involved providing a listening ear, comfort and encouragement. Tugade et al.'s (2004) work on resilience suggests that positive emotions evoked by such relationships contribute to resilience through broadening one's mindset, helping to down-play negative emotion (which can narrow one's thought-action repertoire) and cope with stressors in a flexible, positive way. With repeated experience they theorise that it becomes habitual, increasing personal resources that can be drawn on in times of stress and adversity which enhances wellbeing in an upwards spiral. Not losing sight of the environmental factors supporting resilience (Davydov et al., 2010), consistent early relationships with a caring adult are important to consider in early childhood education (Nolan et al., 2014) – particularly as young children today are spending the majority of their time in early education settings.

What can be drawn from this section so far then is the important role of positive relationships (Nah et al., 2020; Drake et al., 2019; Nolan et al., 2014; Werner, 2013) and sociocultural environment (Shonkoff & Phillips, 2000; Bronfenbrenner & Morris, 1998) during the early years of life. Taken together, in ECE in England, this directly connects with two of the Early Years Statutory Framework's (EYFS: DfE, 2021) overarching principles: 'Positive Relationships' and 'Enabling Environments'.

Teachers in Early Education

Just as environments can support or not a child's resilience, so can they support or not adults' resilience. ECE work is complex and often stressful in nature. This can impact both educators' capacity to provide the aforementioned close, responsive caring relationships (Elfer, 2015) and their own wellbeing. Particularly under the weight of performativity pressures (Roberts-Holmes & Bradbury, 2016) and other micro-stressors, such as low pay, long working hours and meetings the needs of multiple children (Bonetti, 2019; EYA, 2021; Social Mobility Commission, 2020), educators often drawing upon their resilience in order to cope (Andrew, 2015). Therefore, though I must stress the conditions causing the latter should not be overlooked nor tackled, resilience is also valuable for teachers themselves as a protective factor for their own wellbeing, ability to model resilience and capacity to offer responsive positive relationships. As aspects underlying resilience can be strengthened at any age (CDCHU, 2010), the experience of positive relationships and environments for the practitioners themselves can support them in their daily practice (Culshaw & Kurian, 2021). It is here I suggest that viewing resilience in an ECE community of compassion may go some way in contributing to the wellbeing of children and teachers alike, which in turn supports resilience and vice versa (the processes of which are elaborated later).

Wellbeing

What Is Wellbeing?

The wellbeing of people is inscribed in SDG 3 'Health and Well-being' and the World Health Organisation's view of mental health as a basic human right (WHO, 2022a) – a state of wellbeing where individuals can cope with stressors in life and contribute to their community. From this perspective, wellbeing is fundamental to our collective and individual ability to think, emote, act and build relationships (WHO, 2022a, 2002b). On a personal level, a high sense of subjective wellbeing from a eudemonic perspective enables one to positively and meaningfully engage with world and from a hedonic perspective enjoy life.

It is important to note however that this 'state' of wellbeing is dynamic, fluid and subjective, describing points in time which can vary from context to context (Mguni et al., 2011) as well as culture, with the eudemonic and hedonic perspectives presenting a primarily Western philosophical understanding. Moving away from individuals as a point of departure, Kavedžija (2021) presents an anthropological perspective on wellbeing as an ongoing process which draws into focus the enmeshed nature of human–nonhuman, with wellbeing playing out in particular within caring relations. Similar to resilience therefore, attention to environmental influence should not go unwarranted. Recall the thought that 'our inner lives influence our environments, and at the same time are deeply affected by them' (United Nations Educational, Scientific and Cultural Organization [UNESCO, 2019], p. 51) – we are always in relationship. With this in mind, O'Toole and Simovska (2022) argue for wellbeing to be recognised as one of the purposes or goals of education in regard to the transformative role education can play in enhancing lives. Through *Bildung*, an educational concept recognising the interplay between 'inner' and 'outer' worlds, where reference to inner life encapsulates critical reflection on social issues and social order, O'Toole and Simovska (2022) demonstrate that concern for individual wellbeing should go alongside its socio-ecological determinants. These include the educational setting's environment and children's daily experiences of it, which points towards consideration of both individual wellbeing, and supporting the wellbeing of others in promotion of being and living well together. With an understanding that embodied feelings and emotions act as means of orientation within the world and support our meaningful engagement with it, here they stipulate that promotion of wellbeing should be enacted, and done so as more than discrete intervention that places it on the individual. In doing so they highlight, and I concur, a **need to educate compassionately** which involves engaging holistically with compassion in daily life as a whole education community.

Why Is Wellbeing Important in ECE?

As mentioned earlier, we are part of an interconnected web of relations and for a child in their early years of life their environment and relations affect regulation of stress responses and overall health, with long-lasting effects on their wellbeing (CDCHU, 2010). In England's educational policy, the importance of supporting children's wellbeing is increasingly recognised (DfE, 2021) with implications for their learning, development and forming of relationships. This places early years teachers as key influencers in ensuring their early learning community provides an environment that promotes and supports children's wellbeing. Though this governmental view often driven by economic imperative in terms of later outcomes and wider society, I emphasise that children's experiences in the moment matter too in their own right. As Dunn and Layard point out (2009, p. 153), 'children are not "incomplete adults"; their current quality of life is as important as the future adults they will become'. Furthermore, previous research has linked ECE work place stressors such as poor work conditions and the ebbs and flows of emotional labour that the job entails with teachers capacity to provide warm, consistent responsive relations with the children in their charge (Brace, 2020; Seaman & Giles, 2019). These ideas point towards one of the reasons wellbeing is important for the self and important as part of educational experience.

A holistic, whole setting approach should therefore be taken when considering supporting children's emotional resilience and wellbeing in the daily rhythms of one's ECE setting. It is here I believe that compassion can play a pivotal role in an ECE community.

Compassion

What Is Compassion?

Compassion refers to a relational process which as part of an ethic of care (Tronto, 1993) unfolds in regard to supporting and sustaining the wellbeing and living of oneself or others (human and nonhuman). This involves concern for, courage and behaviours directed towards alleviating and preventing distress, pain, hurt and so on, in promotion of one's one or others' welfare. In this understanding, compassion is thought to promote pro-social and pro-environmental behaviours and connectedness, with the way in which compassion unfolds being contextually contingent on the people, places and 'things' (their relations and histories) entangled (proximally and distally) in an encounter.

In context of ECE, compassion can be understood as an integral aspect of daily life (Broadfoot & Pascal, 2020; Lipponen, 2018; Taggart, 2016) which previous research illuminated is experienced in a dynamic, multifaceted manner supporting children and adults needs, rights, capabilities and welfare. This includes (1) acknowledgement and acceptance seen in for example acknowledgement of need, distress or cause, which can lead to raising others awareness to enable collective compassion, and acceptance which manifests in feeling seen, heard and included; (2) offering and feeling security and protection (emotionally and physically), for example through presence of a person or nonhuman object or gesture such as defence against or tackling injustice; and/or (3) facilitation/enablement of relationships, participation and development in promotion of thriving for overall wellbeing (Broadfoot, 2019; Broadfoot & Pascal, 2020).

Compassion's Connection With Wellbeing and Resilience

In this chapter, I argue for the importance of compassion in ECE and positioning compassion as a catalyst for supporting and sustaining emotional resilience, which in turn protects a sense of 'being well' and vice versa. For example, Saarinen and colleagues (2019) in their longitudinal investigation of the relationship between compassion and wellbeing of children found that experiencing compassion heightened sense of wellbeing and predicated higher affective wellbeing over a period of 15 years. This echoes Chan et al.'s (2022) recent study which found a positive correlation between compassion from others and heightened sense of wellbeing and thriving. In terms of resilience, findings from research into compassion training point towards the pivotal role compassion plays in strengthening an individual's emotional resilience (Klimecki & Singer, 2017) and providing protection from stress (Vachon et al., 2015), which in turn promotes and protects subjective wellbeing as described earlier.

Empirical studies focused on compassion explain this through the up-regulation of positive affect which generates positive emotion and feelings of warmth when experiencing compassion that 'buffer' the negative affect simultaneously experienced (Engen & Singer, 2015; Singer & Klimecki, 2014). Further to this, a nerve connecting the brain with the heart called the vagus nerve is activated. This influences emotional expression and slows heart rate, resulting in a calm state of being (Bornemann et al., 2016; Stellar & Keltner, 2017) and protection from negative affect that might be experienced in stressful circumstances (Vachon et al., 2015). These occurrences enable one to turn towards, rather than away from what might appear overwhelming and/or distressing. In other words, compassion enables a resilience that makes space for actively supporting oneself or others to 'be-well'. On a theoretical level (Fredrickson, 2001), these positive emotions generated, while promoting emotional wellbeing, are thought to better allow for cognitive flexibility through broadening one's attention around the pain/distress/fear (rather than narrowing into it) – enabling a wider range of thinking – which studies have shown fosters healthy adaptive responses (Ong et al., 2010); and as mentioned earlier, young children need frequent experiences that nurture these (Masten, 2001).

Why Is Compassion Important in ECE?

Understanding learning as occurring through lived experiences in one's environment, in a collective context such as an early years environment, this points to the benefit of repeated experiences of compassion with others to foster its embodiment (Gilbert, 2018; Gluschkoff et al., 2018). Importantly for children, repeated experiences of compassion in positive relationships have been found to better enable them to cope well in stressful situations in the long term (Mikulincer & Shaver, 2017) and preserve their subjective wellbeing through supporting development of emotion regulation (Hofmeyer et al., 2020; Preckel et al., 2018) and strengthening capacity for resilience (Hofmeyer et al., 2020; Singer & Klimecki, 2014), thereby facilitating healthy adaptive relating styles carried into adulthood (Mikulincer & Shaver, 2017). Where compassion is part of the climate of an early years community, this might be seen in the co-regulation practices carried out by practitioners in instances a young child maybe experiencing overwhelm, fear or distress. With benefit for their own as well other's wellbeing (explored further later), the compassionate approach adopted can help foster children's embodiment of compassion, facilitating their own emotional self-regulation skills (Mikulincer & Shaver, 2017) and strengthening their capacity for resilience. Noted by Darwin and reiterated in evolutionary perspectives since, compassion is also central to bonding and connectedness (Goetz et al., 2010; Spikins, 2017), which is an increasingly recognised aspect of wellbeing and a fundamental part of early human development.

However in light of the realities and complexities of daily ECE practice, often referred to as 'emotional labour' (as mentioned earlier), for ECE teachers working in a compassionate environment is also important for supporting their wellbeing (Culshaw & Kurian, 2021; Jennings, 2015; Rajala & Lipponen, 2018). Early work focusing on compassion in ECE through a sociocultural lens has highlighted daily practices, the institutional ethos, rules and routines influence how compassion unfolds and manifests (Broadfoot & Pascal, 2021; Lipponen, 2018; Rajala & Lipponen, 2018). Therefore, for what I have discussed here to be realised in practice, I advocate for a whole community approach wherein compassion is infused throughout all aspects of a setting. This could better enable teachers to turn towards rather than away (which can unconsciously occur as a means of self-protection) from supporting children during emotionally intense scenarios (Quinones & Cooper, 2022) or repeated episodes of crying such as during the settling-in period (Brace, 2020), thereby helping protect their capacity to provide responsive care and model compassion (Masten, 2018).

Summary and Reflections for Practice

Summary

Resilience is a dynamic process (Nolan et al., 2014) influenced by environmental factors (Ungar, 2013). As a concept, it has been widely applied on collective (e.g. organisation or community) material and individual levels and varies in conceptualisation depending upon the context to which it is applied. Valuable to both children (Werner, 2013) and practitioners (Andrew, 2015), research points towards resilience not only enhancing wellbeing through its protective and promotive factors (Wang et al., 2015) but also that wellbeing acts as an antecedent of resilience, buffering psychological distress (Ong et al., 2010). Further to this, compassion has been found to strengthen resilience and separately increase positive affect (Klimecki & Singer, 2017), thereby presenting as a precursor for both. Though illuminated in psychological and neuroscientific fields, this link has yet to be made in education which this chapter has sought to address. Particularly given the influential nature of early education environments and importance of recognising that compassion, a relational process that unfolds in regard to supporting and sustaining the well-being and living of oneself or others (human and nonhuman), is an integral aspect of the daily lived experiences within ECE communities (Broadfoot & Pascal, 2020; Lipponen, 2018; Taggart, 2016). Without wishing to detract from or overly simplify the complex and dynamic nature of the concepts explored through this chapter, for heuristic purposes, the illustration in the Figure 7.1 provides a brief overview of the linkages between them.

In the context of the pressing need to rethink education in an increasingly complex globalised world and the challenges it presents, underpinning this chapter is thought to an alternative narrative in early education that places value on individual and collective wellbeing. In relation to which I have presented resiliency and compassion as foundational capacities and important embodied modes of being essential for thriving, connectedness and wellbeing, while supporting that of human and nonhuman others. These are also identified by United Nations Educational, Scientific and Cultural Organization [UNESCO] (2020, 2019) and others (Giangrande et al., 2019; Lambrechts, 2020) as key features of and global competencies for sustainability; sustainability being a much debated concept which I have considered here in broad terms as holistic wellbeing and living well together.

Reflections

Holding the threads running through this chapter together requires balancing consideration of children's experiences of compassion, their wellbeing and thriving both in the here-and-now and the future, and viewing this in context of their place in the interconnected world in which they are situated. The past three years have been a stark reminder of this with the adverse, catastrophic implications for both human and nonhuman life brought on by climate change, the COVID-19 pandemic, injustices of war and mass migration, as well as continued biodiversity and species loss. Conceiving of sustainability as having holistic wellbeing at its heart in this manner, expands thought to children's resilience, compassion and wellbeing as they move forwards as global citizens in this context – thriving through and positively addressing whatever challenges and changes they may encounter, and living in harmony with human and nonhuman others. This is particularly of relevance when it comes to issues of social, economic and environmental sustainability, encapsulated

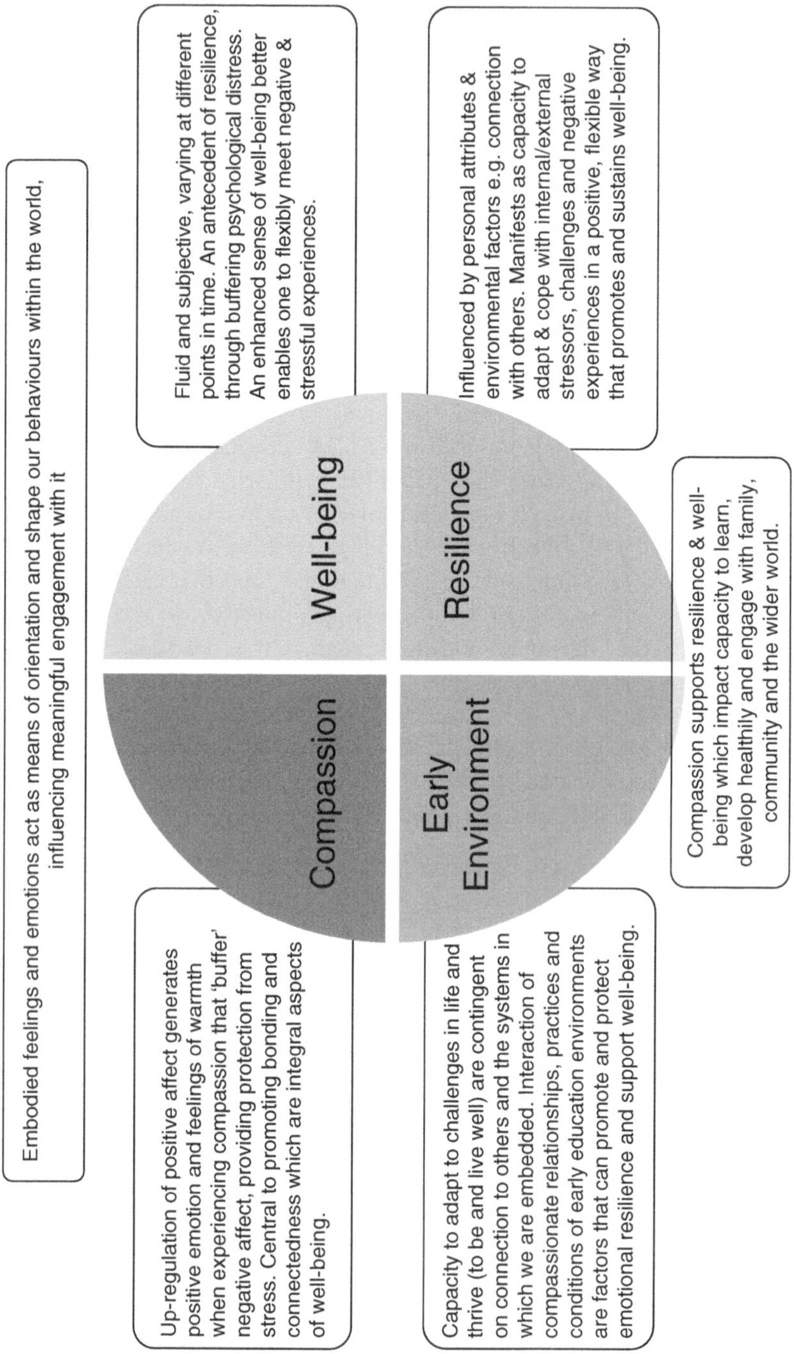

124 Harriet Broadfoot

Embodied feelings and emotions act as means of orientation and shape our behaviours within the world, influencing meaningful engagement with it

Well-being: Fluid and subjective, varying at different points in time. An antecedent of resilience, through buffering psychological distress. An enhanced sense of well-being better enables one to flexibly meet negative & stressful experiences.

Resilience: Influenced by personal attributes & environmental factors e.g. connection with others. Manifests as capacity to adapt & cope with internal/external stressors, challenges and negative experiences in a positive, flexible way that promotes and sustains well-being.

Compassion: Up-regulation of positive affect generates positive emotion and feelings of warmth when experiencing compassion that 'buffer' negative affect, providing protection from stress. Central to promoting bonding and connectedness which are integral aspects of well-being.

Early Environment: Capacity to adapt to challenges in life and thrive (to be and live well) are contingent on connection to others and the systems in which we are embedded. Interaction of compassionate relationships, practices and conditions of early education environments are factors that can promote and protect emotional resilience and support well-being.

Compassion supports resilience & well-being which impact capacity to learn, develop healthily and engage with family, community and the wider world.

FIGURE 7.1 Overview illustration of linkages

in the Sustainable Development Goals which ultimately seek to ensure the wellbeing of all.

So what does this interconnected view mean for practice? With compassion, resilience and wellbeing in mind in early education, children may be better assured to be and live well, while at the same time empowered to live well *together with* and in *active support of* the interconnected world and all those within it (human and nonhuman).

Immersing children in early environments of compassion – in a community of compassion – where it is a way of being in a setting, may go some way in fostering children's innate capacity for and embodiment of it, while supporting emotional resilience and enhancing wellbeing. As opposed to an individualistic intervention, envisioned here is a whole ECE setting approach where the individual is viewed in a collective context in which living, playing and learning as a community of compassion ripples through daily rhythms. Realising this in practice to avoid approaching compassion, resilience and wellbeing as other 'things to do' within education with the pitfalls of implemented approaches appearing as tokenistic or swept to the wayside for the new 'on trend' approach, requires collective dialogue, exploration and deep reflection of the opportunities within a setting for fostering compassion. With this rethink, an alternative narrative is presented which offers hope for a better world for all.

References

Andrew, Y. (2015). What we feel and what we do: Emotional capital in early childhood work. *Early Years, 35*(4), 351–365.

Asah, S. T., & Singh, N. C. (2019). Why social and emotional learning (SEL) is necessary to achieve the sustainable development goals (SDGs). *UNESCO The Blue Dot: Exploring New Ideas for a Shared Planet, 10,* 54–59.

Banerjee, R., McLaughlin, C., Cotney, J., Roberts, L., & Peereboom, C. (2016). *Promoting emotional health, wellbeing and resilience in primary schools.* Public Policy Institute for Wales. https://dera.ioe.ac.uk/32543/1/PPIW-Report-Promoting-Emotional-Health-Well-being-and-Resilience-in-Primary-Schools-Final.pdf

Bonetti, S. (2019). *The early years workforce in England: A comparative analysis using the labour force survey.* Education Policy Institute (EPI).

Bornemann, B., Kok, B. E., Boeckler, A., & Singer, T. (2016). Helping from the heart: Voluntary upregulation of heart rate variability predicts altruistic behavior. *Biological Psychology, 119,* 54–63.

Brace, D. (2020). 'Settling in': Exploring the complexities of observing and responding to young children's communications of distress as they start day care. *Infant Observation, 23*(3), 133–148.

Broadfoot, H. (2019). *Batmens and jumping lion: Exploring experiences of compassion in the daily rhythms of one preschool community* [MA thesis, Centre for Research in Early Childhood].

Broadfoot, H., & Pascal, C. (2020). Exploring experiences of compassion in the daily rhythms of one early childhood community. *European Early Childhood Education Research Journal, 28*(4), 457–474.

Broadfoot, H., & Pascal, C. (2021). An exploration of what conditions facilitate experiences of compassion in one early childhood community. *European Early Childhood Education Research Journal*, *29*(6), 910–924.

Brogaard-Clausen, S., & Robson, S. (2019). Friendships for wellbeing?: Parents' and practitioners' positioning of young children's friendships in the evaluation of wellbeing factors. *International Journal of Early Years Education*, *27*(4), 345–359.

Bronfenbrenner, U., & Morris, P. A. (1998). The ecology of development of development processes. In W. Damon & R. M. Lerner (Eds.), *Handbook of child psychology: Vol. 1. Theoretical model of human development* (pp. 993–1027). John Wiley.

Center on the Developing Child at Harvard University [CDCHU]. (2010). *The foundations of lifelong health are built in early childhood*. http://www.developingchild.harvard.edu

Chan, K. K. S., Lee, J. C. K., Yu, E. K. W., Chan, A. W., Leung, A. N. M., Cheung, R. Y., Chin, W. L., Ho-Man Kong, R., Chen, J., Wan, S. L. Y., Tang, C. H. Y., Yum, Y. N., Jiang, D., Wang, L., & Tse, C. Y. (2022). The impact of compassion from others and self-compassion on psychological distress, flourishing, and meaning in life among university students. *Mindfulness*, 1–9.

Conkbayir, M. (2017). *Early childhood and neuroscience. Theory, research and implications for practice*. Bloomsbury.

Culshaw, S., & Kurian, N. (2021). Love as the lifeblood of being-well: A call for care for teachers in England's schools. *Pastoral Care in Education*, *39*(3), 269–290.

Davydov, D., Stewart, R., Ritchie, K., & Chaudieu, I. (2010). Resilience and mental health. *Clinical Psychology Review*, *30*(5), 479–495. Elsevier. http://doi.org/10.1016/j.cpr.2010.03.003ff.ffinserm00534325f

Department for Education. (2021). *Early years foundation stage*. Retrieved May 12, 2020, from www.gov.uk/government/publications/early-years-foundation-stage-framework-2

Drake, G., Edenborough, M., Falloon, J., Fattore, T., Mason, J., & Mogensen, L. (2019). Is there a place for children as emotional beings in child protection policy and practice? *International Journal of Emotional Education*, *11*(1), 115–134.

Dunn, J., & Layard, R. (2009). *A good childhood: Searching for values in a competitive age*. Penguin.

Early Years Alliance. (2021). *Breaking point: The impact of recruitment and retention challenges on the early years sector in England*. Early Years Alliance.

Einarsdottir, J., Juutinen, J., Emilson, A., Ólafsdóttir, S. M., Zachrisen, B., & Meuser, S. (2022). Children's perspectives about belonging in educational settings in five European countries. *European Early Childhood Education Research Journal*, *30*(3), 330–343.

Elfer, P. (2015). Emotional aspects of nursery policy and practice: Progress and prospect. *European Early Childhood Education Research Journal*, *23*(4), 497–511.

Engdahl, I., & Furu, A. C. (2022). Early childhood education: A vibrant arena in the complex transformation of society towards sustainability. *International Journal of Early Childhood*, 1–12.

Engen, H. G., & Singer, T. (2015). Compassion-based emotion regulation up-regulates experienced positive affect and associated neural networks. *Social Cognitive and Affective Neuroscience*, *10*(9), 1291–1301.

Fredrickson, B. L. (2001). The role of positive emotions in positive psychology: The broaden-and-build theory of positive emotions. *American Psychologist*, *56*(3), 218.

Giangrande, N., White, R. M., East, M., Jackson, R., Clarke, T., Saloff Coste, M., & Penha-Lopes, G. (2019). A competency framework to assess and activate education for sustainable development: Addressing the UN sustainable development goals 4.7 challenge. *Sustainability*, *11*(10), 2832.

Gilbert, P. (2018). Explorations into the nature and function of compassion. *Current Opinion in Psychology, 28,* 108–114.

Gluschkoff, K., Oksman, E., Knafo-Noam, A., Dobewall, H., Hintsa, T., Keltikangas-Järvinen, L., & Hintsanen, M. (2018). The early roots of compassion: From child care arrangements to dispositional compassion in adulthood. *Personality and Individual Differences, 129,* 28–32.

Goetz, J. L., Keltner, D., & Simon-Thomas, E. (2010). Compassion: An evolutionary analysis and empirical review. *Psychological Bulletin, 136*(3), 351.

Hayashi, A., & Tobin, J. (2015). *Teaching embodied: Cultural practice in Japanese preschools.* University of Chicago Press.

Hofmeyer, A., Kennedy, K., & Taylor, R. (2020). Contesting the term 'compassion fatigue': Integrating findings from social neuroscience and self-care research. *Collegian, 27*(2), 232–237.

Holt-Lunstad, J., Smith, T. B., & Layton, J. B. (2010). Social relationships and mortality risk: A meta-analytic review. *PLoS Medicine, 7*(7). http://dx.doi.org/10.1371/journal.pmed.1000316

Ives, C. D., Freeth, R., & Fischer, J. (2019). Inside-out sustainability: The neglect of inner worlds. *Ambio, 49,* 208–217.

Jennings, P. A. (2015). Early childhood teachers' well-being, mindfulness, and self-compassion in relation to classroom quality and attitudes towards challenging students. *Mindfulness, 6*(4), 732–743.

Kaveďija, I. (2021). *The process of wellbeing: Conviviality, care, creativity.* Cambridge University Press.

Kim-Cohen, J., Moffitt, T., Caspi, A., & Taylor, A. (2004). Genetic and environmental processes in young children's resilience and vulnerability to socioeconomic deprivation. *Child Development, 75,* 651–668.

Klimecki, O. M., & Singer, T. (2017). The compassionate brain. In E. M. Seppala, E. Simon-Thomas, S. L. Broan, M. C. Worline, C. D. Cameron, & J. R. Doty (Eds.), *The handbook of compassion science* (pp. 109–120). Oxford University Press.

Lambrechts, W. (2020). *Learning 'for' and 'in' the future: On the role of resilience and empowerment in education* [Paper presentation]. Paper Commissioned for the UNESCO Futures of Education Report. https://unesdoc.unesco.org/ark:/48223/pf0000374088

Lipponen, L. (2018). Constituting cultures of compassion in early childhood educational settings. In S. Garvis & E. E. Ødegaard (Eds.), *Nordic dialogue on children and families* (pp. 39–50). Routledge.

Masten, A. S. (2001). Ordinary magic: Resilience processes in development. *American Psychologist, 56*(3), 227–238.

Masten, A. S. (2018). Resilience theory and research on children and families: Past, present, and promise. *Journal of Family Theory and Review, 10*(1), 12–31.

Masten, A. S., & Barnes, A. J. (2018). Resilience in children: Developmental perspectives. *Children (Basel, Switzerland), 5*(7), 1–16. https://doi.org/10.3390/children5070098

Mguni, N., Bacon, N., & Brown, J. F. (2011). *The wellbeing and resilience paradox.* The Young Foundation.

Mikulincer, M., & Shaver, P. R. (2017). An attachment perspective on compassion and altruism. In P. Gilbert (Ed.), *Compassion: Concepts, research and applications* (pp. 187–202). Routledge, Taylor & Francis Group.

Moss, P., & Robert-Holmes, G. (2021). Now is the time! Confronting neo-liberalism in early childhood. *Contemporary Issues in Early Childhood, 23*(1), 96–99.

Nah, K., Bjørgen, K., Go, Y. M., & Yoo, Y. E. (2020). A comparative study of ECEC practitioners' perceptions of children's wellbeing and their roles in South Korea and Norway. *European Early Childhood Education Research Journal, 28*(6), 847–863.

Nolan, A., Taket, A., & Stagnitti, K. (2014). Supporting resilience in early years classrooms: The role of the teacher. *Teachers and Teaching, 20*(5), 595–608.

Ong, A. D., Zautra, A. J., & Reid, M. C. (2010). Psychological resilience predicts decreases in pain catastrophizing through positive emotions. *Psychology and Aging, 25*(3), 516–523.

O'Toole, C., & Simovska, V. (2022). Wellbeing and education: Connecting mind, body and world. In R. McLellan, C. Faucher, & V. Simovska (Eds.), *Wellbeing and schooling: Cross-cultural and cross-disciplinary perspectives* (pp. 21–33). Springer.

Pascal, C., & Bertram, T. (2021). *Young voices on COVID project*. The Centre for Research in Early Childhood.

Preckel, K., Kanske, P., & Singer, T. (2018). On the interaction of social affect and cognition: Empathy, compassion and theory of mind. *Current Opinion in Behavioral Sciences, 19*, 1–6.

Quinones, G., & Cooper, M. (2022). Infant–toddler teachers' compassionate pedagogies for emotionally intense experiences. *Early Years*, 1–17.

Rajala, A., & Lipponen, L. (2018). Compassion in narrations of early childhood education student teachers in Finland. In S. Garvis, S. Phillipson, & H. Harju-Luukkainen (Eds.), *Early childhood education in the 21st century: An international* perspective (Vol. I, pp. 64–75). Routledge.

Roberts-Holmes, G., & Bradbury, A. (2016). The datafication of early years education and its impact upon pedagogy. *Improving Schools, 19*(2), 119–128.

Rogoff, B., Dahl, A., & Callanan, M. (2018). The importance of understanding children's lived experience. *Developmental Review, 50*, 5–15.

Rutter, M. (2012). Resilience as a dynamic concept. *Development and psychopathology, 24*(2), 335–344.

Saarinen, A. I., Keltikangas-Järvinen, L., Pulkki-Råback, L., Cloninger, C. R., Elovainio, M., Lehtimäki, T., Raitakari, O., & Hintsanen, M. (2019). The relationship of dispositional compassion with well-being: A study with a 15-year prospective follow-up. *The Journal of Positive Psychology, 15*(6), 806–820.

Seaman, H., & Giles, P. (2019). Supporting children's social and emotional well-being in the early years: An exploration of practitioners' perceptions. *Early Child Development and Care, 191*(6), 861–875.

Shonkoff, J. P., & Phillips, D. A. (2000). *From neurons to neighborhoods: The science of early childhood development*. National Academy Press.

Singer, T., & Klimecki, O. M. (2014). Empathy and compassion. *Current Biology, 24*(18), R875–R878.

Social Mobility Commission. (2020). The stability of the early years workforce in England. *Gov.UK*. Retrieved December 5, 2021, from https://www.gov.uk/government/publications/the-stability-of-the-early-years-workforce-in-england

Spikins, P. (2017). Prehistoric origins: The compassion of far distant strangers. In *Compassion* (pp. 16–30). Routledge.

Stellar, J. E., & Keltner, D. (2017). Compassion in the autonomic nervous system: The role of the vagus nerve. In P. Gilbert (Ed.), *Compassion* (pp. 120–134). Routledge.

Taggart, G. (2016). Compassionate pedagogy: The ethics of care in early childhood professionalism. *European Early Childhood Education Research Journal, 24*(2), 173–185.

Tronto, J. (1993). *Moral boundaries: A political argument for an ethic of care* (1st ed.). Routledge.

Tugade, M. M., & Fredrickson, B. L. (2004). Resilient individuals use positive emotions to bounce back from negative emotional experiences. *Journal of Personality and Social Psychology, 86*(2), 320–333. https://doi.org/10.1037/0022-3514.86.2.320

Tugade, M. M., Fredrickson, B. L., & Barrett, L. F. (2004). Psychological resilience and positive emotional granularity: Examining the benefits of positive emotions on coping and health. *Journal of Personality, 72*(6),1161–1190.

Ungar, M. (2013). Resilience, trauma, context, and culture. *Trauma, Violence, & Abuse, 14*(3), 255–266. https://doi.org/10.1177/1524838013487805

United Nations Educational, Scientific and Cultural Organization [UNESCO]. (2017). *Education for sustainable development goals: Learning objectives* [e-book]. Retrieved October 6, 2018, from https://unesdoc.unesco.org/ark:/48223/pf0000247444

United Nations Educational, Scientific and Cultural Organization [UNESCO]. (2019). *Educational content up close: Examining the learning dimensions of education for sustainable development and global citizenship education*. UN.

United Nations Educational, Scientific and Cultural Organization [UNESCO]. (2020). Education for sustainable development: A roadmap. Retrieved May 15, 2021, from https://unesdoc.unesco.org/ark:/48223/pf0000374802

Vachon, D. D., Krueger, R. F., Rogosch, F. A., & Cicchetti, D. (2015). Assessment of the harmful psychiatric and behavioral effects of different forms of child maltreatment. *JAMA Psychiatry, 72*(11), 1135–1142.

Wang, J. L. Zhang, D. J., & Zimmerman, M., A. (2015). Resilience Theory and its Implications for Chinese Adolescents. *Psychological Reports.* 117(2), 354–375.

Weare, K. (2022). Foreword. In R. McLellan, C. Faucher, & V. Simovska (Eds.), *Wellbeing and schooling: Cross-cultural and cross-disciplinary perspectives* (pp. v–x). Springer.

Werner, E. (1996). Vulnerable but invincible: High risk children from birth to adulthood. *European Child & Adolescent Psychiatry*, (1), 47–51. https://doi.org/10.1007/BF00538544

Werner, E. (2013). What can we learn about resilience from large-scale longitudinal studies. In S. Goldstein & R. Brooks (Eds.), *Handbook of resilience in children* (pp. 87–102). Springer.

Werner, E., & Smith, R. S. (1992). *Overcoming the odds: High risk children from birth to adulthood*. McGraw Hill.

Windle, G. (2011). What is resilience? A review and concept analysis. *Reviews in Clinical Gerontology, 21*(2), 152–169.

World Health Organisation [WHO]. (2022a). *World mental health report: Transforming mental health for all*. World Health Organization.

World Health Organisation [WHO]. (2022b). *Mental health: Strengthening our response*. https://www.who.int/news-room/fact-sheets/detail/mental-health-strengthening-our-response

8

TOWARDS A PEDAGOGY OF HOPE

Creating a Listening Culture for Nurturing Children's Wellbeing

Naomi McLeod, Diane Boyd, Catrina Luz Aniere and Suzanne Axelsson

Introduction

In creating a socio-cultural discourse that nurtures children's wellbeing, this chapter unpicks the current early education context and the need for deep listening (by adults) as a reflexive, strength-based approach, in the same way that Freire (1994) promoted his Pedagogy of Hope and also in line with Sustainable Development Goal (SDG) 3, United Nations Educational, Scientific and Cultural Organisation (UNESCO, 2015). Two community-based reflexive pedagogies of hope for promoting a deep listening culture and nurturing children's wellbeing are provided. The first is from Western Australia working respectfully with Indigenous children (*On Country*). The second involves a Palestinian refugee camp that utilises the principles of '*Philosophy for/with Children*' which is best understood as an educational praxis (an action that is consciously committed to human wellbeing and behaving ethically). The endeavour of P4C in practice is participatory and democratic in nature and focuses on the importance of creating a safe, caring, critical, creative, collaborative space (Stanley & Lyle, 2017). Both pedagogies require engaging respectfully and reflexively 'with' communities from other cultures and countries. Here, an 'ethics of care' is significant and is concerned with a relationship that includes both caring as a general habit of mind (Tronto, 1993) characterised by a deep respect for the 'Other' and an emphasis on the importance of relationships which respect alterity (the otherness of the Other) and resist attempting to make the Other into the same (Dahlberg & Moss, 2005, p. 6).

The Current Climate

There is growing realisation and concern that society (including education) in its current form is in crisis (Moss, 2017, 2019) and is inadequate for meeting the needs of the 21st century and for shaping a sustainably well future (International Panel on Climate Change) (IPCC Report, 2022). The current top-down government pressures associated with an over emphasis on assessment, accountability and measured outcomes encourages a technical approach to teaching based on a transmission and reproduction of knowledge (Urban, 2017). Moss (2017, 2019) considers this the result of wider economic competition, profit making and global consumer markets of neoliberalism, associated with greed that creates a power imbalance. As a result, in education, there is often no room for creativity, experiential learning, listening to children or authentic consideration of children's wellbeing and mental health. According to Hickham (2019), children are anxious, distressed and angry at the troubling disconnect between what adults say and what adults do.

In response, this chapter draws on Freire's pedagogy of hope as an alternative narrative, that is socially just and democratic (1994, 1970). Only when educators are aware of the 'politics' that surround education, can education really make sense and become a 'practice of freedom' (Mayo County Council, 2019, p. 5). At the heart of this process is the need to be reflexive which starts by being open and willing to question and develop an awareness of personal values and biases in the context of education. This consciousness can in turn lead to a more deliberate scrutinising of assumptions that underpin pedagogy as a whole. Viewing through different lenses (McLeod, 2019; Brookfield, 2017) can empower educators to be open to (an)other way of seeing and being and make informed decisions about issues associated with power and control (Moss, 2019). This process of deep listening, however, can be both difficult and uncomfortable and requires a space or conditions that allow for being brave and honest, so accepted norms can be challenged.

Children's Holistic Wellbeing

Positive characteristics associated with wellbeing include self-worth, confidence, courage, resilience and the ability to face challenges and learn from mistakes and develop a sense of belonging as part of a family and community (Kingdon et al., 2017; Jelic, 2014; Brooker & Woodhead, 2008). As Laevers (2005) indicates, children's emotional wellbeing is closely linked with enjoyment, feeling connected with themselves and identity (Underdown, 2007).

UNESCO (2015) highlights wellbeing as a key aspect of Sustainable Development Goal 3: Good Health and Wellbeing, with wellbeing identified as 'a feeling of satisfaction with life, a state characterised by health, happiness, and prosperity' (UNESCO, 2021, line 1), initiated through a holistic approach to learning. In defining wellbeing, the DfE (2020, p. 18) in England, as part of the '*State of the Nation 2020: children and young people's wellbeing*' defined good wellbeing as 'the hallmark of a caring and just society' and important for ensuring all children reach their true potential. This resonates with O'Brien (2016, p. 14) who suggests that wellbeing is 'inextricably associated with the wellbeing of others and the natural environment'. Historically, wellbeing is recognised as crucial to good living. Aristotle's philosophical thinking (384–322 BC) was concerned with the pursuit of happiness and well living as associated with what was morally good, contributed to human flourishing as part of a good life. For Aristotle, this was not possible to develop from one's own virtues without benefitting others. His philosophy was therefore for everyone as part of an interrelated society. As Aristotle (1925, p. 11) stated, in seeking good in one's life, 'we call that which is in itself worthy of pursuit more final than that which is worthy of pursuit for the sake of something else'. That something was happiness, suggesting that 'the happy man lives well' (Noddings, 2003, p. 151). Happiness flows as a result of individual happiness, wellbeing and pleasure. This resonates with Narvaez (2015) and Noddings (2003) who link wellbeing with flourishing and happiness within the context of a person's socio-moral capacities and networks.

Building on this the British Columbia Ministry of Education (2019, p. 69) identifies wellbeing as linked to both joy and belonging, with the idea of joy in relationships with people and places. This resonates with Moss (2013, p. 82) who notes that places give 'constant hope to wonder and surprise, magic moments and goose bumps, and a source of hope and renewed belief in the world'. Moss highlighted that happiness and wellbeing stems from the awe and wonder, and love of place, which as a result gives a strong sense of belonging, and as a result, wellbeing.

In contrast, a negative sense of wellbeing and view of the self have been linked to mental health issues such as anxiety, stress, low self-esteem and a lack of confidence (McLean et al., 2010). For example, a growing body of research suggests that current societal issues, such as climate change, are leading to 'eco-anxiety' with children feeling worthless, afraid and angry. There is little confidence in adult rhetoric or inaction, and their low self-esteem and stress are a result of their 'overwhelming sense of responsibility to deal with something so huge it becomes paralysing' (The Lancet Child, 2021, p. 91)

Indigenous communities have always associated the interconnectedness of the land and people, with the reality that we *are* the environment. Indigenous thinking draws on the land, by listening to it, is one with the land, and has a deep cultural immersion of both body and soul and is key to wellbeing (Ward et al., 2021). The First Peoples Principles of Learning in British Columbia, for example, highlight that not only is learning holistic but also is reflexive, relational and experimental, while recognising that there is a connectedness of *all*, when considering wellbeing. It states that 'learning ultimately supports the wellbeing of the self, the family, the community, the land, the spirits and the ancestors' (BC, Early Learning Framework 2019, p. 14) which requires a deep level of listening. This deep level of listening requires an openness or reflexivity about how we view the world and the cultural, historical, political influences that shape who we are and a sense of what is right. Ward et al. (2021) acknowledge that as well as listening to the land, listening to, and interacting with 'Tshenut' (the Elders) a cultural practice to access the wisdom of past generations, is viewed as significant in contributing to Innu wellbeing, a strong identity that fosters a sense of freedom. While wellbeing is often associated with happiness globally, O'Brien (2016) cautions that in contrast to indigenous communities, a western consumer society happiness can become extrinsically entangled. As Kasser (2006, p. 200) states, happiness should be 'the path to the good life' but is often confused with 'goods life'.

Deep Listening and Self-Reflection

Through deep, respectful listening as an authentic, rights-based, relational pedagogical approach, children can feel valued and heard, which in turn can nurture a sense of wellbeing and feeling connected. Listening or attending to the other person is not always comfortable. The words 'attend' and 'tension' share a common root, tendere, which means 'to stretch'. To really attend to another or to pay attention to another person, we must stretch ourselves; we must really strain to listen, to see, to feel that it is not a casual process (British Columbia Ministry of Education, 2019, p. 48). At the heart of this pedagogy of listening (Rinaldi, 2006; Malaguzzi, 1994), creating a safe, trusting, open, caring, respectful space, so children feel comfortable expressing themselves is essential (Laevers, 2005; Stanley & Lyle, 2017). This requires adults who are reflexive and value children's voice as part of democratic, relational pedagogy. Being ready to engage in internal listening and self-awareness of unconscious bias through questioning of personal assumptions is crucial here for appreciating other perspectives and tuning into the many ways that children communicate and display their feelings (Edwards et al., 2012; McLeod, 2019).

Creating a safe, open, respectful space begins when adults take children's perspectives seriously in line with Articles 12 and 13 of the United Nations (1989) and offer opportunities that are active rather than passive as part of processes that matter to them (Clark, 2017, 2005; Rinaldi, 2006). To interpret accurately what is being communicated by another person (child or adult), there is the need to start with ourselves and develop self-awareness of our own listening (McLeod, 2019).

As Scharmer (2009) reminds us, the tendency is to hear what is familiar to us based on our personal experiences and biases. In reality, 'very little is heard other than what we have heard before' (ibid. p. xiv). Most situations remain the same because our awareness 'renders it invisible' (p. xiv). There is a lack of response to the subtle powers that influence us. As a result, when we listen, we selectively hear or over generalise what is familiar to us based on our views, experiences and feelings, so the 'other' (the new) is taken and turned into the familiar (McLeod, 2019). For Rinaldi, the pedagogy of listening requires openness at its core and a welcoming of differences which Schön (1987) referred to as a 'convergence of meaning' – an honest and accurate interpretation. Here, Levinas identifies the need to check the accuracy of our interpretation, so there is not a mis-representation or as Rinaldi called it 'the ethics of an encounter' (2006, p. 14), which is particularly important for supporting children's wellbeing. This reflexive active listening process begins by being ready to engage in internal listening and self-awareness of unconscious bias and behaviours (McLeod, 2015), which can happen through personal questioning and disciplined noticing (Mason, 2002).

Internal or multiple listening as part of Rinaldi's pedagogy of listening (2006) is complex and needs to be visible as a daily commitment to nurture children's wellbeing. As part of our daily experiences, noticing is something we constantly do. It is unlikely however that we are aware of sensory noticing as part of experiences, for example, how we hold a book and the sensation of it in our hands, or how we read it, and sounds around us, unless these features have been brought to our attention. In a world that is busy, hectic and pressurised, finding time to listen or notice on a basic level is challenging, never mind engaging with listening on a deeper level so it includes our senses. And yet, our greatest needs as human beings, such as belonging, being loved, having a sense of identity and wellbeing, require us to listen. Developing our listening, or 'noticing' as Mason (2002) refers to it, is not easy because we are not in the habit of noticing on a deeper, sensory level. As Mason (2002) suggests, noticing needs to become a discipline that involves researching or noticing from the inside as an internal process. In this way, the discipline of noticing involves being sensitive to a situation through self-awareness so we can be awake to possibilities and respond appropriately.

In the context of wellbeing, sensory noticing is key in terms of being able to observe things that might otherwise be overlooked to demonstrate authentic empathy, show we care and be able to offer appropriate support. It requires 'being present and sensitive in the moment' (p, 1). Until we notice with our senses and become aware of our hidden assumptions, dispositions and behaviours, we are not in a position to relate to others. Central to this is 'harnessing emotion as the source of pycho-socio-cultural energy' (Mason, 2002, p. 96). As Maturana (1988) said, 'Reason drives us only through the emotions which arise in us'. Such practice offers hope for creating a listening culture for nurturing children's wellbeing.

A Pedagogy of Hope

In the same way that Aristotle recognised the need for praxis as a moral disposition to act truthfully and rightly and have a concern to further human wellbeing and the good life, Freire (1994) speaks of 'praxis' as action supported by reflection (examining one's own experiences and views). In praxis, there is a continual interplay between ends and means so that action is informed with a moral intent. When resistance is combined with movement, there is hope, in the same way that Freire (1970, 1994) promoted in his Pedagogy of Hope. Hope is the necessary ingredient for a new reality that embraces an alternative democratic discourse in the context of neoliberalism, decolonisation, ongoing conflict and the impact of global pandemic and nurturing a positive sense of wellbeing. Creating a safe, open, respectful dialogical space enables children to make connections between their sociocultural contexts, and the relationship with personal thoughts, feelings, wellbeing and the confidence to take action (Hilppö et al., 2016). Such an approach is central to an ethical, socially just way of learning and wellbeing. This requires effective participation with children, so adults can access their viewpoints, anxieties and experiences. Our conceptualisation of a positive wellbeing is therefore inextricably linked to democratic participatory practice and deep listening. Such qualities are valued as part of Philosophy with/for Children which is best understood as an educational praxis (an action that is consciously committed to human wellbeing and behaving ethically (Stanley & Lyle, 2017). The endeavour of P4C in practice is participatory and democratic in nature and incorporates thinking critically, creatively and collaboratively in a caring manner for supporting young children's wellbeing and identity (Clark, 2017). The teacher's role is to listen, respond respectfully to children's contributions and facilitate open-ended enquiries (Haynes & Murris, 2013).

As part of this chapter, and our hope for nurturing wellbeing through deep listening, we also recognise the importance of listening to the land, listening to, and interacting with 'Tshenut' (the Elders) who are recognised as wisdom keepers or cultural custodians, an Indigenous cultural practice to access the wisdom of past generations that supports the wellbeing of Indigenous children. Blenkinsop and Fettes (2020) note that Indigenous cultures value land relationally, and the importance of listening on a deeper level. This deeper level is demonstrated through 'respectful listening and silent, attentive observation' stressing that these values should be embedded from the earliest years (2020, p. 1041). Jickling et al. (2018) further suggest that to listen deeply with the land, in fact changes your relationship with the it and your 'being in the world'. Blenkinsop and Fettes (2020, p. 1042) liken this 'being with the world' as a consequence of 'spending time on the land, coming to know its rhythms and ways of speaking', which they describe as the 'intellectual rigour required to listen well', thus implying it is a disciplined requirement (similar to Mason, 2002) as well as relational. Nesterova (2020) reflects that through this relational and ethical acknowledgement of the land through listening, a spiritual connection develops organically, which teaches people to listen to nature and be protective of the health and wellbeing of the natural environment. In this way, wellbeing and good health (SDG 3) are intrinsically linked with listening and relationships between human and non-humans.

Two Community-Based Approaches

Next we explore two community-based approaches as pedagogies of hope for promoting a listening culture and nurturing children's wellbeing. First, Catrina Luz Aniere provides insight into the '*Kids on Country*' programme implemented in the Goldfields within the Woodlands in Western Australia; an indigenous intergenerational community-based pedagogy associated with decolonisation and intergenerational trauma (The Wilderness Society, 2020). We deconstruct socio-cultural dimensions associated with holistic listening as a reflexive and strength-based approach against the colonial backdrop that Australia has experienced. Given a Western understanding of the environment as separate to people, using this relational understanding, we demonstrate why and how Indigenous sustainability knowledge can help heal environments (Yunkaporta, 2019). Second, Suzanne Axelsson demonstrates respectful listening working as part of a Palestinian refugee camp community in Jenin and the importance of creating a safe, caring, critical, creative, collaborative space for nurturing children's wellbeing.

Case Study 1 'Kids on Country' in Western Australia: Reflections on Deep Listening and Wellbeing (by Catrina Luz Aniere)

Right time
Right people
Right place

I have been walking through the woodland
Deep listening
Listening and learning
Reflection
At the heart of it.

Turn your mind
Inside out
And hear the trees, the wind, the sand
The flowers
Turning their

Heads to speak to
You
More than words.
It is the sounds, the sun
The past, the future, the now.

Acknowledging different ways of thinking
Listening
The learning
Together
Two way.

Context to the Case Study

Catrina Luz Aniere is CEO of *Millennium Kids Inc.*, a youth-led environmental organisation, where young people can tackle big societal issues. She has a passion for youth voice and engagement and has 27 years of experience of working with young people to change their world. '*Kids on Country*' is a collaborative project between '*Millennium Kids*' and the community of Traditional Indigenous Owners in remote Western Australia.

As the author, I Catrina respectfully acknowledge Betty and Maxine as the Traditional Indigenous Owners and Elders/cultural custodians, who live in Western Australian, Coolgardie. Through *Kids on Country*, we fully respect Indigenous intergenerational knowledge, attitudes and practices of sustainability and place-based, family-focused learning which is fundamental to this programme.

This pedagogical case study highlights the importance of telling the story around Indigenous concepts and ideas which rely upon a deep, reflexive relational way of understanding people as reciprocal carers of place. For example, the term '*Country*' is often capitalised in Australian Indigenous contexts to denote an understanding of one's spiritual and cultural homeland, which is relational and more inclusive than is understood by 'country' in English. The English language tends to see environment and people as separate, but Indigenous language speakers and knowledge holders see these 'categories' as inseparable.

However, the expectation in western Australian state classrooms is that children will conform to a set of established behaviours, rules from the dominant white culture. Children are expected to listen to learn. But as part of *On Country*, we talk openly about wellness, children's rights and being culturally responsive.

Kids on Country acknowledges that all children have the right to practice their own culture, language and religion in line with the United Nations Convention on the Rights of the Child (1989, article 3). The programme is developing a wellness framework based on deep listening and reflection, working alongside Traditional Owners and children, scientists and artists on Country. The framework is based on guidelines for building positive, culturally appropriate learning experiences and educators, who can build relationships in the community to support the mental health and wellbeing of children. Wellness for us is about learning together in a safe environment, eating food together, having conversations, listening and laughing together. This reflects a deep all-encompassing mutual respect in line with the Sustainable Development Goals (UNESCO, 2015) (SDG 3: Good Health and Wellbeing and SDG 4: Quality Education) underpin this wellness framework, based on guidelines for building positive, culturally appropriate learning experiences and educators, who can build relationships in the community to support the mental health and wellbeing of children.

In the following case study, the children were listened to as they spoke through their actions.

On Country Case Study: Listening With Our Hearts

After a two-hour bus journey to the campsite, we set up camp by lighting a fire, cooking our food and organising our beds. There was lots laughter and smiles. We had torches for a night walk to the red rock, where children could explore independently and organically, lie under the night sky, point out the stars and tell sky stories. Cultural custodians (Betty and Maxine) shared important cultural stories around the gnamma (a natural hole in a rock in which rainwater collects). *These natural cavities are commonly found in hard rock, particularly granite outcrops which acts as natural water tanks, which are replenished from underground stores and rainwater run-off.*

However, three children walked away from the gnamma, agitated and loud, throwing sticks and skimming stones. If we want children to listen, to speak out about the big issues in their world, we need to role model with our actions, so we show we are listening, and acting on what they tell us. Their behaviour was telling. This was not the right time, right place and right people. Being *On Country* is complex. There are things as non-Indigenous people we do not know and so do not see or feel. For whatever reason, the children were not comfortable in this place, at this time.

A car was arranged and the three children went back to town. It was not a punishment. There was no reprimanding. It was their right to feel uncomfortable, to 'speak' up and determine their place in the world. For them to 'speak' without words. To shout '*This is not my place*'. To know they had been heard was important.

The next day at the pool the bus came back for the children who waved when the bus pulled in. All smiles. They jumped on.

While the children are *On Country*, the children move freely across the landscape. Some swim in the rocky pool, others look for critters in the shallow waters. There may be frogs and a frog story, depending on the time of year. Some collect sticks and make the fire. Others sit under the trees and draw and paint, and share stories of the important places they visit, to make sense of their world. We all walk into the area burnt by bushfire and talk of the malleefowl. We find the big old nest and wonder whether the birds will come back. We talk of fire (kala) and use symbols and signs to make maps in the sand, so we can find the place again. Learning their way is important and shows respect.

Reflecting on these experiences *On Country*, the children say 'We love it when that "koonyi" white bus comes around the corner'. Deep listening and reflection have engaged these youngsters in '*On Country*' experiences when ordinary state classrooms don't. As a result of this programme over the last nine years, the children have developed a sense of belonging and empowerment. The health and wellbeing of our Indigenous children need educators to engage in deep listening and include culturally appropriate learning styles that are deeply embedded in Indigenous ways. *Kids on Country* is responsive. It is inclusive. Decision-making is participatory with involvement from all members of our intergenerational team reflecting a meaningful interpretation of SDG 17.

Reflecting upon the start of the programme, in our first meeting together, we stood in a circle, each of us introducing ourselves by name, family, country and place of birth. The Elder/cultural custodian, Betty stood there and said: '*I was born here. This is my Country. My parents and grandparents were born here. I can trace my family back*'.

This resonates then and it resonates now as we continue to work with the oldest living culture in the world. We should listen with our hearts and with our feet, to people *On Country*, wherever we are. If we want wellness, we must become the learners.

Case Study 2   A Palestinian Refugee Camp Community (Suzanne)

By Suzanne Axelsson

I was asked by The Freedom Theatre to work with Palestinian educators in Jenin to deepen their understanding of a play pedagogy for preschool children as their early years curriculum had been updated to be play based, and there was a thirst for knowledge. I was aware of my privilege, my lack of knowledge of Islamic pedagogical traditions (Shofi, 2003), the Arabic language, and lack of experience in this part of the world. I realised that in order to be a meaningful pedagogical advisor, I would have to listen to the educators, the children, the urban, natural landscapes, the history weighing heavily on the present and the continued story of conflict.

As an educator of young children in Sweden, I had been using 'Philosophy with Children' aged two to five as a listening and dialogue tool as part of a democratic space (Axelsson, 2020). By democracy, I mean that everyone is able to participate and have influence, to the best of their ability, as well as feeling valued. When I first started developing this approach, I discovered that listening was key for supporting children's wellbeing (Biggeri & Santi, 2012). This involved my ability as an educator to listen without an agenda and to scaffold the children's ability to listen to each other. This is active listening in order to understand, rather than just expecting the children to be quiet while waiting their turn to talk. I visited kindergartens and schools in Jenin, in Palestine and noticed the rules, routines and hierarchies within the group of teachers that became visible over time, including between those that lived in the camp and those who did not.

Change is not an easy process. It means uprooting what you know and planting new seeds. It requires trust, so creating safe, caring, creative and brave spaces for the teachers was essential. Many of the educators lacked a holistic understanding of play, as they did not have the opportunity to play when they were young; their childhoods marred with violence, displacement and occupation. I listened to their stories. I cried with them, for their past, their present and for the fears they have for their children. The lack of resources in schools, personal loss, violence and lack of hope that there will be peace are negatively impacting on the children's wellbeing (Mahamid & Berte, 2020).

Through listening, it became clear that what I needed to provide were opportunities:

- to play, so they understand how it feels,
- to truly listen to them, so they know how being valued feels, and
- to ensure everything I share is safe to put into practice.

This meant that I did not talk about gender equality, as Palestinian society was not ready for these dialogues, and change could endanger the children they taught, even some of the educators could be negatively affected by encouraging this kind of equality (Jarrar, 2015). I listened with my whole body. I moved differently (no hopping and skipping as usual in public), I dressed differently and, as I walked around the town, my senses were bombarded with what felt like chaos compared to the well-ordered Stockholm I call home. There was rubbish everywhere, vehicles and people jostled in the streets with a noisy equality, and every evening the sound of guns and booms would fill the air, sometimes to celebrate a wedding or the return of an incarcerated family member, sometimes as violent, even fatal, altercations. This would be followed by the sound of children crying who were woken up by the noise. Every educator I met has been woken up during the middle of the night by Israeli soldiers to search their homes; the family, including the children, who are required to stand in the living room (Veronese et al., 2010). I am aware of how sleep deprivation negatively impacts cognitive development and wellbeing (Hill et al., 2007). The children are learning on a sleep deficit. The teachers are teaching on one too.

When visiting kindergartens, I observed how many of the educators would hit children who were not behaving as expected, which included when the children were hitting each other. As classes and groups had a low adult ratio (100:4 among three- to five-year-olds), it seemed to increase the frequency to use a hitting strategy as the default tool for control and correcting the children's behaviour. Hitting was also an expected punishment by parents for children who neither behaved nor succeeded as expected.

I made the decision to listen and not pass or make judgement, so I could try and understand the process from other perspectives. This was far from easy. Building trust rather than me making suggestions was important if the teachers were to be open to listening and change. After getting to know them for six months, one of the educators asked me:

How can we stop the children from hitting each other?
I replied, '*I don't think it helps that you hit them.*'

This was met with various voices saying how they did not hit hard, yet previously they had shared stories about how they, as children, had been hit by teachers and how they hated it, and some were hit hard. I explained that while adults might not hit hard, the children learned that when they did something a teacher didn't like, they were hit. So naturally, when a peer does something that they do not like, they hit too, lacking the self-regulation to make it gentle. This eventually spiralled out of control. My 17-year-old daughter was with me at the time, and they all considered her well-raised and polite. They asked her if I had ever hit her. Rather shocked, she shook her head. It was a powerful moment. This was new knowledge to them. They did not know that this was possible.

Afterwards, I was on my way into town with one of the educators and her daughter. The mother raised her hand as a reflex when her daughter swerved into the road, but then paused and marvelled at the fact her daughter self-corrected.

This simple pause provided the time to notice her child's competence. All of this reality needed to be listened to and resulted in me weaving trauma-informed play activities based on 'Philosophy with Children' into our sessions together. I spent many hours carefully listening and noticing the educators, and then planning, depending on how the educators had responded. The rhythm of our play responsive 'Philosophy with Children' sessions were predictable, calm, filled with joy, stories and sensory play (including shadows, light, water and ice). New things were always introduced together with the familiar, such as local resources and approaches to teaching, and it was important I was attuned to the teachers' responses to scaffold a positive, caring, calm and creative learning environment for the children. After a while, these strategies were discussed as a model for the educators to use with the children.

Using 'Philosophy with Children' strategies (Axelsson, 2020), I created a space of listening and respect for the educators, where sniggering and belittling comments were not allowed and that *all* questions, comments and ideas were welcome as they could be the seed of change if we worked collectively at cultivating it. The teachers from Jenin camp came to me at the end of our first three weeks, telling me the joy of feeling listened to and valued for the first time.

It's such a small thing.

Listening

But the impact genuine listening has on wellbeing is huge.

I was given the nickname 'Shukran' which is Arabic for thank you. Apparently, the other teachers would use 'yalla' to get their attention and *make* them learn. Instead, I waited quietly until they were ready and then said *'thank you'* when they were ready to listen. A lot of time initially seemed wasted, but I felt that sometimes their talks together were just as vital as what I had to offer. My agenda was to facilitate their understanding of playful learning; it was not to teach them a set number of facts. It was also a way to create a sense of equity and to ease the hierarchy I had observed. We *all* came to the space as equals, with different knowledges and experiences and using 'Philosophy with Children', we shared these with each other so that a more democratic approach could be translated into a Palestinian context. The aim was to nurture their understanding about the importance of listening first hand by experiencing:

- how it feels to be listened to
- practising listening through play and dialogue
- engaging in play that enables transdisciplinary learning
- listening to children with all their senses

This enabled the teachers to gain a deeper understanding of how they could recreate this in their classrooms.

By encouraging the teachers to play and mess about, they began to decode the language of childhood (Hawkins, 2003) and play became an act of listening and wellbeing. By laughing together as we played, joy and curiosity, instead of competition and being right, became the driving forces of finding out more and making unexpected discoveries. Fear and trauma can force children to lose this language of play, having to put energy into surviving rather than thriving (Stone & Bray, 2015). For many in Palestine, this is a transgenerational problem.

Summary

The aforementioned case studies demonstrate powerfully how deep reflective listening can facilitate respectful understandings of other less familiar cultural perspectives to promote relational ways of being as a pedagogy of hope. For children growing up in the 21st century (particularly in the context of war, a global pandemic, decolonisation, climate change and neoliberalism), creating a listening culture for nurturing children's wellbeing and a space to deal with anxieties is essential. Bourn and Hatley (2022) highlight that both the UN and UNESCO have consistently called for the voices and needs of children and young people to be recognised and central to any policy, suggesting that listening is key to this success. Children and young people's anxieties about the future of their families, communities and their planet are a direct result of recognition that these societal issues affect them more than any other sector within society. As Rinaldi (2006, p. 80) notes 'listening is not easy' but this can only be achieved with deep awareness of (an)other perspective, a recognition of any unconscious bias and essentially an 'openness to change'.

Wellbeing is inextricably linked to cultural knowledge, knowing Country, understanding family and belonging in the world. Good health and wellbeing (SDG 3) (UNESCO, 2015) require that all children and young people have healthy lives and wellbeing at all ages, regardless of culture, gender and socio-economic status. With the rise of eco-anxiety, authentic deep listening, as the case studies demonstrate, offers an approach that has the power to transform and offer hope for shaping a sustainably well future.

References

Aristotle. (1925). *The Nicomacheon Ethics*. Oxford University Press.
Axelsson, S. (2020). *Philosophy with children in a pandemic*. https://www.interactionimagination.com/post/philosophy-with-children-during-a-pandemic
Biggeri, M., & Santi, M. (2012). The missing dimensions of children's wellbeing and Well-becoming in education systems: Capabilities and philosophy for children.

Journal of Human Development and Capabilities, 13(3), 373–395. https://doi.org/10.1080/19452829.2012.694858

Blenkinsop, S., & Fettes, M. (2020). Land, language and listening: The transformations that can flow from acknowledging indigenous land. *Journal of Philosophy of Education, 54*(4), 1033–1046. https://doi.org/10.1111/1467-9752.12470

Bourn, D., & Hatley, J. (2022). *Target 4.7 of the sustainable development goals: Evidence in schools in England. Research for our shared world.* Development Education Research Centre, Institute of Education Research Paper No 2.

British Columbia Ministry of Education. (2019). *British Columbia early learning framework* [Online]. early_learning_framework.pdf gov.bc.ca

Brooker, L., & Woodhead, M. eds. (2008). Developing positive identities: Diversity and young children. *Early childhood in focus (3)*. Milton Keynes: Open University.

Brookfield, S. D. (2017). *Becoming a critically reflective teacher* (2nd ed.). Jossey-Bass A Wiley Company.

Clark, A. (2005). Listening to and involving young children: A review of research and practice. *Early Child Development & Care, 175*(6), 489–505. https://doi.org/10.1080/03004430500131288.

Clark, A. (2017). *Listening to young children, expanded: A guide to understanding and using the Mosaic approach* (3rd ed.). Kingsley Publishers.

Dahlberg, G., & Moss, P. (2005). *Ethics and politics in early childhood education*. Routledge.

DfE. (2020). *State of the nation: Children and young people's wellbeing*. Government Social Research, Crown Publications.

Edwards, C., Gandini, L., & Forman, G. E. (2012). *The hundred languages of children: The Reggio Emilia experience in transformation* (3rd ed.). Praeger.

Freire, P. (1970). *Cultural action for freedom* (M. Bergman, Trans.). Penguin.

Freire, P. (1994). *Pedagogy of hope*. Continuum.

Hawkins, D. (2003). *Messing about in science: Informed vision*. Algora Publishing.

Haynes, J., & Murris, K. (2013). The Realm of meaning: Imagination, narrative and playfulness in philosophical exploration with young children. *Early Child Development and Care, 183*(8), 1084–1100. https://doi.org/10.1080/03004430.2013.792256

Hickham, C. (2019, September 15). I'm a psychotherapist–here's what I've learned from listening to children talk about climate change. *The Conversation* [Online]. Retrieved May 25, 2022, from https://theconversation.com/im-a-psychotherapist-heres-what-ive-learned-from-listening-to-children-talk-about-climate-change-123183

Hill, C. M., Hogan, A. M., & Karmiloff-Smith, A. (2007). To sleep, perchance to enrich learning? *Archives of Disease in Childhood, 92*, 637–643. https://doi.org/10.1136/adc.2006.096156.

Hilppö, J. Lipponen, L., Kumpulainen, K., & Rainio, A. (2016). Children's sense of agency in preschool: A sociocultural investigation. *International Journal of Early Years Education, 24*(2), 157–171. https://doi.org/10.1080/09669760.2016.1167676

International Panel on Climate Change (IPCC) Report. (2022). *Climate change 2022: Impacts, adaptation and vulnerability. Summary for policymakers* [Online]. https://www.ipcc.ch/report/ar6/wg2/downloads/report/IPCC_AR6_WGII_FinalDraft_FullReport.pdf

Jarrar, N. (2015). *A study of to what extent the national early childhood development strategy and kindergarten in public school in regard to gender sensitivity in West Bank* دراسة مدى مراعاة الاستراتيجية الوطنية لتطوير الطفولة المبكرة، ومشروع الصف التمهيدي الحكومي للنوع الاجتماعي، في الضفة الغربية. https://hdl.handle.net/20.500.11888/8775

Jelic, M. (2014). Developing a sense of identity in pre schoolers. *Mediterranean Journal of Social Sciences, 22*(5), 225–234.

Jickling, B., Blenkinsop, S., Morse, M., & Jensen, A. (2018). *Wild pedagogies: Six initial touchstones for early childhood environmental educators.* Springer.

Kasser, T. (2006). Materialism and its alternatives. In M. Csikszentmihalyi & I. Csikszentmihalyi (Eds.), *Life worth living; Contributions to positive psychology* (pp. 200–214). Oxford University Press.

Kingdon, Z., Gourd, J., & Gasper, M. (2017). *Flourishing in the early years – contexts, practices and futures.* Routledge.

Laevers, F. (2005). *Well-being and involvement in care settings. A process-oriented self-evaluation instrument.* http://www.kindengezin.be/img/sics-ziko-manual.pdf

The Lancet Child & Adolescent Health. (2021). A climate of anxiety (editorial). *The Lancet Child & Adolescent Health, 5*(2), 91. https://www.thelancet.com/journals/lanchi/article/PIIS2352-4642%2821%2900001-8/fulltext

Mahamid, F., & Berte, D. Z. (2020). Happiness, sadness, and hope for the future in narratives of Palestinian refugee children. *International Journal of Mental Health Addiction, 18*, 1638–1651. https://doi.org/10.1007/s11469-020-00303-2

Malaguzzi, L. (1994). Listening to children. *Young Children, 49*(5), 55. https://www.jstor.org/stable/42725534

Mason, J. (2002). *Researching your own practice: The discipline of noticing.* Routledge Falmer.

Maturana, H. (1988). Reality: The search for objectivity or the quest for a compelling argument. *Irish Journal of Psychology, 9*(1) 25–82. https://doi.org/10.1080/03033910.1988.10557705

Mayo County Council. (2019). *Climate ready Mayo: Climate adaptation strategy* [Online]. Mayo-Climate-Adaptation-Strategy. https://www.mayo.ie/getmedia/ede67b0c-a4e4-4e7c-a40b-fb1fcbdfd00c/Mayo-Climate-Adaptation-Strategy.pdf

McLean, K. C., Breen, A. V., & Fournier, M. A. (2010). Constructing the self in early, middle, and late adolescent boys: Narrative identity, individuation, and wellbeing. *Journal of Research on Adolescence, 20*(1), 166–187. https://doi.org/10.1111/j.1532-7795.2009.00633.x

McLeod, N. (2015). Reflecting on reflection: Improving teachers' readiness to facilitate participatory learning with young children. *Professional Development in Education, 41*(2), 254–272. https://doi.org/10.1080/19415257.2013.805306

McLeod, N. (2019). Chapter 2 the reflexive educator. In N. McLeod & P. Giardiello (Eds.), *Empowering early childhood educators: International pedagogies as provocation* (pp. 36–62). Routledge.

Moss, P. (2013). *Transformative change and real utopias in early childhood education: A story of democracy, experimentation, and potentiality.* Routledge.

Moss, P. (2017). Power and resistance in early childhood education: From dominant discourse to democratic experimentalism. *Journal of Pedagogy, 8*(1), 11–32. DOI 10.1515/jped-2017-0001

Moss, P. (2019). *Alternative narratives in early childhood: An introduction for students and practitioners.* Routledge.

Narvaez, D. (2015). Understanding flourishing: Evolutionary baselines and morality. *Journal of Education, 44*(3), 253–262. https://doi.org/10.1080/03057240.2015.1054619

Nesterova, Y. (2020). Rethinking environmental education with the help of indigenous ways of knowing and traditional ecological knowledge. *Journal of Philosophy of Education, 54*(4), 1047–1052. https://doi.org/10.1111/1467-9752.12471

Noddings, N. (2003). *Happiness and education.* Cambridge University Press.

O'Brien, C. (2016). *Education for sustainable happiness and wellbeing.* Routledge.

Rinaldi, C. (2006). *In dialogue with Reggio Emilia: Listening, researching and learning.* Routledge.

Scharmer, C. O. (2009). *Theory U: Leading from the future as it emerges.* Berrett-Koehler Publishers.

Schön, D. A. (1987). *Educating the reflective practitioner toward a new design for teaching.* Jossey-Bass.

Shofi, M. (2003, March). *Islamic education: A brief history of madrassas with comments on curricula and current pedagogical practices.* Draft Report.

Stanley, S., & Lyle, S. (2017). Philosophical play in the early years. In M. R. Gregory, J. Haynes, & K. Murris (Eds.), *The Routledge international handbook on philosophy for children* (Part II, Chapter 7). Routledge.

Stone, J., & Bray, S. (2015). Trauma and young children: How the problem plays out. *Discussions on Sensitive Issues. Advances in Early Education and Day Care, 19,* 177–211. Emerald Group Publishing Limited. https://doi.org/10.1108/S0270-402120150000019012

Tronto, J. C. (1993). *Moral boundaries: A political argument for an ethic of care.* Psychology Press.

Underdown, A. (2007). *Young children's health and wellbeing.* Open University Press.

UNESCO. (2015). *Sustainable development goals.* https://www.globalgoals.org/3-good-health-and-well-being

UNESCO. (2021). *SDG resources for educators – Good health and wellbeing.* https://en.unesco.org/themes/education/sdgs/material/03

United Nations. (1989). *Convention on the rights of the child. UN general assembly document A/RES/44/2.* United Nations.

Urban, M. (2017). We need meaningful, systematic evaluation, not a preschool PISA. *Global Education Review, 4*(2), 18–24 https://www.academia.edu/35674680/We_Need_Meaningful_Systemic_Evaluation_Not_a_Preschool_PISA

Veronese, G., Said, M., & Castiglioni, M. (2010). Narratives from Jenin refugee camp: Children as extreme defence against the disintegration of family and community. *International Journal of Human Sciences. 7,* 85–104. https://www.researchgate.net/publication/230729750_Narratives_from_Jenin_Refugee_Camp_Children_as_extreme_defence_against_the_disintegration_of_family_and_community

Ward, L. M., Hill, M. J., Antane, N., Chreim, S., Olsen Harper, A., & Wells, S. (2021). The land nurtures our spirit: Understanding the role of the land in Labrador Innu wellbeing. *International Journal of Environmental Research. Public Health, 18*(10), 5102. https://doi.org/10.3390/ijerph18105102

The Wilderness Society. (2020). *Now or never.* https://www.wilderness.org/

Yunkaporta, T. (2019). *Sand talk: How indigenous thinking can save the world.* Text Publishing.

9
PLAY IN THE EDUCATION AND CARE OF YOUNG AUTISTIC CHILDREN

Jenny Louise Gibson and Sinéad Máire McNally

Introduction

In this chapter, we argue for the importance of prioritising play as a proactive and naturalistic way of supporting the wellbeing of young autistic children in Early Childhood Education (ECE). We present arguments showing that as well as being a right for all children; play presents an important opportunity in the education and care of young autistic children to celebrate neurodiversity and to promote meaningful social engagement for all children. We focus on play as a support for social and communication differences in autism as these are often framed as a significant challenge for autistic children (Lyall et al., 2017), compounded by the social demands of education (Parsons et al., 2013). However, more recent conceptualisations in the field of autism studies emphasise that successful communication is a two-way street, arguing that communication challenges are not inherent to autism but rather a property of interactions in which diversity of communicative styles is not considered (Williams et al., 2021). We argue that play provides a powerful and protective context for the development of all children's social and communication skills, making play an important strategy in early education to foster communication between children of all neurotypes (Gibson et al., 2021; Barnett, 2018). We conclude this chapter by discussing research evidence on the potential of play in interventions aimed at supporting autistic children within educational contexts (e.g. Kossyvaki & Papoudi, 2016; Wolfberg et al., 2015) and highlighting key take-aways for contemporary approaches to Early Childhood Education for autistic children. By supporting a strength-based and inclusive perspective on play, we propose that families, early childhood educators and the broader community can directly impact children's resilience and wellbeing.

DOI: 10.4324/9781003345664-12

Play in Inclusive Early Childhood Education

The United Nations Convention on the Rights of the Child (United Nations, 1989) recognises the right to play for all children. In addition to being a fundamental right, play has been identified as a 'universal design to promote inclusion' (UNCRC, 2013) providing the ideal context in which to promote a culture of acceptance and inclusion in education and as a way to help all children to reach their full potential. Indeed, play has been adopted as central to early childhood curricula across the globe (in the *Te Whāriki* curriculum in New Zealand for example and in the *Aistear* curriculum in Ireland). In Early Childhood Education (ECE) practice, this means providing play opportunities and play-based learning while also adapting play in the classroom to meet children's developmental level and individual interests (Carrero et al., 2014; Papoudi & Kossyvaki, 2018).

While the right to play is recognised and increasingly at the heart of early childhood curricula, gaining consensus on how play can and should be used in pedagogical practice is more challenging (O'Keeffe & McNally, 2021, 2022). To begin with, there is no one definition of play (Jensen et al., 2019; Zosh et al., 2018). Play has been defined in terms of both objective characteristics (e.g. active engagement (Wolfberg, 1995; Wolfberg & Schuler, 1999) and subjective characteristics (e.g. playfulness (Barnett, 1990; Eberle, 2014), as well as different in terms of the different types of play (e.g. object, symbolic, pretend, games with rules; Whitebread et al., 2012, 2017). Increasingly, there has been a move towards a broader understanding of play as a continuum (Broadhead, 2010; Wood, 2010) or a spectrum recognising the value of different types of play (Wood, 2010; Jensen et al., 2019). For the purposes of this chapter, we adopt a spectrum view of play to reflect the multifaceted nature of the construct while capturing the heart of play and its important characteristics for learning (Zosh et al., 2018). Within a spectrum view, play ranges from free play (with no adult guidance or explicit learning goals) to guided play and games, to playful instruction ((with some purposeful adult support and learning goals) and to playful instruction (Zosh et al., 2018).

Play to Foster Social and Communication Skills for Wellbeing

Research on the play of autistic children has historically regarded autistic play as 'abnormal' (Jarrold et al., 1993, p. 295) or 'impoverished' (Riguet et al., 1981), yet more contemporary research highlights the need to acknowledge children's differences in play (Jordan, 2003) and to recognise the play of autistic children as different, not less (Grandin, 2012). Psychological definitions of resilience emphasise children's ability to adapt and cope in the face of challenges (Ameis et al., 2020) and, importantly, link the process of resilience to both children's psychological makeup and socio-ecological contexts (Ungar,

2015). In this approach to resilience, children's social and communication skills and early educational contexts are protective factors that work to support children's wellbeing and build resilience through the development of peer relationships, which are especially important for wellbeing in later childhood.

We focus on early educational settings as key socio-ecological contexts that help to build resilience and support the wellbeing of autistic children by supporting social and communication skills, skills which are often framed as a significant challenge (Lyall et al., 2017) in socially demanding educational contexts (Parsons et al., 2013). For example, autistic children experience challenges in forming and maintaining friendships (Bauminger & Shulman, 2003; Locke et al., 2010), which in turn are associated with loneliness (Bauminger & Kasari, 2000; Deckers et al., 2017) and bullying and victimisation (Cappadocia et al., 2012). However, recent conceptualisations in the field of autism studies emphasise that successful communication is a negotiated process, and highlight that communication challenges are not inherent to autism but rather a property of interactions (Williams et al., 2021). Increased social difficulties as autistic children progress through formal schooling (Bauminger-Zviely, 2014) highlight the need for early supports for social and communication development among autistic children within naturalistic educational contexts (Fuller & Kaiser, 2019; Boyd et al., 2019; Goldberg et al., 2019; Sutton et al., 2019).

Playful activities and behaviour often prompt or motivate social engagement, which can take a variety of forms. Examples commonly encountered in ECE contexts include exercise play, rough and tumble play, social role play, shared pretence, and engagement in simple, rule-based turn-taking games. Such activities require children to attend to and 'read' the social environment, as well as playing their part in constructing it through self-regulation and co-operation. It is therefore unsurprising that an established literature suggests strong links between different types of play and social communication development (Lillard et al., 2013; Uren & Stagnitti, 2009; Pellegrini et al., 2002; Veiga et al., 2016). Play also has a role in children's agency, meaning-making and emotional processing (Rao & Gibson, 2019) and has been linked to mental health and wellbeing (Zhao & Gibson, 2022; Dodd & Lester, 2021). These social and emotional corollaries of play map closely to established psychological components of resilience, for example, social supports, locus of control, a sense of self-efficacy, and acceptance (Iacob et al., 2020).

Links between play and social-emotional development have been shown to apply to autistic children. For example, Zhao and Gibson (2022) found a longitudinal association between peer role play behaviours at three years and aspects of language and communication skill aged seven years in a sample of autistic children, and Wilson and colleagues (2017) report that play behaviours from as early as 15 months are predictive of status on later behavioural assessments used to diagnose autism. Early intervention approaches aiming to support development of social communication skills and wellbeing in autistic young people have used such associations to leverage the power of play as both a context for intervention delivery and a key mechanism designed to promote beneficial outcomes (see Francis et al., 2022; O'Keeffe & McNally, 2021). Of particular interest in the current volume is a view of play as providing an authentic context for social communication interactions embedded within the classroom (Reifel, 2014; Shire et al., 2020), and researchers have emphasised the potential of play in supporting the social communication skills of autistic pupils within educational contexts (Jordan, 2003; Kossyvaki & Papoudi, 2016; Manning & Wainwright, 2010; Wolfberg et al., 2015).

Given that many ECE settings and many early childhood educators have a strong play ethos (O'Keeffe & McNally, 2021), we here outline some key considerations that can help settings to adjust their play offer to the needs of autistic children and help to support their wellbeing. First, the social and relational aspects of resilience point towards friendship and peer relations as an important aspect of the ECE environment. The role of play with peers in supporting play of autistic children has also been underestimated in previous research (Yang et al., 2003). Play contributes to peer acceptance levels within early years classrooms and is essential in the formation of classroom social hierarchies (Flannery & Watson, 1993; Ladd et al., 1988). Play and peer acceptance are thus likely to be important considerations for young autistic children who often remain on the periphery of classroom social networks (Chamberlain et al., 2007) and who may experience isolation and rejection which can continue through to adulthood (Rotheram-Fuller et al., 2010). Given the centrality of play in influencing peer acceptance levels, it is likely that play is an important context for supporting peer acceptance though more research is needed on the potential of play to support peer acceptance (e.g. Santillan et al., 2019).

Alongside these relational considerations, and consistent with recognising play as a human right for all children (UNCRC, 1989; Davey & Lundy, 2011), we advocate that individual preferences and differences in play should be respected. The neurodiversity approach is a helpful framework to reference here, given its emphasis on understanding that many different ways of experiencing and processing the world exist across the spectrum of human cognition (Dwyer, 2022). The corollary of this for education settings is an understanding that we need to design for universal inclusion to accommodate everyone (Aitken & Fletcher-Watson, 2022), and we believe that this applies to play. From both rights-based and neurodiversity perspectives, playtime should never be curtailed or withheld in an effort to ensure behavioural compliance (BPS, 2021). Such practices are inappropriate for all children, but may be particularly harmful for autistic children who need time for rest and self-regulation as they are frequently in environments that are not designed with support for neurodivergent individuals in mind (McAllister & Sloan,

2016). While withholding playtime/recess can be more of an issue in primary school settings, it is not uncommon in Early Childhood Education settings for preferred play items (e.g. spinning tops, favourite objects or toys) to be withheld from autistic children and offered as 'rewards' for engagement or compliance (Charlop-Christy & Haymes, 1998; Cló & Dounavi, 2020). We argue that use of preferred play items as a reward for compliance is unlikely to build confidence or intrinsic motivation and is contrary to the spirit of play and playfulness. Instead, we encourage settings to consider choice of behavioural support (if indicated) together with children and their families, and to consider how time can be made available for play with favourite activities and objects without framing them as contingent 'reward'.

A further observation is that both solitary and social aspects of play can be beneficial for social engagement and development. Rather than solitary play, parallel play and social play representing discrete stages of a developmental hierarchy, research shows us that these manifestations of play are states that children step into and out of during single play episodes and over developmental time (Howes & Mathieson, 1992). Fine-grained observational research has shown that although autistic children, in contrast to neurotypical peers, may spend longer periods in 'disengaged', 'repetitive' or 'sensory seeking' behaviours, these less socially oriented states can in fact be precursors to re-engagement and more socially oriented play behaviour (Farr et al., 2010; Francis et al., 2019). Reflections from autistic adults shed light on potential reasons for this (Dawson et al., 2017). In an interview study, Pritchard-Rowe et al. (2023) found that autistic adults reported that solitary and sensory play was essential for recharging social batteries and self-regulating in busy and overwhelming environments. Crucially, many adults in this study reported social play activities to be desirable and nourishing, stressing the need for an approach that balanced balances demands and capacities.

The implications of these insights for ECE settings are that adults who are in charge have responsibility for shaping autistic children's play opportunities; materials and spaces should be mindful that autistic wellbeing may depend on activities having multiple entry and exit points. For example, a block play set up can allow for collaborative activity as well as independent activity, and engagement can be fostered by adults supporting showing and sharing of creations. Adults may also need to adjust their perception of what constitutes purposeful play. Allowing time, space and patience for meeting sensory needs and encouraging self-regulation may mean adults taking a step back from redirecting children into what is often considered more meaningful or 'appropriate' play. This is not to say that adults should not encourage and support autistic children to engage with peers in social play. Indeed, some research with autistic individuals has demonstrated a desire for interventions that build friendship and social understanding (e.g. Bauminger & Kasari, 2000). Rather, we are arguing for a more flexible approach that does not immediately judge or curtail autistic play behaviours and is sensitive to the self-regulatory function that 'atypical' play engagement may serve.

Environmental considerations are key to enabling inclusive play in this way. Classroom setups that provide variety, with easy access from one zone to the next, can be helpful: for example, provision of quiet corners and sensory spaces that can be accessed independently by children who need them (McAllister & Maguire, 2012). Outdoor spaces, too, can be beneficial environments to support autistic children's play and engagement. Setting up outdoor play areas with large loose parts (e.g. milk crates, tyres, tarpaulins) can create an 'affordance' for engagement and collaboration between children with different social profiles and skill sets (Gibson et al., 2017). Beyond typical ECE premise settings, Friedman et al. (2022) found that Forest School could be beneficial in promoting wellbeing of autistic children as viewed through the lens of self-determination theory. Crucially, however, this study also observed that a 'one-size fits all' approach is unhelpful, and some autistic children found forest school overwhelming. Again, a personalised approach to understanding and supporting individual needs is essential for creating a context that can help build resilience.

Implications for Practice: Key Messages

What is autistic play?

- Autistic play can look different to neurotypical play. Play activities that may appear 'purposeless' to non-autistic adult observers often have a meaning to the player and may fulfil important self-regulation needs.
- Autistic children are likely to need a mix of solitary, sensory and social play opportunities to meet their needs.
- Like all children, autistic children have a right to play.

What are the connections between play, autism and resilience?

- Resilience is an interaction between individual characteristics, social relationships and environmental contexts that helps promote positive outcomes and protect against negative outcomes.
- Play is a crucial medium that early childhood educators can use to boost resilience and build wellbeing for autistic children.
- Play provides contexts that are intrinsically motivating and that help support the development of self-regulation and social competencies for all children. It also supports the expression of emotion and skills in coping with uncertainty. These aspects of development are associated with having higher quality friendships and with better wellbeing and mental health.

What can practitioners do?

- Autistic children have a right to play, and it is inappropriate to use play as a reward or punishment
- Play is a crucial medium that early childhood educators can use to boost resilience and build wellbeing for autistic children
- Autistic children are likely to need a mix of solitary, sensory and social play opportunities to meet their needs
- Early childhood educators are encouraged to recognise that autistic play can look 'different' and activities that may appear 'purposeless' to adult observers can fulfil important self-regulation needs
- Autistic children have a right to play and it is inappropriate to use play as a reward or punishment
- Early childhood educators should take an individualised approach to planning to meet the play needs of autistic children, bringing together insights from individual preferences, social relationships and environmental contexts.
- Recognise that it is inappropriate to use play as a reward or punishment, including withholding play opportunities.
- Acknowledging that autistic and non-autistic children alike may benefit from help and strategies to support them in creating enjoyable and inclusive social play opportunities with each other.
- Respect that autistic children may choose solitary, sensory and/or repetitive play over social play.
- Celebrate difference and diversity in play, encouraging all children to express themselves through play and to respect the playful preferences of others.

Conclusion

The neurodiversity approach encourages us to recognise that diversity of human cognition, and experience is valuable and desirable, while recognising that neurodivergent individuals may need different kinds of support to the majority of learners. There is growing research evidence on the potential of play in interventions aimed at supporting autistic children within educational contexts (e.g. Kossyvaki & Papoudi, 2016; Wolfberg et al., 2015) and specifically on social and communication development (see O'Keeffe and McNally (2021) for a review of the research evidence on play for social communication in educational contexts and Gibson et al. (2021) for a review of play for the social communication development of young autistic children). By advocating a neurodiversity-informed approach and highlighting the right of all children to play in ways that they prefer, we argue that autistic play should be fostered and encouraged to thrive. We have illustrated that autistic play can sometimes have a different presentation to that of the neurotypical majority and can serve important self-regulatory functions that can help build resilience processes.

It is important to note that these perspectives have *not* led us to conclude that play should never be used as part of interventions. There is growing research evidence on the potential of play in interventions aimed at supporting autistic children within educational contexts (e.g. Kossyvaki & Papoudi, 2016; Wolfberg et al., 2015) and specifically on social and communication development (see O'Keeffe and McNally (2023) for a review) of the research evidence on play for social communication in educational contexts and Gibson et al. (2021) for a review of play for the social communication development of young autistic children. Our core message is that interventions must be respectful of difference, inclusive and, above all, desirable and acceptable to the children involved.

References

Aitken, D., & Fletcher-Watson, S. (2022). Neurodiversity-affirmative education: Why and how? *The Psychologist*.

Ameis, S. H., Lai, M. C., Mulsant, B. H., & Szatmari, P. (2020). Coping, fostering resilience, and driving care innovation for autistic people and their families during the COVID-19 pandemic and beyond. *Molecular Autism*, *11*, 61. https://doi.org/10.1186/s13229-020-00365-y

Barnett, J. H. (2018). Three evidence-based strategies that support social skills and play among young children with autism spectrum disorders. *Early Childhood Education Journal*, *46*(6), 665–672. https://doi.org/10.1007/s10643-018-0911-0

Barnett, L. A. (1990). Playfulness: Definition, design and measurement. *Play & Culture*, *31*, 319–336.

Bauminger, N., & Kasari, C. (2000). Loneliness and friendship in high-functioning children with autism. *Child Development*, *71*(2), 447–456. https://doi.org/10.1111/1467-8624.00156

Bauminger, N., & Shulman, C. (2003). The development and maintenance of friendship in high-functioning children with autism: Maternal perceptions. *Autism*, *7*(1), 81–97. https://doi.org/10.1177%2F1362361303007001007

Bauminger-Zviely, N. (2014). School age children with ASD. In F. R. Volkmar (Ed.), *Handbook of autism and pervasive developmental disorders* (4th ed., pp. 148–175). John Wiley and Sons Inc.

BPS. (2021). *Position paper on the right to play. BPS division of education and child psychology*. London

Boyd, B. A., Dykstra Steinbrenner, J. R., Reszka, S. S., & Carroll, A. (2019). Research in autism education: Current issues and future directions. In R. Jordan, J. Roberts, & K. Hume (Eds.), *The SAGE handbook of autism and education* (pp. 595–605). SAGE Publications.

Broadhead, P., Howard, J., & Wood, E. (2010). *Play and learning in the early years: From research to practice*. SAGE Publications.

Cappadocia, M. C., Weiss, J. A., & Pepler, D. (2012). Bullying experiences among children and youth with autism spectrum disorders. *Journal of Autism and Developmental Disorders*, *42*(2), 266–277. https://doi.org/10.1007/s10803-011-1241-x

Carrero, K. M., Lewis, C. G., Zolkoski, S., & Lusk, M. E. (2014). Research-based strategies for teaching play skills to children with autism. *Beyond Behavior*, *23*(3), 17–25. https://doi.org/10.1177/107429561402300304

Chamberlain, B., Kasari, C., & Rotheram-Fuller, E. (2007). Involvement or isolation? The social networks of children with autism in regular classrooms. *Journal of Autism and Developmental Disorders, 37*(2), 230–242. https://doi.org/10.1007/s10803-006-0164-4

Charlop-Christy, M. H., & Haymes, L. K. (1998). Using objects of obsession as token reinforcers for children with autism. *Journal of Autism and Developmental Disorders, 28*(3), 189–198.

Cló, E., & Dounavi, K. (2020). A systematic review of behaviour analytic processes and procedures for conditioning reinforcers among individuals with autism, developmental or intellectual disability. *European Journal of Behavior Analysis, 21*(2), 292–327. https://doi.org/10.1080/15021149.2020.1847953

Davey, C., & Lundy, L. (2011). Towards greater recognition of the right to play: An analysis of article 31 of the UNCRC. *Children and Society, 25*(1), 3–14.

Dawson, M., Courchesne, V., Mineau, S., Mottron, L., & Jacques, C. (2017). *Repetitive behavior and object exploration in young autistic children: How are they associated?* [Paper presentation]. Paper presented at International Meeting for Autism Research. San Francisco, USA.

Deckers, A., Muris, P., & Roelofs, J. (2017). Being on your own or feeling lonely? Loneliness and other social variables in youths with autism spectrum disorders. *Child Psychiatry & Human Development, 48*(5), 828–839. https://doi.org/10.1007/s10578-016-0707-7

Dodd, H. F., & Lester, K. J. (2021). Adventurous play as a mechanism for reducing risk for childhood anxiety: A conceptual model. *Clinical Child and Family Psychology Review, 24*, 164–181. https://doi.org/10.1007/s10567-020-00338-w

Dwyer, P. (2022). The neurodiversity approach(es): What are they and what do they mean for researchers? *Article Human Development, 66*, 73–92. https://doi.org/10.1159/000523723

Eberle, S. G. (2014). The elements of play: Toward a philosophy and a definition of play. *American Journal of Play, 6*(2), 214–233.

Farr, W., Yuill, N., & Raffle, H. (2010). Social benefits of a tangible user interface for children with autistic spectrum conditions. *Autism The International Journal of Research and Practice, 14*(3), 237–252.

Flannery, K. A., & Watson, M. W. (1993). Are individual differences in fantasy play related to peer acceptance levels? *The Journal of Genetic Psychology, 154*(3), 407–416. https://doi.org/10.1080/00221325.1993.10532194

Francis, G., Farr, W., Mareva, S., & Gibson, J. L. (2019). Do tangible user interfaces promote social behaviour during free play? A comparison of autistic and typically developing children playing with passive and digital construction toys. *Research in Autism Spectrum Disorders, 58*, 68–82. https://doi.org/10.1016/j.rasd.2018.08.005

Friedman, S., Gibson, J., Jones, C., & Hughes, C. (2022). 'A new adventure': A case study of autistic children at forest school. *Journal of Adventure Education and Outdoor Learning*, 1–17.

Fuller, E. A., & Kaiser, A. P. (2019). The effects of early intervention on social communication outcomes for children with autism spectrum disorder: A meta-analysis. *Journal of Autism and Developmental Disorders*, 1–18. https://doi.org/10.1007/s10803-019-03927-z

Gibson, J. L., Cornell, M., & Gill, T. (2017). A systematic review of research into the impact of loose parts play on children's cognitive, social and emotional development. *School Mental Health, 9*, 295–309. https://doi.org/10.1007/s12310-017-9220-9

Gibson, J. L., Pritchard, E., & de Lemos, C. (2021). Play-based interventions to support social and communication development in autistic children aged 2–8 years: A scoping review. *Autism & Developmental Language Impairments*. https://doi.org/10.1177/23969415211015840

Goldberg, J. M., Sklad, M., Elfrink, T. R., Schreurs, K. M., Bohlmei-jer, E. T., & Clarke, A. M. (2019). Effectiveness of interventions adopting a whole school approach to enhancing social and emotional development: A meta-analysis. *European Journal of Psychology of Education, 34*(4), 755–782. https://doi.org/10.1007/s10212-018-0406-9

Grandin, T. (2012). *Different not less.* Future Horizons.

Howes, C., & Mathieson, C. C. (1992). Sequences in the development of competent play with peers: Social and social pretend play. *Developmental Psychology, 28*(5), 961–974. https://doi.org/10.1037/0012-1649.28.5.961

Iacob, C. I., Avram, E., Cojocaru, D., & Podina, I. R. (2020). Resilience in familial caregivers of children with developmental disabilities: A meta-analysis. *Journal of Autism and Developmental Disorders, 50*(11), 4053–4068. https://doi.org/10.1007/s10803-020-04473-9.

Jarrold, C., Boucher, J., & Smith, P. (1993). Symbolic play in autism: A review. *Journal of Autism and Developmental Disorders, 23*(2), 281–307.

Jensen, H., Pyle, A., Zosh, J. M., Ebrahim, H. B., Scherman, A. Z., Reunamo, J., & Hamre, B. K. (2019). *Play facilitation: The science behind the art of engaging young children.* The LEGO Foundation.

Jordan, R. (2003). Social play and autistic spectrum disorders: A perspective on theory, implications and educational approaches. *Autism, 7*(4), 347–360. https://doi.org/10.1177/1362361303 007004002

Kossyvaki, L., & Papoudi, D. (2016). A review of play interventions for children with autism at school. *International Journal of Disability, Development and Education, 63*(1), 45–63. https://doi.org/10.1080/1034912X.2015.1111303

Ladd, G. W., Price, J. M., & Hart, C. H. (1988). Predicting preschoolers' peer status from their playground behaviors and peer contacts. *Child Development, 59*, 986–992.

Lillard, A. S., Lerner, M. D., Hopkins, E. J., Dore, R. A., Smith, E. D., & Palmquist, C. M. (2013). The impact of pretend play on children's development: A review of the evidence. *Psychological Bulletin, 139*(1), 1. https://www.psycnet.apa.org/doi/10.1037/a0029321

Locke, J., Ishijima, E. H., Kasari, C., & London, N. (2010). Loneliness, friendship quality and the social networks of adolescents with high-functioning autism in an inclusive school setting. *Journal of Research in Special Educational Needs, 10*(2), 74–81. https://doi.org/10.1111/j.1471-3802.2010.01148.x

Lyall, K., Croen, L., Daniels, J., Fallin, M. D., Ladd-Acosta, C., Lee, B. K., Park, B. Y., Snyder, N. W., Schendel, D., Volk, H., & Windham, G. C. (2017). The changing epidemiology of autism spectrum disorders. *Annual Review of Public Health, 38*, 81–102.

Manning, M. M., & Wainwright, L. D. (2010). The role of high level play as a predictor social functioning in autism. *Journal of Autism and Developmental Disorders, 40*(5), 523–533. https://doi.org/10.1007/810803-009-0899-9

McAllister, K., & Maguire, B. (2012). Design considerations for the autism spectrum disorder-friendly key stage 1 classroom. *Support for Learning, 27*(3), 103–112.

McAllister, K., & Sloan, S. (2016). Designed by the pupils, for the pupils: An autism-friendly school. *British Journal of Special Education, 43*, 330–357. https://doi.org/10.1111/1467-8578.12160

O'Keeffe, C., & McNally, S. (2021). 'Uncharted territory': Teachers' perspectives on play in early childhood classrooms in Ireland during the pandemic. *European Early Childhood Education Research Journal, 29*(1), 79–95.

O'Keeffe, C., & McNally, S. (2022). Teacher experiences of facilitating play in early childhood classrooms during COVID-19. *Journal of Early Childhood Research, 20*(4), 552–564. https://doi.org/10.1177/1476718X221087064

O'Keeffe, C., & McNally, S. (2023). A systematic review of play-based interventions targeting the social communication skills of children with autism spectrum disorder in educational contexts. *Review Journal of Autism Developmental Disorders*, *10*, 51–81. https://doi.org/10.1007/s40489-021-00286-3

Papoudi, D., & Kossyvaki, L. (2018). Play and children with autism: Insights from research and implications for practice. In P. Smith & J. L. Roopnarine (Eds.), *The Cambridge handbook of play: Developmental and disciplinary perspectives* (pp. 563–579). Cambridge University Press. https://doi.org/10.1017/9781108131384.031

Parsons, S., Charman, T., Faulkner, R., Ragan, J., Wallace, S., & Wittemeyer, K. (2013). Commentary–bridging the research and practice gap in autism: The importance of creating research partnerships with schools. *Autism*, *17*(3), 268–280. https://doi.org/10.1177%2F1362361312472068

Pellegrini, A. D., Kato, K., Blatchford, P., & Baines, E. (2002). A short-term longitudinal study of children's playground games across the first year of school: Implications for social competence and adjustment to school. *American Educational Research Journal*, *39*(4), 991–1015. https://doi.org/10.3102%2F00028312039004991

Pritchard-Rowe, E., de Lemos, C., Howard, K., & Gibson, J. (2023). Diversity in autistic play: Autistic adults' experiences. *Autism in Adulthood*. http://doi.org/10.1089/aut.2023.0008

Rao, Z., & Gibson, J. (2019). The role of pretend play in supporting young children's emotional development. In D. Whitebread, V. Grau, & K. Kumpulainen (Eds.), *The SAGE handbook of developmental psychology and early childhood education* (pp. 63–79). SAGE Publications.

Reifel, S. (2014). Developmental play in the classroom. In E. Brooker, M. Blaise, & S. Edwards (Eds.), *The SAGE handbook of play and learning in early childhood* (pp. 157–168). SAGE Publications.

Riguet, C. B., Taylor, N. D., Benaroya, S., & Klein, L. S. (1981). Symbolic play in autistic, Down's, and normal children of equivalent mental age. *Journal of Autism and Developmental Disorders*, *11*(4), 439–448. https://doi.org/10.1007/BF01531618

Rotheram-Fuller, E., Kasari, C., Chamberlain, B., & Locke, J. (2010). Social involvement of children with autism spectrum disorders in elementary school classrooms. *Journal of Child Psychology and Psychiatry*, *51*(11), 1227–1234. https://doi.org/10.1111/j.1469-7610.2010.02289.x

Santillan, L., Frederick, L., Gilmore, S., & Locke, J. (2019). Brief report: Examining the association between classroom social network inclusion and playground peer engagement among children with autism spectrum disorders. *Focus on Autism and Other Developmental Disabilities*, *34*(2), 91–96.

Shire, S. Y., Shih, W., Bracaglia, S., Kodjoe, M., & Kasari, C. (2020). Peer engagement in toddlers with autism: Community implementation of dyadic and individual joint attention, symbolic play, engagement, and regulation intervention. *Autism*, *24*(8), 2142–2152. https://doi.org/10.1177%2F1362361320935689

Sutton, B. M., Webster, A. A., & Westerveld, M. F. (2019). A systematic review of school-based interventions targeting social communication behaviors for students with autism. *Autism*, *23*(2), 274–286. https://doi.org/10.1177/1362361317753564

Ungar, M. (2015). Practitioner review: Diagnosing childhood resilience – a systemic approach to the diagnosis of adaptation in adverse social and physical ecologies. *Journal of Child Psychology and Psychiatry*, *56*(1), 4–17.

United Nations. (1989). *Convention on the rights of the child*. United Nations.

United Nations Committee on the Rights of the Children. (2013). *General comment no. 17 on the right of the child to rest, leisure, play, recreational activities, cultural life and the arts*. United Nations.

Uren, N., & Stagnitti, K. (2009). Pretend play, social competence and involvement in children aged 5–7 years: The concurrent validity of the child-initiated pretend play assessment. *Australian Occupational Therapy Journal*, 56(1), 33–40. https://doi.org/10.1111/j.1440-1630.2008.00761.x

Veiga, G., Neto, C., & Rieffe, C. (2016). *Preschoolers' free play: Connections with emotional and social functioning* 8(1), 48–62.

Whitebread, D., Basilio, M., Kuvalja, M., & Verma, M. (2012). *The importance of play*. Toy Industries of Europe.

Whitebread, D., Neale, D., Jensen, H., Liu, C., Solis, S. L., Hopkins, E., Hirsh-Pasek, K., & Zosh, J. (2017). *The role of play in children's development: A review of the evidence*. LEGO Fonden.

Williams, G. L., Wharton, T., & Jagoe, C. (2021). Mutual (mis) understanding: Reframing autistic pragmatic 'impairments' using relevance theory. *Frontiers in Psychology*, 12, 616664.

Wilson, K. P., Carter, M. W., Wiener, H. L., DeRamus, M. L., Bulluck, J. C., Watson, L. R., Crais, E. R., & Baranek, G. T. (2017). Object play in infants with autism spectrum disorder: A longitudinal retrospective video analysis. *Autism & Developmental Language Impairments*, 2. https://doi.org/10.1177/2396941517713186.

Wolfberg, P., DeWitt, M., Young, G. S., & Nguyen, T. (2015). Integrated play groups: Promoting symbolic play and social engagement with typical peers in children with ASD across settings. *Journal of Autism and Developmental Disorders*, 45(3), 830–845. https://doi.org/10.1007/s10803-014-2245-0

Wolfberg, P. J. (1995). Supporting children with autism in play groups with typical peers: A description of a model and related research. *International Play Journal*, 3, 38–51.

Wolfberg, P. J., & Schuler, A. L. (1999). Fostering peer interaction, imaginative play and spontaneous language in children with autism. *Child Language Teaching and Therapy*, 15(1), 41–52.

Wood, E. (2010). Developing integrated pedagogical approaches to play and learning. In *Play and learning in the early years* (pp. 9–26). Sage.

Yang, T. R., Wolfberg, P. J., Wu, S. C., & Hwu, P. Y. (2003). Sup- porting children on the autism spectrum in peer play at home and school: Piloting the integrated play groups model in Taiwan. *Autism*, 7(4), 437–453. https://doi.org/10.1177/1362361303007004009

Zhao, Y. V., & Gibson, J. L. (2022). Solitary symbolic play, object substitution and peer role play skills at age 3 predict different aspects of age 7 structural language abilities in a matched sample of autistic and non-autistic children. *Autism & Developmental Language Impairments*, 7. https://doi.org/10.1177/23969415211063822

Zosh, J. M., Hirsh-Pasek, K., Hopkins, E. J., Jensen, H., Liu, C., Neale, D., Solis, S. L., & Whitebread, D. (2018). Accessing the inaccessible: Redefining play as a spectrum. *Frontiers in Psychology*, 9, 1124.

10
HOLISTIC EDUCATION AS SUPPORT FOR WELLBEING AND RESILIENCE

Tansy Watts

What Is Resilience and Why Is Awareness Important?

Resilience is understood differently across various fields, but in early education, the focus has predominantly been on the child and their exposure to risk but potential for positive psychological outcomes (Nolan et al., 2014). Although the focus is on the child, their capacity for resilience is understood as a dynamic process and involving "the child as a whole", their "multi-dimensional and ecological" context and support that "takes into consideration children's lives, contexts and relationships" (Naidoo, 2016, p. 2). A focus on resilience has been accompanied by growing insight into trauma impacts on whole body systems with lifelong implications (Felitti et al., 1998). Insight into mitigating factors is important in counteracting risk impacts, and resilience promotion holds value in a context characterised by multiple social, economic, and environmental risks (Thomas, 2021).

The Role of Early Education in Resilience Promotion

Literature demonstrates scope for a reactive or proactive approach to promoting resilience in early childhood education. Such an activity can support good outcomes, stress resistance, and recovery from trauma in individuals (Luthar & Cicchetti, 2000). Early education can offer a well-timed intervention in responding to the trauma of abuse or neglect in young children (Shonkoff & Levitt, 2010) and positive outcomes include mitigation of developmental impacts in the child along with support and respite to families in difficulty (Ellenbogen et al., 2014). Quality early education is an important component of an effective resiliency intervention along with delivery

DOI: 10.4324/9781003345664-13

in conjunction with family services that build social support networks and reduce family isolation (Hurlburt et al., 2013; Suchman et al., 2011). Such insights can raise questions about the connective value of early years services with recognition given to the unique position these hold as community-based meeting places. Thomas (2021) has identified that early years settings offer grounds for systemic support though community connectedness and asserts the relevance in rethinking early education according to a "family resiliency" model. Such a model moves away from education that is "child-centred and involving or partnering with parents, to one that encompasses and positions early childhood educational services at the heart of the community" (Thomas, 2021, p. 3). Associated new discourses would understand early education according to its development of links, relationships, and opportunities for networking at micro- and meso-levels (Duncan, 2011). Such a model orients to a strength-based rather than a deficit model and enables universal support meaning those that need it most can access this without feeling stigmatised (Thomas, 2021). A "family resiliency" model aims to empower families and communities in supporting children and to work through associated values of "belonging, confidence and fairness" (Vandenbroeck, 2017, p. 412). This chapter will now introduce a holistic pedagogy that aligns with such a view and sits at the historical roots of early educational practice. The pedagogy can offer a connection through familiar and well-established early years principles and practices to a "resiliency" model of early education.

The Holistic Educational Paradigm

Holistic education orients to a vision of life as a whole and connective parts. There are a range of philosophies that align with this paradigm and orient to common principles applied in diverse ways. The holistic paradigm shapes the educational aim as "learning to belong to the whole" (Mahmoudi et al., 2012, p. 182) and shapes practice to support this in a balanced development of and relationship between

> different aspects of the individual (intellectual, physical, spiritual, emotional, social and Aesthetic), as well as the relationships between the individual and other people, the individual and natural environment, the inner-self of students and external world.
>
> *(Mahmoudi et al., 2012, p. 178)*

The individual can learn to appreciate their place within a whole social-ecological system with an overall aim to promote "harmonious biocultural interactions" (Ungar & Theron, 2020).

Froebelian Pedagogy

The holistic pedagogy explored in this research is that of Friedrich Froebel whose establishment of the first kindergarten in 1837 was influential within the historical development of early education at global scale (Brehony, 2009). Froebel's early years practice was shaped by an underpinning holistic philosophy of Unity through which all life was considered in continuity and connection, but human learning within this through experience of its diverse forms and processes. The natural world was held up as a source of guidance for human activity and described as the means for the "removal of obstacles to growth and the elimination of force in pedagogy" (Roseman, 1965, p. 331). The garden was determined as a central feature of kindergarten practice and could facilitate children's experience of the natural world, supported by sympathetic educational practices. The following historical example of kindergarten pedagogy illustrates this sense of continuity and connection between humanity and natural world.

> This nurturing of flora and fauna simulated the nurturing they themselves received from their teachers and was reiterated in the way they were encouraged to serve each other and their community: not just making their playroom clean but pouring water for the next child when they took turns to wash after dinner.
>
> *(Darling, 2017, p. 368)*

Such an approach can be considered a pedagogy of care expressive through relations within human community and natural world. The underpinning law of unity was considered expressive through human life alongside that in surrounding life and shaped attendance to each individual as they "unfold their essence" and learn through "self-determination and freedom" (Froebel, 1887, p. 2). In this way, Froebel's holistic education oriented to the potential to experience relational balance through an ongoing process of making "the outer inner – and the inner, outer" (Froebel, 1887, p. 32). Play was determined as a relational language supportive to the ongoing growth and development of child into adult and when "recognised and rightly fostered" could unite "the germinating life of the child attentively with the ripe life of experiences of the adult and thus fosters the one through the other" (Froebel, cited by Liebschner, 1992, p. 24). Play equally enabled an experience of balance with surrounding life, and this could be experienced as "joy, freedom, contentment, inner and outer rest, peace with the world" (Froebel, 1887, p. 55). It is the wellbeing and development of all life that is in focus in holistic education and support for human development within it. Froebel's holistic vision of learning that is lifelong and continuous can be seen in the following description of educational purpose.

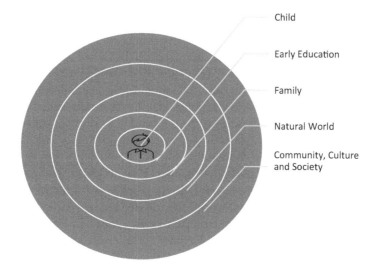

FIGURE 10.1 Early years practice can facilitate children's relations with the natural world while building supportive connections between family, community, culture, and society. This is within a relational pedagogy that recognises mutual influence between child and whole context

> Let us impart life to ourselves, to our children; let us through them give meaning to our speech and life to the things about us! Let us live with them, and let them live with us; thus, shall we obtain from them what we all need.
>
> *(Froebel, 1887, p. 88)*

The contemporary contribution of this pedagogy has been explored in this research and shared here in considering its support for family wellbeing and resilience. The following model (Figure 10.1) illustrates the holistic educational context, and its consideration not of the child within an educational setting, but "every child in relation to family, community, nature, culture, and society" (The Froebel Trust, 2023)

A Contemporary Exploration of Froebelian Pedagogy

The research explored preschool organised family trips to local natural environments developed in response to family-identified barriers to green space through urbanisation as reflected in current literature (Soga et al., 2018). I wondered as the preschool manager in this context about its' environmentally and community-connective function and drew on Froebel Trust funding to explore inspiration from Froebel's relational pedagogy. For the purposes of this research in a suburban context, a natural environment was understood as space to "engage with and follow natural processes but . . . (can be) typically designed, constructed, regulated, and maintained" (Hartig et al., 2014, p. 208). Access for all families was facilitated through lift-sharing and a third of all those registered at preschool attended each trip. Ten families became the focus of research activity during trips, and this was framed with a sensory ethnography approach (Pink, 2009). The data collection centred on offering children an opportunity to wear a GoPro™ video camera on trips, and use of this footage as the basis for shared reflections with parents. This research design sought to amplify children's voice for adult attendance in exploring relational learning between child, adult, and environment during trips. In this way, to respond to a call to "live with our children" (Froebel, 1887, p. 89) and explore contemporary means to do so through digital media that can recover "the prelinguistic, somatic relation to others of infancy, a capacity that still remains accessible to us in adulthood" (MacDougall, 1998, p. 53). The child-led video and recorded parent reflections were analysed through use of a vocabulary of holistic relations as an analytical lens. The vocabulary was identified in the theory of the evolution of human consciousness (Gebser, 1949) previously used in child and natural world research and determined as a means for drawing attention to "otherwise difficult-to-acknowledge aspects of children's experience" (Chawla, 2002, loc. 2602). The research design sought to explore what Froebel's holistic perspective might contribute to supporting a contemporary wellbeing agenda through education. This approach is supported by a growing body of research demonstrating the health benefits of nature contact and connection (Defra, 2018).

Research Findings

The findings illuminated scope for rich multi-directional influence between child, adult, and environment when viewed through a holistic lens. Insight will be given into finding that highlight parent reflections on the value of a holistic educational context, the benefits of environmentally connective pedagogy, and the opportunities for mutual influence between adult, child, and environment.

Holistic Context: Parent Reflections on the Value of Preschool Trips

The following comments highlight the way these parents' valued trips for facilitating social and environmental connections along with insight into their child's education. Such comments might raise questions about families in which their relations are challenged but can highlight connective opportunities that can be educationally valued and celebrated.

Parent 1:

It's all very well – you can learn things in the classroom – but I think going out of the classroom – you can learn about nature in the classroom – but to be out in nature to listen to feel . . . is a completely different way of learning. I think you learn so much more outside the classroom – it's vital really . . . and to interact with the whole group outside the school is another way of learning. And as a parent on a school trip to see your child learning adds another level . . . to see what she does.

Parent 2:

Harry really enjoyed it. He was very excited because we told him about where he was going beforehand . . . but he really enjoyed it. He's still talking about it now, about going on the school trip. He's very keen on school anyway, so he enjoyed the association of doing something with the school. I really enjoyed it as well. Took time off to go – 'cause I'm very into seeing what he does. . . . And doing everything on the trip. He enjoyed the activity and being there, being outside. If it was done indoors . . . it wouldn't be so . . . it opens new opportunities. Exploring, his senses, interaction with everything.

Parent 3:

Been to all the pre-school trips bar one. I think they're good . . . can't speak for other parents. If they'd been more regular, I'd have tried to go to them more. It's good for the kids and gets them out of the same environment as well. I think it should be encouraged – for both kids and parents to be more social and make new friends and stuff. Honestly so many people are so shy and struggle with making conversation. . . . I think it's quite a big issue.

The comments highlight the links, relations, and opportunities for networking this activity promoted for families. This included not only contact with a natural environment but also the sense of being part of a community for children and families. I identified a significance as participant observer in moving this practice beyond the preschool setting, as this could enable educational the staff, children, and families to become "explorers" of their locality together. Such activity could facilitate children's voice through environments enabling their exploration, and for family funds of knowledge to be shared informally through relations with their local context. In this way for connective relations to be considered in terms of children, families, community, culture, and environment and the scope for education to facilitate supportive networks between them. These parent comments might be considered indicative of those choosing to take part in trips and therefore not representative of the whole preschool population. However, the responses do offer some insight into the types of connective opportunities important to children and families. The following comment highlights how for some families the social contact could be more challenging but might also raise questions about the significance of such practices as a regular feature of education.

Parent 4:

It's schools – you've gotta behave yourself a bit. If they're doing things sometimes you feel you can't really speak to your kids how you would sometimes. I'm quite funny about who I meet. I find it really difficult. I'm just too busy. I've got friends and family.

Such a comment highlights the importance of considering cultural capital within education and the relevance of inclusive practices celebrating diverse home cultures. Measures protective to children's wellbeing and resilience include "peer relationships, nonfamily member relationships and nonfamily member social support" (Afifi & MacMillan, 2011, p. 268). These reflections highlight the potential contribution of early education that attends to the value of community-building around the setting.

Holistic Pedagogy: Human and Environment Relations

Play

The preschool trips offered activities to support social and environmental relations in a new context, and this included storytelling, a walk, shared snack, and craft using found resources. The activities were optional and allowed for the environment and social relations to be influential and represented well-established early years practice to support learning from life in surroundings (DfE, 2021). Links can be traced between these activities and Froebel's original "mother songs", "gifts", and "occupations" underpinned by a holistic aim to support "learning to belong to the whole" (Mahmoudi et al., 2012, p. 182). It is a progression in cultural and philosophical influences over time that have shaped an understanding of these activities as supportive to individual development (Chung & Walsh, 2000). However, it is their consideration through a holistic analytical lens that raises questions about who and how we may be learning. The following short extract is taken from four-year-old Jack and his dad while spending 20 minutes together creating a clay model of a caterpillar using found objects.

Dad: There we go. Lovely (pushes caterpillar model slightly)
Jack: My Marshall's all slipping. (Jack is holding a small world play figure)
Dad: Has the caterpillar finished eating yet?
Jack: No!
Dad: Do we need to get the caterpillar some more food to eat later? Shall we go into the jungle? What do you think the caterpillar might like? Maybe some sticks and stuff? (Dad is referring to a walk in the woods on offer during trips)
Jack: Yeah
Dad: We can put him in this bag, right?
Nanna: Shall we put him in the bag nice and flat, so he doesn't get broken?
Jack: In
Nanna: Put Marshall in there too?
Jack bends down and picks up stick: A little stick.
Nanna: Put it in there for him to eat.
Dad framed his reflection on this activity in terms of the learning for his son.
Dad: He loved that – making the caterpillar. Getting them to make a caterpillar there gets them thinking about it as a creature and relating that to outdoors more and caring for things and the world and stuff.

However, Froebel's holistic perspective promotes consideration of play as a language supportive to the ongoing balanced development of child, adult, and environment. The value of such activity for Dad might be considered in terms of a more recent definition of play as "free activity standing quite consciously outside 'ordinary' life as being 'not meant', but at the same time absorbing the player intensely and utterly" (Huizinga, 1955, p. 13). Play can offer an "intermezzo, an interlude in our daily lives" (Huizinga, 1955, p. 13), and perhaps a brief disruption to the "becoming" associated with adulthood with an experience of "being" associated with the child (James & James, 2012). Holistic pedagogy disrupts a linear orientation to individualised development with a vision of wellbeing and resilience supported through interconnection. Play might be considered in terms of experiential relations between adult and child with additional relational support through nature contact and connection (Pretty et al., 2009; Richardson, 2023).

Nature Contact and Connection

Nature contact has been found restorative to attention and self-regulation (Kaplan & Kaplan, 1989) and linked with stress-reducing psychophysiological responses (Ulrich et al., 1991). Studies have demonstrated an association between nature contact and gaining a sense of freedom to be one's authentic self (Fredrickson & Anderson, 1999) and a greater sense of vitality (Nisbet &

Zelenski, 2011; Ryan et al., 2010). There is also a significant relationship between measures of nature connectedness and happiness indicators such as positive affect and life satisfaction (Capaldi et al., 2015), along with psychological resilience identified as key to managing stress and maintaining positive mental health (Ingulli & Lindbloom, 2013). Family-based nature activity can offer the symbolic communication of being "away" from a daily environment and a revitalising effect through engagement with the spontaneity of the natural world (Izenstark & Ebata, 2016). Such benefits might be contemplated in relation to understanding childhood resilience in terms of behavioural, emotional, social, and academic competences (Walsh et al., 2010) and for these to be influenced by individual, familial, and community factors (Afifi & Macmillan, 2011). Such benefits are currently finding a place in therapeutic interventions (Jordan & Hinds, 2016), but are integral to a holistic educational approach. The qualities of experience promoted through shared child, adult, and natural environment experiences will now be outlined as highlighted through use of a vocabulary of holistic relations.

Holistic Relations

The "vocabulary" of holistic relations in the theory of the evolution of human consciousness offers five terms named archaic, magic, mythic, mental, and integral consciousness. These terms represent "generalizations that help us to orient our understanding of human experience" (Yiangou, 2017, p. 432) when giving equal value to all relational qualities. The findings include a brief introduction to each term that draws from relevant scholars and its highlighting of the interactions led by adult and child. The findings illuminate the experiential depths in fleeting moments and might raise questions about what quality early education in conjunction with family support might look like. This is of course always mindful of the need to remain sensitive to risk or need for family support.

Moments of Archaic Consciousness

Archaic consciousness concerns the operations of our autonomic nervous system as a "vital exchange" with the world and framed as a foundation for wisdom (Chawla, 2002). It is highlighted as the dominant consciousness of animals and infants that we may re-enter in later life when "in repose or reverie, when we are simply absorbed in our body and our place" (Chawla, 2002, loc. 2629). Drawing on this descriptor highlighted children's absorption in embodied, emplaced experiences and its potential to influence the adults accompanying them. Children could be seen to lead adults off pathways through wilder spaces and into direct contact with undergrowth or woodlands. This child-led activity could be understood as motivated by environmental affordances for whole bodied exploration (Heft, 1988) and enabled by judgement of such spaces as safe for their free movement but requiring adults to keep children within sight. Through this, adults had their attention drawn towards children's fascinations and examples included the qualities of puddles, soft feathers, sticky mud, echoes, shadows, self-set challenges and an invitation to move freely in open space. The following parent comment highlights the opportunity to value such experiences and was voiced by a Mum after watching footage of a walk along a slippery, muddy path from her three-year-old daughter's point-of-view.

Walking back was even better . . . dunno . . . it just got even thicker mud . . . our boots were getting stuck. You know when you lift your foot up and your boot gets left behind! You've got to think about every step. It's just there. It's just there for you. The more you get out and experience, the more they want to get out and do it again.

Such a comment might be considered significant within a contemporary urbanisation process shaping an "extinction of experience" of "direct, intimate encounters with places and organisms" (Pyle, 2003, p. 209). Archaic consciousness has been drawn on to describe young children as "baptized in the world by immersion . . . close to the ground and up against the full sensory qualities of things . . . that adult height and habits will later remove them from" (Chawla, 2002, loc. 2635). This research animated the benefit in following guidance to "live with our children" as a route to reconnecting with a "sensory nutrition" in surroundings (Oldfield, 2012, p. 103). This might be contemplated in relation to the role of early education in promoting wellbeing and resilience through mitigating developmental impacts on the child, facilitating supportive relations with families (Ellenbogen et al., 2014) and gaining relational benefits through engagement with the spontaneity of the natural world (Izenstark & Ebata, 2016).

Moments of Magic Consciousness

Magic consciousness describes a pre-verbal sense of self that is in separation to other described as a "silent intuition of the world's power and our own" (Chawla, 2002, loc. 2646). This consciousness is associated with hearing through which we "belong – to what we hear, we attune" (Johnson, 2019, loc. 1016), and is a state in which we "make with" surroundings in reciprocal relations. Drawing on this descriptor highlighted nature play motifs understood as recurring play patterns children engage in "when they have safe free time in nature" (Sobel, 2008, loc. 307). The observed nature play motifs included "animal allies", which highlights the strong feelings children can demonstrate towards animals and was seen in these families' encounters with the insects, birds, and mammals within natural environments. Children raised "big questions" (Meehan, 2017) about whether the animal was a friend or foe, and adults demonstrated a responsibility to convey positive relations that might be accompanied by more bio-phobic emotional responses. The following short extract is from an interaction between four-year-old Noah and his Mum as pigeons fly away when Noah runs closer. Such everyday encounters can highlight core issues at play in balancing the need for self-protection with recognition that "the other" embodies a life just like our own.

Noah: Do they like eating leaves? (As he excitedly runs across grass covered in leaves towards the pigeons) Do they? (Gasps) They flied away?!
Mum: Never mind (mum reinforces her statement with the expression of a shrug)
Noah: (Gasps) Only one (a very disappointed voice)
Mum: Don't worry.
Noah: (Gasps, as he continues to walk towards them) The others are walking away? (Disappointment)
Mum: Why are they flying away? (Mum asks this as a reflective question whilst demonstrating a shrug)
Noah: Cos they didn't want to see me (sounds very sad)
Mum: It's not that darling, it's because you're bigger than them so perhaps they're a little bit scared of you. They don't know that you're a very nice person.

Mum described seeing from Noah's perspective as a "golden nugget", and her protective impulse was evident in seeking to support his self-image. However, Mum was also prompted to consider "we as adult don't think whether they like us or not, they're a different species – but for a child it might be "Why can't I be friends with a bird?". Such a comment highlights the perspective offered by children's "fresh eyes" on the world, and Froebel's holistic philosophy promotes awareness of its support for an adult relational vitality. A consideration of wellbeing and resilience in these terms engages with the interconnection of self-efficacy and life satisfaction (Hyman & Williams, 2001), support for home relations (Afifi & MacMillan, 2011) and a resilience supported through the development of micro- to meso-level networks (Duncan, 2011).

Moments of Mythic Consciousness

Mythic consciousness describes the use of language and symbol in story, song, and rhyme. Such language is described as "associative, metaphorical thinking that is known through the voice" (Chawla, 2002, loc. 1081) and is allied with oral cultures. Mythic consciousness thereby engages with language and symbol use to support affective relations and for this to be associated with the creation of "complimentary" rather than "contradictory opposites" (Johnson, 2019, loc. 1081). Use of this "vocabulary" drew attention to the way that all the families used familiar stories from home as a shared language to form relations in their wider context. Examples were both child- and adult-led, and a psychoanalytic perspective highlighted differing drives to imaginatively face fears or present the world as a safe place. The following example involves four-year-old Tom as he enters a park and knows he is now safe to run.

Tom: Run, run, run as fast as I can, you can't catch me I'm the gingerbread man (he speaks in a "gingerbread man voice"). You can't catch me! You can't catch me!
Dad: I can't catch you. (Tom laughs excitedly as he continues running, and his sister over-takes him).
Sara: You can't catch me.
Tom: Yes, I can (his sister runs ahead. Tom stops and turns back towards Dad who is pushing the buggy along the path behind them) I need your speed. (He starts to walk back towards Dad) I need your speed.
Dad: You need speed?
Tom: Yeah
Dad: Ready? (He holds out his hand to him, they touch hands) "Pzzzh-hhhhhhh- Go!" (Tom starts to run, then stops and turns around again).
Sara: You can't catch me! (She is flapping her arms as she runs like wings)
Tom: Yes, I can – I got speed! (He then stops and turns back)

A psychoanalytic perspective highlights how repetitive story patterns from "brief rhymes . . . into whole structures of incident" (Warner, 2014, p. 42) offer children clearcut motifs through which to make sense of their relations with the world (Bettelheim, 1976). This family interaction references superhero play seen in other examples of data and demonstrates how story language narrates Tom's body movement as he plays with the danger of running away but within the safety of family relations. Dad later described their current context as the "centre of the universe" in appreciating surroundings facilitating family needs after moving from a city. Such "everyday adventures" and "ordinary magic" (Gill, 2012) might seem inconsequential and only of importance to children. However, a holistic perspective suggests these express a deep-seated need to feel embedded in sources of relational support. "Storying the outdoors" is an educational approach aiming to "nourish habits such as noticing, listening, touching and feeling that children may need to build a kinship with the outdoor places" (Witt, 2017, p. 69). The GoPro™ footage illuminated family interactions in which these occurred spontaneously and highlight the relevance of considering educational practices oriented to relations between people and place.

Moments of Mental Consciousness

Mental consciousness highlights use of language and symbol in association with the dominance of the visual sense. Such capacities enable "paradox, abstraction, rational reflection, and self-assertion" but also the potential creation of "precarious dualities" and sense of separation (Chawla, 2002, loc. 2665). Drawing on this descriptor highlighted adult perceptions oriented to sights at a distance, future events, and pre-formed knowledge, but for their attention to be drawn back to immediate surroundings and language in forming relations. Examples in GoPro™ footage were fleeting but included children picking wildflowers and discovering a "whitebell" among bluebells which they asked dad to name. A further example included a mum's suggestion to count buttercups in a field which the GoPro™ demonstrated that her son couldn't see. Instead, for their shared attention to be drawn by the wiggling whiskers of a nearby horse which they laughed at together. Such subtle differences in attention and language-use might go unnoticed and aligns with the assertion that instances when our "discourse rests on intercourse with life and nature" are rare (Froebel, 1887, p 88). However, this is accompanied by guidance to live with children as means to give "meaning to our speech and life to the things about us!" (Froebel, 1887, p. 88). Measures of wellbeing and resilience include aspects of mental health, social capacity, and support through accessible relations (Walsh et al., 2010), and there may be additional avenues to explore when considering multi-directional influence between all relations.

An Integral Consciousness

Integral consciousness highlights scope for holistic experience. Humanity has a capacity for holistic relations, and their integration can support a sense of belonging to the whole. A holistic vocabulary has illuminated a rich influential potential between child, adult, and environment, and sensory, co-creative capacities as connective experiences (Lumber et al., 2017). Such moments might be fleeting and not noticed unless highlighted, and a holistic perspective suggests that it is important to do so. This is for support offered to the individual in learning to be, become, and belong in the world as a lifelong, relational learning process. A holistic perspective can offer connective support for a collective wellbeing and resilience. Insights from lockdown responses taken during the COVID-19 pandemic have highlighted the importance of family access to green space for their wellbeing and resilience (Natural England, 2020; ONS, 2020). Such understandings in local contexts might highlight the importance now in revisioning education according to collective support for a connective resilience (Sterling, 2021).

Conclusion

The healthy balance of a whole system is in focus in holistic education and the promotion of a sense of belonging understood as integral. Our individual resilience is important but considered in terms of broad scope for social and environmental support in relations. This view can align with the recently developed socio-bio-ecological "one health" model in understanding human, animal, and biosphere health as interwoven in a single, interdependent system (Barrett & Osofsky, 2013). Its application to early education has shaped its consideration as a "community-based healthy ecosystem" that could be developed through "naturalising" outdoor spaces in community involvement processes (Moore & Cosco, 2014, p. 168). The example shared here of family trips to local natural environments offers a further example of early years practice shaped by similar holistic considerations. Such practices align with understanding the early years setting as a site for active community-building (Early Years Coalition, 2021) and children as "cultural brokers" between social contexts. However, a reconnection of current understanding of early years practice with Froebel's holistic vision gives rise to considering children as the "cultural brokers" of environmental relations. The holistic paradigm orients to the wellbeing of a whole ecological system and offers educational guidance towards this through balancing a process of making "the outer inner – and the inner, outer" (Froebel, 1887, p. 32). It is in considering the individual as interconnected with their whole context that links, relations, and opportunities for networking become a firmer measure of quality in education.

References

Afifi, T., & MacMillan, H. (2011). Resilience following child maltreatment: A review of protective factors. *Canadian Journal of Psychiatry*, 56(5), 266–272.

Barrett, M., & Osofsky, S. (2013). One health: Interdependence of people, other species, and the planet. In D. Katz, J. Elmore, D. Wild, & S. Lucan (Eds.), *Jekel's epidemiology, biostatistics, preventive medicine, and public health* (4th ed., pp. 364–377). Elsevier.

Bettelheim, B. (1976). *The uses of enchantment: The meaning and importance of fairy tales*. Penguin Press.

Brehony, K. (2009). Transforming theories of childhood and early childhood education: Child study and the empirical assault on Froebelian rationalism. *Paedagogica Historica*, 45(4–5), 585–604.

Capaldi, C., Passmore, H., Nisbet, E., Zelenski, J., & Dopko, R. (2015). Flourishing in nature: A review of the benefits of connecting with nature and its application as a wellbeing intervention. *International Journal of Wellbeing*, 5, 4. https://internationaljournalofwellbeing.org/index.php/ijow/issue/view/19 on 29.6.17

Chawla, L. (2002). Spots of time: Manifold ways of being in nature in childhood. In P. Kahn & S. Kellert (Eds.), *Children and nature: Psychological, sociocultural, and evolutionary investigations*. MIT Press.

Chung, S., & Walsh, D. (2000). Unpacking child centredness: A history of meanings. *Journal of Curriculum Studies, 32*(2), 215–234.

Darling, E. (2017). Womanliness in the slums: A free kindergarten in early twentieth-century Edinburgh. *Gender & History, 29*(2). 359–386.

Department for Environment, Food and Rural Affairs. (2018). *A green future: Our 25-year plan to improve the environment.* https://www.gov.uk/government/publications/25-year-environment-plan

Department of Education. (2021). *The early years foundation stage framework.* https://www.gov.uk/government/publications/early-years-foundation-stage-framework-2

Duncan, J. (2011). Building communities: Begins in the early years with early childhood services and professional teachers. *Pacific Early Childhood Education Research Association.* https://ir.canterbury.ac.nz/handle/10092/5898

Early Years Coalition. (2021). *Birth to 5 matters: Non-statutory guidance for the early years foundation stage.* https://birthto5matters.org.uk

Ellenbogen, S., Klein, B., & Wekerle, C. (2014). Early childhood education as a resilience intervention for maltreated children. *Early Child Development and Care, 184*(9–10), 1364–1377.

Felitti, M., Anda, R., Nordenberg, M., Williamson, D. F., Spitz, A. M., Edwards, V., & Marks, J. S. (1998). Relationship of childhood abuse and household dysfunction to many of the leading causes of death in adults: The adverse childhood experiences (ACE) study. *American Journal of Preventative Medicine, 14*(4): 245–258.

Fredrickson, L. M., & Anderson, D. H. (1999). A qualitative exploration of the wilderness experience as a source of spiritual inspiration. *Journal of Environmental Psychology, 19*(1), 21–39.

Froebel, F. (1887). *The education of man* (W. Hailmann, Trans.). Dover.

The Froebel Trust. (2023). https://www.froebel.org.uk/.

Gebser, J. (1949). *The ever-present origin.* Ohio University Press.

Gill, T. (2012). *Celebrating ordinary magic and everyday adventures.* https://rethinkingchildhood.com/2012/04/26/everyday-adventures/

Hartig, T., Mitchell, R., de Vries, S., & Frumkin, H. (2014). Nature and Health. *Annual Review of Public Health, 35*(1), 207–228.

Heft, H. (1988). Affordances of children's environments: A functional approach to environmental description. *Children's Environments Quarterly, 5*(3), 29–37.

Huizinga, J. (1955). *Homo ludens; a study of the play-element in culture.* Beacon Press.

Hurlburt, M. S., Nguyen, K., Reid, J., Webster-Stratton, C., & Zhang, J. (2013). Efficacy of the incredible years group parent program with families in Head Start who self-reported a history of child maltreatment. *Child Abuse & Neglect, 37*(8), 531–543.

Hyman, B., & Williams, L. (2001). Resilience among women survivors of child sexual abuse. *Affilia, 16*, 198–219.

Ingulli, K., & Lindbloom, G. (2013). Connection to nature and psychological resilience. *Ecopsychology, 5*(1), 52–55.

Izenstark, D., & Ebata, A. T. (2016). Theorizing family-based nature activities and family functioning: The integration of attention restoration theory with a family routines and rituals perspective. *Journal of Family Theory & Review, 8*, 137–153.

James, A., & James, A. (2012). *Key concepts in childhood studies.* SAGE Publications.

Johnson, J. (2019). *Seeing through the world.* Revelore Press.

Jordan, M., & Hinds, J. (2016). *Ecotherapy: Theory, research and practice.* Palgrave Press.

Kaplan, R., & Kaplan, S. (1989). *The experience of nature: A psychological perspective.* Cambridge University Press.

Liebschner, J. (1992). *A child's work: Freedom and guidance in Froebel's educational theory and practice.* The Lutterworth Press.

Lumber, R., Richardson, M., & Sheffield, D. (2017). Beyond knowing nature: Contact, emotion, compassion, meaning, and beauty are pathways to nature connection. *PLoS One, 12*(5), 1–24.

Luthar, S., & Cicchetti, D. (2000). The construct of resilience: Implications for interventions and social policies. *Development and Psychopathology, 12*(4), 857–885.

MacDougall, D. (1998). *Transcultural cinema*. Princeton University Press.

Mahmoudi, S., Jafari, E., & Liaghatdar, M. (2012). Holistic education: An approach for 21 century'. *International Education Studies, 5*(2), 178–186.

Meehan, C. (2017). Where do I come from? Young children engaging with 'big' questions and the role of adults. *School Science Review*. https://repository.canterbury.ac.uk/item/88256/where-do-i-come-from-young-children-engaging-with-big-questions-and-the-role-of-adults

Moore, R., & Cosco, N. (2014). Growing up green: Naturalization as a health promotion strategy in early childhood outdoor learning environments. *Children, Youth and Environments, 24*(2), 168–191.

Naidoo, J., & Muthukrishna, N. (2016). Child well-being in a rural context: Shifting to a social sustainability lens. *South African Journal of Childhood Education, 6*(2), 1–9.

Natural England. (2020). *The people and nature survey for England: Children's survey (experimental statistics)*. https://www.gov.uk/government/statistics/thepeople-and-nature-survey-for-england-child-data-wave-1-experimental-statistics/the-peopleand-nature-survey-for-england-childrens-survey-experimental-statistics

Nisbet, E., & Zelenski, J. (2011). Underestimating nearby nature: Affective forecasting errors obscure the happy path to sustainability. *Psychological Science, 22*(9), 1101–1106.

Nolan, A., Taket, A., & Stagnitti, K. (2014). Supporting resilience in early years classrooms: The role of the teacher. *Teachers and Teaching, 20*(5), 595–608.

Office of National Statistics. (2020). *Children's views on well-being and what makes a happy life*. https://www.ons.gov.uk/peoplepopulationandcommunity/wellbeing/articles/childrensviewson wellbeingandwhatmakesahappylifeuk2020/2020-10-02

Oldfield, L. (2012). *Free to learn*. Hawthorn Press.

Pink, S. (2009). *Doing sensory ethnography*. SAGE Publications.

Pretty, J., Angus, C., Bain, M., Barton, J, Gladwell, V., Hine, R., Pilgrim, S., Sandercock, S., & Sellens, M. (2009). Nature, childhood, health and life pathways. In *Interdisciplinary centre for environment and society occasional paper*. University of Essex.

Pyle, R. (2003). Nature matrix: Reconnecting people and nature. *Oryx, 37*(2), 206–214.

Richardson, M. (2023). *Reconnection*. Pelagic Publishing.

Roseman, N. (1965). A note on Froebel's conception of personal freedom. *Educational Theory, 15*(4), 265–350.

Ryan, R., Weinstein, N., Bernstein, J., Brown, K., Mistretta, L., & Gagne, M. (2010). Vitalizing effects of being outdoors and in nature. *Journal of Environmental Psychology, 30*, 159–168.

Shonkoff, J., & Levitt, P. (2010). Neuroscience and the future of early childhood policy: Moving from why to what and how. *Neuron, 67*(5), 689–691.

Sobel, D. (2008). *Childhood and nature: Design principles for educators*. Stenhouse Publishers.

Soga, M., Takahiro Yamanoi, T., Tsuchiyaa, K., Koyanagi, T. F., & Kanaib, T. (2018). What are the drivers of and barriers to children's direct experiences of nature? *Landscape and Urban Planning, 180*, 114–120.

Sterling, S. (2021). Concern, conception, and consequence: Re-thinking the paradigm of higher education in dangerous times. *Frontiers in Sustainability, 2*, 743806. https://doi.org/10.3389/frsus.2021.743806

Suchman, N. E., Decoste, C., McMahon, T. J., Rounsaville, B., & Mayes, L. (2011). The mothers and toddlers' program, an attachment-based parenting intervention for substance using women: Results at 6-week follow-up in a randomized clinical pilot. *Infant Mental Health Journal, 32*(4), 427–449.

Thomas, T. (2021). Family resiliency: A strengths-based, relational and community approach to early education. *He Kupu*, 6(4), 32–39.
Ulrich, R., Simons, B., Losito, E., Fiorito, L., Miles, M., & Zelson, M. (1991). Stress recovery during exposure to natural and urban environments. *Journal of Environmental Psychology*, 11(3), 201–230.
Ungar, M., & Theron, L. (2020). Resilience and mental health: How multisystemic processes contribute to positive outcomes, *The Lancet Psychiatry*, 7(5), 441–448.
Vandenbroeck, M. (2017). Supporting (super) diversity in early childhood settings. In L. Miller, C. Cameron, C. Dalli, & N. Barbour (Eds.), *The SAGE handbook of early childhood policy* (pp. 403–417). SAGE Publications.
Walsh, W., Dawson, J., & Mattingly, M. (2010). How are we measuring resilience following childhood maltreatment? Is the research adequate and consistent? What is the impact on research, practice, and policy? *Trauma Violence Abuse*, 11, 27–41.
Warner, M. (2014). *Once upon a time: A short history of the fairy tale*. Oxford University Press.
Witt, S. (2017). Storying the outdoors. In E. Pickering (Ed.), *Teaching outdoors creatively* (pp. 59–70). Routledge Press.
Yiangou, N. (2017). Is a new consciousness emerging? Reflections on the thought of Ibn 'Arabi and the impact of an integral perspective. *World Futures*, 73(7), 27–441.

11
BUILDING A CIRCLE OF CARING SUPPORT FOR OUR CHILDREN WITH DIVERSE ROOTS

Nurturing Young Children's Resiliency

Wilma Robles-Melendez, Berta Capo and Eric G. Robles

Working with children is a learning journey where every day more is realized about their unfolding development that is witnessed right in our classrooms and communities. Born with an eagerness to learn, they also experience a world where multiple challenges continue to define life in current times. Today, growing and developing in a society where multiple changes and challenges are happening, children's wellbeing continues as a main priority for childhood educators and advocates. While changes and different challenges are a constant in society, many more seem to be taking place these days. Upholding the commitment to support children's optimal development to guide efforts of education, we are today aware of the many issues threatening the world of the child (UNICEF, 2021; National Association for the Education of Young Children, 2020). More than ever, children are under the threat of conflict, violence, social insecurity, poverty, and social disparities menacing their own future. Together with children, at risk is also the future of society. Just as UNICEF states, "We must be silent no longer" (2021, p. 4), and take steps to respond today with actions for children's sake.

The need is now, for centering efforts that will thoughtfully nurture children's development and empower them to be successful. Society itself has made it urgent to address the challenges facing children. How it happens and what supports it? This is what we discuss ahead in this chapter. In particular, we address practices that can help us make our classrooms become a place where they can find themselves supported. A working framework to encourage children's resiliency of young children with diverse backgrounds is presented as a tool to create that circle of support children need.

DOI: 10.4324/9781003345664-14

Children Are Faced With Many Challenges

The report on the *State of Children 2021* (UNICEF, 2021) clearly revealed the difficult conditions that are experienced by children in our society. It points out to the multiple situations that are placing children at risk everywhere in the world. Beyond the statistical data, it is a reminder that all children are vulnerable for childhood is in itself a most vulnerable time for the developing child. Making us aware about the risk, it also calls attention to the impact these situations, disparities, and sociopolitical conflicts, have on childhood's wellbeing and particularly in the mental health of children. Much of the realities they face have been a fact continuing to be present for decades and that are now becoming more evident after humanity experienced the 2020 COVID-19 pandemic. Among those most impacted were susceptible families and their children from marginalized groups and those living in economically challenged communities who were faced with unimaginable challenges (Frisco et al., 2022; Pittalwalla, 2022).

Concerned with the conditions experienced by many children during and post-pandemic time, the United Nations has cautioned society about the impact on children, stating, "they risk being among its biggest victims. . . . This is a universal crisis, and, for some children, the impact will be lifelong" (United Nations, 1989, n.p.). Everyone, we must say, has been impacted, including many children who affected by the feelings of uncertainty characterizing these times that continue to be questioned by society. Compounding the situation faced at present by children is the ongoing presence of armed conflict and war, most recently in Eastern Europe, and the urgent conditions and status of families and children forced to seek refuge in many parts of the globe (Figure 11.1). To these challenges, we must add the existing unfair circumstances faced by many children and adults with diverse ethnic roots, who are

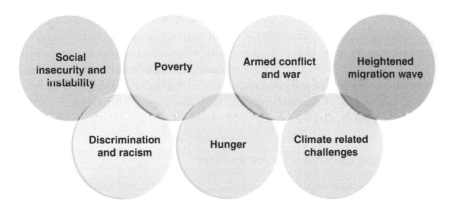

FIGURE 11.1   World challenges faced by children

experiencing discriminatory practices. Their realities, happening across global contexts, further add to the panorama of risk defining children's experiences in simply too many places.

Children are never alone, and concerns for their wellbeing remain a priority for everyone seeking their integral development and wellbeing. Across communities, voices of researchers, early childhood educators and advocates have already pointed out to the need to protect children and to secure the future of a generation faced with many difficult challenges (Shonkoff et al., 2012; UNICEF, 2021). Concerns particularly emerge about the increase in experiences that, stressful and distressing in nature, are placing at risk their healthy development, both physically and socioemotionally (Clark et al., 2020; Sorrels, 2015). With more challenges emerging from prevailing social violence, poverty, and a myriad of inequities, the need for efforts intentionally guided at addressing the wellbeing of the child is recognized.

We Know They Need Support

Conversations with educators and observations in early childhood classrooms have shown us how children, in their own way, alert us with their behaviors about the difficulties faced in what becomes a call for their support. Some of the authors of this chapter have actually experienced the impact of current situations through the responses of the younger members in their families (Box 1). These experiences have further cemented the fact that current societal issues leave a mark on the child. In what way we can respond and build their ability to overcome difficult realities is what drives efforts of educators pursuing the child's healthy and positive wellbeing. The fact is that pursuing the welfare of children is a mandate for society that must be recognized and moved into actions for the child. With growing situations that adversely impact children, we must also remember that every child has a right to a safe and positive development as declared by the Convention on the Rights of the Child (United Nations, 1989). In these times, it is imperative to recognize that society must always respond with what is in the best interest of the child. Today, that premise demands greater attention to effectively establish determined efforts that will promote child development and respond with the support needed for children confronted with challenges (Eismann et al., 2020; Erdman & Colker, 2020).

There Is Hope! Children Who Are Resilient

Amid the challenges experienced in society, we still find and marvel at children continuing to thrive despite the immense challenges that some faced in their young lives. Developmentalists and educators agree that those who can overcome difficult events and realities demonstrate an ability to be resilient. We all have met or currently know of children whose ability to overcome and thrive reveals an impressive strength despite the difficulties faced. How they can rise and succeed remains as an example of the human power to defeat obstacles. Described as resilient individuals, resiliency has been defined as the capacity to effectively overcome and adapt to conditions threatening an individual's wellbeing (Masten, 2021; Sorrels, 2015). Resiliency is a multidimensional and complex concept. It is a human capacity that can be developed and strengthened, which calls for intentional efforts at home and in the classroom. The study of resiliency emerged in response to a need for understanding the varied response of children facing difficult experiences (Masten & Barnes, 2018; McKenzie, 2021). It has since been the focus of attention for researchers who continue to investigate its many factors and impact on the individual. As a complex concept, some of the key characteristics depicting resiliency are the following:

- Resiliency is best defined as "a multisystemic dynamic process of successful adaptation or recovery in the context of risk or a threat" (Mesman et al., 2021, p. 587). A variety of factors influence and contribute to building resilient behaviors.
- Resiliency is revealed through the positive patterns of adaptation that an individual displays in the context of difficult and adverse conditions (Masten & Obradovic, 2007).
- Research reveals that resilient children have "the ability to adapt well to adversity, trauma, and other sources of stress".
- Resiliency is associated with positive mental health especially when faced with a variety of risk factors and threats (American Psychological Association [APA], 2020a; Masten et al., 2021).
- People who are resilient have the ability to rebound once affected by adverse childhood experiences (Lally & Mangione, 2017)
- There are multiple pathways leading to build and support a child's resiliency. Families, concerned adults, and educators all play an important role in building and supporting a child's resiliency (Robles-Melendez & Capo, 2020).

Studies have shown that resilient children are characterized by their positive perspective and confident ways. Based on research on resiliency (Erdman & Colker, 2020; Masten & Barnes, 2018; Osher et al., 2020; Sorrels, 2015), resilient children share the following characteristics:

- Have caring adults who provide support.
- They are assertive and show optimism even when faced with difficult situations.
- Show confidence despite their challenges.

- Are more successful in school.
- Have a circle of relationships.

We Can and Must Become Resilient

Different from what it was thought before, resiliency is not "necessarily a personality trait that only some people possess" (American Psychological Association [APA], 2020a, para 7). Today, we know that resilience is a capacity that can be developed and strengthened. Influenced by interactions and experiences with parents, families, classroom, peers, and others, resiliency is a capacity that is essential to address successfully challenges and conflicts that can be faced. Studies on resilience have shown that this ability appears to shield the individual from adverse and hostile circumstances, allowing them to thrive in otherwise difficult environments (Masten, 2007; Mesman et al., 2021). It is also known that being resilient does not make us immune to experiencing adverse situations. Rather, what it does is to provide individuals with the tools needed to address challenges emotionally and cognitively.

With increasing social, political, and economic complexity, many today are facing numerous obstacles that influence their development. Considerations to this reality highlight an existing need for efforts guided at building the child's capacity to successfully face difficult situations. Building that armor that protects a child is what many times has been alluded when describing resiliency. Research has shown us that concerted classroom efforts can effectively impact and build a child's resilient behavior (Condly, 2006; Masten, 2007; National Scientific Council on the Developing Child, 2015; Sorrels, 2015). Caring relationships are an influential component promoting the child's ability to respond with resilient behaviors. Relationships are, too, at the core of successful experiences in the classroom. Given the influence of the classroom on the young child, intentional efforts building resiliency are a factor contributing to how children become resilient (Osher et al., 2020).

Social Diversity and the Need for Building Children's Resiliency

Challenging circumstances are a reality that are not absent from childhood and that may be experienced by any child. It is also known that exposure to events and situations deemed traumatic can occur across and beyond social and economic lines (Erdman & Colker, 2020). In societies known for their increasing social, ethnic, and cultural diversity, it is known that presence of unfair and discriminatory experiences may be experienced at some point by children. Research has also revealed that children with diverse cultures and ethnic roots are more prone to experience stressful and difficult realities (APA, 2008). In fact, it is not uncommon for them to have been subjected to experiencing prejudice and unfair treatment (Australian Children's Rights, 2016; Robles-Melendez & Beck, 2019; Society for Research in Child Development, 2011). Sadly, social and economic inequities experienced by children and families continue to be a factor leading many to face multiple risks. These risks challenge their right to opportunities and to a successful development.

Existing disparities uncovered during the 2020 pandemic lockdown clearly showed to society the prevalence of social inequalities across communities. Many of these ranged from access to health services to even internet connectivity issues, which further isolated thousands of children who were left unable to join their virtual classrooms (Carrión-Martínez et al., 2021). Notwithstanding, many were surprised to see how, beyond these and numerous other obstacles, there were children who continue to demonstrate their ability to overcome and succeed. It was clearly their resilient spirit which contributed to defeating the challenge faced. Many more children, however still, need support with many reports later revealing and acknowledging the learning loss experienced by children from socially challenged and marginalized communities (Donnelly & Patrinos, 2022). As a social justice issue, it raises the need for practices and efforts to shield and empower children by building their resiliency. These experiences along with many others also evidence the need for addressing fairness and to direct attention to building the resilient behaviors of children of diverse backgrounds.

There Is Greater Need for Building Children's Resiliency

Life in the first few decades of this century continues to be characterized by its multiple challenges. This is the context where, together with their families, children today grow and develop. This is a time of inexplicable character for everyone and particularly children. While challenges and difficult moments are experiences that, at some point in our lives, we all will experience (American Psychological Association [APA], 2020b). Today we are becoming mindful about the presence of more challenging factors exposing children to traumatic experiences. Violence, poverty, and social injustices including exposure to racial discriminatory practices, they all describe a context that impacts and influences the life of a child. Adding to its many challenges, climate changes are also now contributing to placing many more in challenged situations. Living in contexts where their very own existence is confronted by many difficult happenings leaves a mark in their young lives. We need to be mindful that childhood is not unaffected to what occurs in society. Behaviors and actions in the classroom already tell us much about what they are experiencing. The time is now to become aware and understand that children are not immune witnesses and that such experiences are hurtful and damaging during a time of great vulnerability.

Presence of Adverse Childhood Experiences

Research has made us aware about the presence of challenging living situations in the lives of children. Adverse childhood experiences (ACEs) may negatively affect the child's development. These potentially traumatic situations experienced during a child's most vulnerable time, "can have tremendous impact on future . . . lifelong health and opportunity" (Centers for Disease Control, 2021, n.p.). Early exposure to ACEs can trigger more serious issues for young children since developmental periods build upon each other (Yoon, 2018). This very fact is already a call for action. Bethell (2016) identified nine kinds of ACEs and how they affect the potential for appropriate development of the child. These are comprised by the following:

- Serious economic hardship
- Witnessing or experiencing violence in the neighborhood
- Alcohol, substance abuse
- Living in homes where there is domestic violence,
- Mental health problems in the home
- Parental divorce
- Loss of parents to death or incarceration
- Social rejection through racial and ethnic discrimination.

(Bethell, p. 140)

Being exposed to multiple ACEs increases the prevalence of emotional, mental, or behavioral conditions and affects children's resiliency (Bethell et al., 2016). At the same time, studies about ACEs have brought an awareness about the existence of protective factors that must and should be supported to ensure the child's wellbeing (du Toit et al., 2021; Eismann et al., 2020; Khambati et al., 2018; Worku et al., 2018; Yoon, 2018; Yule et al., 2020).

Challenging Contexts, Challenging Experiences

Violence and instability, along with ensuing inequities still present throughout society, are marking the lived realities of many young children in our schools (Breedlove et al., 2020). Continuing prejudice and racism are among the experiences challenging many children in society and in our own communities (American Psychological Association [APA], 2020b; Bethell, 2016). In the faces and questions of children, experiences with current circumstances defined by dramatic and traumatic nature can be read and heard as these are revealed to us. Presence of difficult situations whether directly experienced or vicariously learned about, are a factor influencing a child's successful development. Frequency of such circumstances in the lives of children are today too familiar to educators who continue to grow worried about their future given the impact on children's health and wellbeing (Moffitt, 2013). How to safeguard the child and promote their positive and resilient development is shared as a focus of efforts across classrooms. A multitude of difficult realities continues to be of concern to educators who zealously aim at what is best for every child to develop and successfully grow. Three of those considered of greater concern especially for children with diverse backgrounds are discussed in the section that follows.

The Pandemic of 2020

The recent global health pandemic brought to society a challenging and traumatic experience. Painful images and reports have emerged across communities evidencing the distressing reality. The impact of the pandemic has also been felt on the lives of young children. They have been faced with an experience that altered daily routines. While conflict and challenges are part of the happenings people may experience, the pandemic has brought to light the resilient nature and response of people. Stories of actions from many families and of children have demonstrated resiliency as a key factor in how they responded. For children with culturally diverse backgrounds, challenges increase given the existence of multiple inequities. Resiliency, the capacity of shielding people and fostering their ability to overcome challenges, emerges during the early years. With traumatic experiences being a fact in life, the need for addressing children's wellbeing calls for nurturing and building their resiliency. This is particularly relevant in a post-pandemic society and in a world where violence and challenging circumstances continue to threaten children's wellbeing and development.

Social, Economic, and Cultural Challenges. Food insecurity, home instability, family life disruption, and lack of access to healthcare are still areas challenging children and families particularly for those in economically challenged communities and minoritized groups. For some, disparities in education and access to quality experiences are also present as challenges. Many are also impacted by continuing cultural misconceptions and misguided views still prevalent in society. The context where children grow and develop is influential in their development during their early years. Community characteristics particularly those where more difficult living conditions exist may expose and challenge children's wellbeing (Casey Family Programs, 2015).

Violence, Conflict, and Insecurity Challenges

Many children are socially and economically challenged during normal times. These challenges were compounded by multiple crisis due to suffering through the years of the COVID-19 pandemic along with ongoing devastating social insecurity, violence, and wars, among other adversities. According to the World Health Organization (WHO), globally, thousands of children ages 2–17 years are victimized by violence in some of its many forms (physical, sexual, or emotional violence or neglect) (WHO, 2022). Violence is considered as one of the most pressing challenges placing children at risk in many communities. Its presence is one of the main and more common reasons causing stressful conditions (Moffitt, 2013). In 2022, a war in Ukraine forced millions of families and children to leave the safety of their homes. Since early in the century, a combined threat of insecurity, armed conflict, and hunger has continuously threatened millions of children and families who have left their homes migrating and seeking refuge all in an effort to survive the surreal realities of the contexts where they live. We are left with an image of difficult experiences for many children of the world were so many are threatened with famine, displacement, terrorism, war, and much more (Lally & Mangione, 2017). Whether directly or indirectly experienced, these are circumstances to consider for their impact on the child's wellbeing.

Caring for Children Is Building Their Resiliency

Within the community of the classroom, educators are uncovering how children experience and make sense of the realities at home, near and far, of times characterized by continuous transformation. Shared through their comments and behaviors, we are learning how they visualize life's realities. We are also learning that they are not shielded from the challenges of violent environments or from local or national events. With incidents of social, economic, and of political nature increasing today, more children are now exposed and affected by their impact on their young lives (Erdman & Colker, 2020; Peña et al., 2018). Heightening the need to find ways to responsively safeguard children is the fact that, as pointed out earlier, their own development and potential for future success are at risk. As many have said before, it is, in fact, a need to urgently understand we are witnessing a generation at risk of being impacted by the multifold nature of adversity. The duty of care that society and education have toward children continues as a reminder of the responsibilities that are needed for children (Clark et al., 2020). Helping them to become resilient is a step to provide children with the tools needed to navigate and face the ongoing issues and challenges in life. More than just a strategy, caring practices in our classrooms are integral to promote and build a child's sense of resiliency. They are also fundamental to supporting the wellbeing of children. Nurtured by the relationships and sense of safety, caring practices are an empowering factor building children's ability to face challenges.

Continuing challenges of today are a reminder about the impact of ACE) on their potential for successful developmental growth. While society finds ways to address social, economic, and political issues, we can respond with practices guided at empowering and building children's resiliency.

Building a Circle of Support

With our commitment to children, and just as Nobel laureate poet, Gabriela Mistral once said, *"Many things we need can wait. The child cannot. Now is the time his bones are formed, his mind developed. To him we cannot say tomorrow, his name is today."* The call for action for children remains as a priority. Mindful consideration to the numerous challenges that children are facing today make us aware about the urgent need to respond with actions to support children. For too many children, their opportunity for successful development is already at risk. Committed to support the child, and upholding our ethical responsibility, we are called for a response aimed and directed to safeguard a safe developmental trajectory for every child. Every child has a right to caring practices that nurture and support children and their integral development anywhere in our global society. Events and challenges of current times highlight the need to establish a circle of supporting developmentally based practices framing actions and strategies to build children's resilient skills and behavior. A caring circle of support for children (Figure 11.2), proposed as a framework to guide actions, must be centered on joined efforts of educators together with families and guided by what is culturally responsive for the child.

Responding With Care and Nurturing Practices

Caring is more than just an action. It is a demonstration of commitment and purpose to ensure the wellbeing of those that one cares for. In the classroom, caring is integral to all the educational experiences we provide to children. Caring and nurturing children contribute to building attachment, which establishes affective bonds that promote a sense of being cared for and of emotional safety (Centers for Disease Control, 2021). Nurturing a child's potential, caring practices are a protective factor (McKenzie, 2021). They are also vital and contributing to building resilient behaviors. In the classroom, caring and nurturing practices are a composite of experiences intentionally directed and seeking to foster resiliency for the child. They include a variety of experiences and supports based on the developmental needs of children and mindful of their contextual realities (National Association for the Education of Young Children, 2020; Erdman & Colker, 2020). Together, they become a circle of caring support for the child (Figure 11.2) and a framework for promoting children's resiliency. Two points are important to consider when using this framework. One, it is developmentally based and responds to the needs

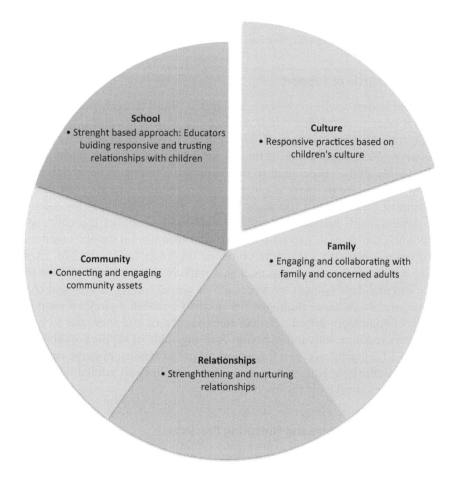

FIGURE 11.2 Circle of support promoting resilience

and cultural realities of the child. Second, it has a strength-based focus and pursues empowering children to successfully respond to the challenges they may find as they grow up.

Protective Factors

Many continue to highlight the role and need of protective factors. These attributes or conditions can contribute to lessen incidence of difficult experiences and may also provide a shield to children when faced with traumatic experiences (Centers for Disease Control, 2021). Numerous research articles focus on protective factors (e.g., du Toit et al., 2021; Eismann et al., 2020; Khambati et al., 2018; Worku et al., 2018; Yoon, 2018; Yule et al., 2020).

Protective factors allow children and families to cope and adapt to adversity (Borge et al., 2016). They help the child and family cope with ACE and thus help promote resiliency. Khambati lists the following protective factors for the child:

- Intelligence
- Having an internal locus of control
- Effective communication skills
- A child's easy temperament
- A caring family

(p. 344)

Caring as a Protective Factor

Relationships are a central component and protective factor for every child. According to the literature, the critical protective factor for children is a responsive caregiver relationship (du Toit, 2021). Harkness and Super (1994) theorized a niche of influence on children where caregivers were one of the main players. Developmentally, educators are one of the influential caregivers of a child and thus the need for efforts in the classroom to nurture children's positive development. Classroom opportunities to show caring support are many, and when intentionally planned, they become a vital factor supporting and building children's resiliency.

There are several other factors that also protect children and support their resilience. For children in marginalized and low-income communities, other critical protective factors include children living with both parents, married parents, and being cared by caregivers whose education is at least 8–12 grades (du Toit, 2021). Collaborative efforts of educators with children's families, particularly those in more challenged communities, are another central protective factor. Connections built by educators with families and in the classroom with children provide a strong circle of support and of caring attention to the child.

A Personal Experience: Caring and Loving Support Is Always Needed to Overcome Challenges

The populations of the world without much warning were suddenly forced into quarantine. Schools closed and students were forced to learn online and on the computer. The abrupt change was difficult for many students. I witnessed the frustration firsthand. My seven-year-old granddaughter was doing her assignments on the computer. She was becoming more and more frustrated with the situation. It was hard for her to understand what was occurring. She finally broke down and refused to do her schoolwork on the computer.

PHOTO 11.1 Working remotely was a stressful and isolating experience for many children

My granddaughter was crying profusely while repeatedly proclaiming "I hate the computer! I want to go back to school"! Seeing that a change of scenery may do her good, I brought her to my house. After hugs, talking, and praise, she began to do her computer homework with me at first and then alone. I made sure not to push her. It was slow going, but she soon settled into the new routine, though she did not like it. Families and I as a grandmother were able to alleviate the situation since a critical protective factor is a loving caregiver (Borge et al., 2016).
We thank our colleague Dr. Berta Capo, for sharing her personal experiences.

Building children's resiliency also brings attention to the need for intentional efforts to strengthen existing protective factors. In particular, according to Eismann et al. (2020), the following protective factors should be strengthened:

1. Direct efforts to build parental resiliency
2. Building and maintaining strong social connections
3. Responding and providing concrete support in time of need
4. Directing efforts to improve and support knowledge of parenting and child development
5. Giving attention to the child's social and emotional development

Classroom Practices That Build Resiliency

The classroom continues to be a place of experiences both formative and socioemotionally supportive for children. Practices guided at building children's resiliency are grounded on a strength-based focus. Within the community of the classroom, educators' attention and mindful support to every child continues to be a fundamental factor contributing to building a child's resiliency (Robles-Melendez & Capo, 2020). Practices are guided to build and enhance their resiliency when these are strength based and see the potential in every child to thrive. Resiliency building practices are directed at:

- Providing supportive experiences with intentionality.
- Capitalizing on the processes and relationships that enhance opportunities for children during difficult times.
- Nurturing the child's ability to succeed.
- Working with the child's family/caring adults.
- Implementing and following culturally responsive practices.

Within the construct of a circle of caring support, there are many classroom practices that are central to building resiliency for all children and particularly for the child with culturally and linguistically diverse heritage. Some of those highlighted here include implementation of developmentally responsive and supportive practices, consciously based attention to building children's resiliency, connection building, and collaborations with families. In each and all of these, the educator-committed effort is the key factor.

Developmentally Responsive and Supportive Practices

Working with children from diverse cultures and languages calls for developmentally focused experiences and attention to their cultural realities. Considerations to what is common and individually needed are essential to provide sensitive and responsive caring. Responsive and developmental caring practices address the child's needs and set a welcoming climate where experiences are responsively planned (National Association for the Education of Young Children, 2020; Sorrels, 2015). Such settings are places characterized by the following:

- Classroom provides a developmentally emotionally supportive environment.
- There is continuity in the supportive climate experienced in the environment.

- Experiences are planned to address children's learning needs in sensitive and engaging ways.
- Educators mindfully address children's feelings.
- They place attention on caring and supporting child's connections and sense of belonging.

Consciously Based Attention to Build Resiliency

Focused and intentional efforts are vitally needed to address and support resiliency. Building resiliency demands conscious efforts to ensure continuity of experiences directed at building and promoting resilient skills and attitudes. Intentionally based, sensitive, and responsive caring happens when attention is placed on the child's holistic needs (Masten & Barnes, 2018). Educators consciously consider and are aware about children's lived experiences (Rogoff et al., 2018). Some of these intentional practices happened are described in the following.

Teachers take time to:

- Listen to the child when they verbalize feelings and when they do not.
- Provide a sense of stability even in uncertain situations.
- Demonstrate interest and attention to the child.
- Consider and focus on emotions exhibited.
- Ensure classroom communication welcomes children to share.
- Address challenging circumstances faced by the child and show honest interest.

Focus on Connections and Relationship Building

Strong relationships and connections are known to be an important factor in the social and emotional development process. Resilient children are characterized by a circle of relationships that provide and offer support. Research shows that "the capacity of an individual to adapt to challenges depends on their connections to other people and systems external to the individual through relationships and other processes" (Masten & Barnes, 2018, p. 4). During the early years, classrooms are one of the important venues where children build and develop relationships that connect them to peers and adults. In times of challenges, connections and positive relationships provide needed guidance and support to overcome and lessen the impact of difficult experiences (National Scientific Council on the Developing Child, 2015). Planning and targeting relationships and connections building in the classroom are essential strategies to foster resiliency. Figure 11.3 shows some of the many ways in which connections can be built and promoted within the community of the classroom.

Building a Circle of Caring Support   191

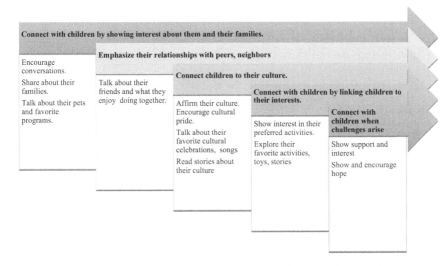

FIGURE 11.3   Building connections that support children's resilient skills

Collaborations With Families

Engaging and collaborating with families are well-established principles in early childhood education (National Association for the Education of Young Children, 2020; Robles-Melendez & Beck, 2019). Working with children to effectively support their wellbeing is a joint effort together with their parents and families. Successful collaborations with families contribute to provide experiences intentionally aimed at addressing the child's needs. Fomenting positive collaborations to support children's resiliency are successful when these are anchored on four main tenets:

- **Know**
  - Educators hold knowledge about the children's families and their realities. They are conscious and mindfully aware about their experiences and challenges.
- **Communicate**
  - Establish culturally respectful communication that promote and build trustful relationships.
  - Keep families informed about the children's needs, their successes and plan together for their wellbeing.
- **Show**
  - They honestly show respect and interest about their children's wellbeing. Interactions are welcoming and foster trust.

- Share
  - Share resources and useful information needed to support children's wellbeing. Share ideas and knowledge to help strengthen parenting skills.

Children Need Us

Every day is another opportunity to make a difference in the life of a child. Building their resiliency is one of those ways that help make a difference in their young lives. The enduring power of resilient behaviors and responses can transform the developmental path of a child contributing to achieve their wellbeing. In the classroom, we have the power to make that happen. We must remember that "Early childhood is both the most critical and the most vulnerable time in any child's development. . . . We cannot fail children in these early years" (Brazelton & Greenspan, 2000, p. x). Children need to feel safe. They need caring and supportive people. We trust that you are already one!

References

American Psychological Association [APA]. (2008). *Children and trauma. Update for mental health professionals.* update.pdf (apa.org)

American Psychological Association [APA]. (2020a). *Building your resilience.* Author. https://www.apa.org/topics/resilience/building-your-resilience

American Psychological Association [APA]. (2020b). *Resilience guide for parents and teachers.* https://www.apa.org/pi/families/resources/children-trauma-update (Original work published 2010)

Australian Children's Rights. (2016, March 16). *Survey finds prejudice and diversity are childhood issues.* https://humanrights.gov.au/about/news/survey-finds-prejudice-and-diversity-are-childhood-issues

Bethell, C., Gombojav, N., Solloway, M., & Wissow, L. (2016). Adverse childhood experiences, resilience and mindfulness-based approaches: Common denominator issues for children with emotional, mental, or behavioral problems. *Child and Adolescent Psychiatric Clinics of North America, 25*(2), 139–156. https://doi.org/10.1016/j.chc.2015.12.001

Borge, A., Motti-Stefanidi, F., & Masten, A. (2016). Resilience in developing systems: The promise of integrated approaches for understanding and facilitating positive adaptation to adversity in individuals and their families. *European Journal of Developmental Psychology, 13*(3), 293–296.

Brazelton, T., & Greenspan, S. (2000). *The irreducible needs of children. What every child must have to grow, learn, and flourish.* Perseus Publishing.

Breedlove, M., Choi, J., & Zyromski, B. (2020). Mitigating the adverse childhood experiences: How restorative practices in schools support positive childhood experiences and protective factors. *The New Educator, 17*(3), 223–241.

Carrión-Martínez, J., Pinel-Martínez, C., Pérez-Esteban, M. D., & Román-Sánchez, I. M. (2021). Family and school relationship during COVID-19 pandemic: A systematic review. *International Journal of Environmental Research and Public Health, 18,* 11710. https://www.ncbi.nlm.nih.gov/pmc/articles/PMC8582909/pdf/ijerph-18-11710.pdf

Casey Family Programs. (2015). *Geography matters.* https://www.casey.org/media/geography-matters.pdf

Centers for Disease Control. (2021). *Adverse childhood experiences (ACEs).* https://www.cdc.gov/violenceprevention/aces/index.html

Clark, H., Coll-Seck, A. M., Banerjee, A, Peterson, S., Dalglish, S. L., Ameratunga, S., Balabanova, D., Bhan, M. K., Bhutta, Z. A., Borrazzo, J., Claeson, M, Doherty, T., El-Jardali, F., George, A. S., Gichaga, A., Gram, L., Hipgrave, D. B., Kwamie, A., Meng, Q., . . . Mercer, R. (2020). A future for the world's children? A WHO-UNICEF-Lancet Commission. *The Lancet, 395*(10224), 605–658. https://doi.org/10.1016/S0140-6736(19)32540-1

Condly, S. J. (2006). Resilience in children: A review with implications for education. *Urban Education, 41*(3), 211–236.

Donnelly, R., & Patrinos, H. (2022). Learning loss during Covid-19: An early systematic review. *Prospects, 51*(4), 601–609.

du Toit, M., van der Linde, J., & Swanepoel, D. W. (2021). Early childhood development risks and protective factors in vulnerable preschool children from low-income communities in South Africa [article]. *Journal of Community Health, 46*(2), 304–312. https://doi.org/10.1007/s10900-020-00883-z

Eismann, E. A., Brinkmann, C., Theuerling, J., & Shapiro, R. A. (2020). Supporting families exposed to adverse childhood experiences within child care settings: A feasibility pilot [article]. *Early Childhood Education Journal, 48*(4), 451–462. https://doi.org/10.1007/s10643-019-01012-9

Erdman, S., & Colker, L. (2020). *Trauma and young children. Teaching strategies that support and empower.* National Association for the Education of Young Children.

Frisco, M., Van Hook, J., & Thomas, K. (2022). Racial/ethnic and nativity disparities in U.S. Covid-19 vaccination hesitancy during vaccine rollout and factors that explain them. *Social Science and Medicine, 307*, 115183. https://doi.org/10.1016/j.socscimed.2022.115183. Epub June 30, 2022. PMID: 35843179; PMCID: PMC9242888.

Harkness, S., & Super, C. (1994). The developmental niche: A theoretical framework for analyzing the household production of health. *Social Science and Medicine, 38*(2), 217–226. https://doi.org/10.1016/0277-9536(94)90391-3.

Khambati, N., Mahedy, L., Heron, J., & Emond, A. (2018). Educational and emotional health outcomes in adolescence following maltreatment in early childhood: A population-based study of protective factors [article]. *Child Abuse & Neglect, 81*, 343–353. https://doi.org/10.1016/j.chiabu.2018.05.008

Lally, J. R., & Mangione, P. (2017). Caring relationships: The heart of early brain development. *YC Young Children, 72*(2), 17–24. http://dx.doi.org/10.1111/dmcn.14911

Masten, A. & Obradovic, J. (2007). Competence and resilience in development. *Annals of the New York Academy of Sciences, 1094*, 1: 13-27.

Masten, A. S. (2007). Resilience in developing systems: Progress and promise as the fourth wave rises. *Development and Psychopathology, 19*(3), 921–930.

Masten, A. S., & Barnes, A. (2018). Resilience in children: Developmental perspectives. *Children, 5*(7), 98. https://doi.org/10.3390/children5070098. PMID: 30018217; PMCID: PMC6069421.

Masten, A. S., Lucke, C., Nelson, K., & Stallworthy, I. (2021). Resilience in development and psychopathology: Multisystem perspectives. *Annual Review of Clinical Psychology, 7*(17), 521–549.

McKenzie, E. (2021). Child resilience in a global pandemic. *Dimensions of Early Childhood, 49*(1), 6–13.

Mesman, E., Vreeker, A., & Hillegers, V. (2021). Resilience and mental health in children and adolescents: An update of the recent literature and future directions. *Current Opinion in Psychiatry, 34*(6), 586–592.

Moffitt, T. (2013). Childhood exposure to violence and lifelong health: Clinical intervention science and stress biology research join forces. *Development and Psychopathology,* 25, 402. https://www.ncbi.nlm.nih.gov/pmc/articles/PMC3869039/#__ffn_sectitle

National Association for the Education of Young Children. (2020). *Developmentally appropriate practices. Position statement.* Author.

National Scientific Council on the Developing Child. (2015). *Supportive relationships and active skill-building strengthen the foundations of resilience: Working paper 13.* http://www.developingchild.harvard.edu

Osher, D., Cantor, P., Berg, J., Steyer, L., & Rose., D. (2020). Drivers of human development: How relationships and context shape learning and development. *Applied Developmental Science,* 24(1), 6–36.

Peña, C., Jones, L., Orange, A., Simieou, F., & Márquez, J. (2018). Academic success and resiliency factors: A case study of unaccompanied immigrant children. *American Journal of Qualitative Research,* 2(1), 161–181. https://doi.org/10.29333/ajqr/5797

Pittalwalla, I. (2022, May). Marginalized communities of color face high COVID-19 risk. *UC Riverside News.* https://news.ucr.edu/articles/2022/05/25/marginalized-communities-color-face-high-covid-19-risk

Robles-Melendez, W., & Beck, V. (2019). *Teaching young children in multicultural classrooms: Issues, concepts and strategies* (5th ed.). Cengage.

Robles-Melendez, W., & Capo, B. (2020). *Circles of caring support for our children with diverse roots: Nurturing young children's resiliency* [Paper presentation]. Paper presentation at the Annual Conference of the Florida Association for the Education of Young Children (Virtual).

Rogoff, B., Dahl, A., & Callanan, M. (2018). The importance of understanding children's lived experience. *Developmental Review,* 50(Part A), 5–15. https://doi.org/10.1016/j.dr.2018.05.006.

Shonkoff, J., Garner, A., & Committee on Psychosocial Aspects of Child and Family Health. (2012). Committee on early childhood, adoption and dependent care, & section on developmental and behavioral pediatrics. *Pediatrics,* 129(1), e232-e246.

Society for Research in Child Development. (2011). Reducing prejudice and promoting equity in childhood. *Policy Brief,* 25(4). https://www.srcd.org/sites/default/files/resources/SPR%20Brief_25-4_2011.pdf

Sorrels, B. (2015). *Reaching and teaching children exposed to trauma.* Gryphon House.

UNICEF. (2021). *The state of the world's children 2021.* UNICEF. https://www.unicef.org/reports/state-worlds-children-2021

United Nations. (1989).*Convention on the rights of the child.* https://www.unicef.org/child-rights-convention/convention-text

Worku, B. N., Abessa, T. G., Franssen, E., Vanvuchelen, M., Kolsteren, P., & Granitzer, M. (2018). Development, social-emotional behavior and resilience of orphaned children in a family-oriented setting [article]. *Journal of Child & Family Studies,* 27(2), 465–474. https://doi.org/10.1007/s10826-017-0908-0

World Health Organization. (2022). *Violence against children. Key facts.* https://www.who.int/news-room/fact-sheets/detail/violence-against-children

Yoon, S. (2018). Fostering resilient development: Protective factors underlying externalizing trajectories of maltreated children [article]. *Journal of Child & Family Studies,* 27(2), 443–452. https://doi.org/10.1007/s10826-017-0904-4

Yule, K., Murphy, C., & Grych, J. (2020). Adaptive functioning in high-risk preschoolers: Caregiver practices beyond parental warmth [article]. *Journal of Child & Family Studies,* 29(1), 115–127. https://doi.org/10.1007/s10826-019-01660-w

12

A SYSTEM IN 'FIGHT MODE'?

Resilience and Social Capital in a Community Emerging From Conflict

Clionagh Boyle

Introduction

The literature on resilience, the capacity of some children to survive and thrive in spite of adverse circumstances, had its emergence in the psychological disciplines. In an early collection of studies, resilience was conceptualised by Anthony (1987), as the phenomenon of the 'invulnerable child' observed in children who appeared to thrive despite a parent's serious mental health challenges. Masten's later study described resilience as the 'ordinary magic' of children growing up in poverty attaining positive outcomes. The focus of resilience research on the child, the parent and the immediate microsystem of home and family has been a dominant shaping force in the field. As a result, in policy and practice, the design of interventions to support resilience in early childhood has principally focused on supporting behavioural change in the parent child dyad (MacLeod & Nelson, 2000; Furlong & McGilloway, 2015; Gardner et al., 2019). This concentration on the capacity of the individual child or parent has been criticised among others by Rutter (2012) who advocated for closer examination of social and environmental factors rather than the child's capacity to navigate these. A socio-ecological approach to interventions aimed at supporting resilience, drawing upon Bronfenbrenner's model (1976) has been conceptualised by Ungar (2008) whose premise is that 'the social ecology surrounding the intervention and the pathways to resilience children travel are as or more important than the qualities of the child him or herself' (Ungar, 2008, p. 55). Drawing from Ungar's work, VanderPlaat (2016) invites researchers to explore resilience through the 'sociological imagination' cautioning that focusing on adversity and resilience as residing only in the immediate domain of home and family not only 'deflects our gaze from

DOI: 10.4324/9781003345664-15

the social structures that cause and maintain these social conditions in the first place, but also limits our capacity to deal with these issues on a broad scale' (p. 191). This chapter will therefore deploy the sociological imagination in the exploration of an ecological case study of early intervention to illuminate the dynamics of resilience not just within the microsystem but at the exosystemic and macrosystemic levels.

Theoretical Framework and Methodology

The theoretical framework for the case study presented employs the 'thinking tools' of habitus, capital and field as identified by Bourdieu (1990, 2004) to better understand the dynamics of interventions aimed at supporting resilience at child, parent, community and political levels alongside Merriam's (1998, 2009) critically informed but pragmatic approach to case study. A case study of a self-identified early intervention city in Northern Ireland at a point where the wider policy focus was on early intervention to support resilience and wellbeing facilitated the exploration of institutional, political and community dimensions of the subject (Burawoy, 1991). Given the documented relationship between social capital and community resilience, these dimensions are considered in relation to Szreter and Woolcock's (2004) definition of social capital involving 'bonding, bridging and linking' (p. 640). In this frame, *bonding* is defined as connecting inward, enmeshing more homogenous group identities, *bridging* describes outward facing networks connecting across social and ethnic groups. *Linking* takes this to the macrosystemic and involves connecting social capital and trust building with wider political structures (Szreter & Woolcock, 2004; Poortinga, 2012).

In the city named for the purpose of the case study as Ballymore, three strategic priorities to support child, family and community resilience were identified as objectives within the action plan for an Early Intervention City. These were first to connect early attachment and communication programmes across the area; second to create a shared commitment to family support and nurturing and third to build the resilience and capacity of children, young people and families to cope with life changes and challenges. Both 'bonding' and 'bridging' aspects of social capital are evident in these priorities. The 'linking' element was also apparent in the connection of the priorities with the policy discourse at governance level in Northern Ireland, for example in the Early Intervention Transformation programme and the Northern Ireland Executive's Child Poverty Strategy as part of the Northern Ireland Office of the First Minister and Deputy First Minister (2013).

Consistent with a critical approach (Lather, 2016), the layers of the system in the case study were considered holistically rather than as separate levels of analysis, with a focus on complex rather than linear relationships. However, consistent with the pragmatic approach Merriam (1998, 2009) advocates, this was underpinned by systematic data collection, utilising interviews and focus groups with key informants at different levels of the system. This data was coded and analysed thematically (Braun & Clarke, 2006). This structure, running alongside critical analysis of the policy discourse (Fairclough, 1995), was employed to manage the process of inquiry.

Outline of Case Study

The case-study context allowed for adversity and resilience to be examined at different parts of the system and the field was constructed through examining community, local commissioning and governance structures involved the Early Intervention Action plan. The four neighbourhoods within Ballymore, named North, South, East and West River also corresponded with the community infrastructure of Sure Start and Neighbourhood Renewal. The different, interconnected levels of enquiry – policy, city, neighbourhood and programme – could thus be explored in a single complex case study. The key informants were those who managed programmes – neighbourhood and Sure Start managers (n = 10); those who delivered interventions, family support workers and health visitors (n = 16); and parents and carers who participated in programmes (n = 86). Regional managers and commissioners in health and social care (n = 2) and early intervention partnership members (n = 4) were also interviewed to establish the connection from policy to practice locally. In this way, purposeful sampling allowed for systematic data collection at each level of the system (Bryman, 2008; Merriam, 1998). The interviews and focus groups were semi-structured (Patton, 1990), with broad areas agreed in advance, while allowing for emergent narratives (Denzin, 2017).

Political Context of the Case Study

In order to contextualise the case study, a summary of the context of policymaking in Northern Ireland is required. During the most recent period of conflict known as the Troubles, Northern Ireland was governed by direct rule from Westminster (Mitchell & Wilford, 1999; Ruane & Todd, 1999). After the peace agreement in 1998, the British government devolved powers to the Northern Ireland Assembly on a consociational governance model – a coalition government with parallel institutions to protect distinct identities (Lijphart, 1975; McGarry & O'Leary, 2004). Policy and legislative decisions therefore have to be supported by an overall majority and, on issues of significance, must also secure a minimum of 40% support from the Unionist and Nationalist blocs (Arthur, 2001; Wilson, 2010).

While implemented as a means to achieve post agreement governance, consociationalism can actually entrench divisions (Horowitz, 2001; Ryan, 1995). The failure to achieve consensus in political decision-making carries risk of policy paralysis or at worst suspension of the institutions of government. Since devolution began, Northern Ireland has been without a functioning government for more than a third of its lifespan (Moriarty & McClements, 2020). In considering resilience at the political level, particularly in regions or states experiencing or emerging from conflict, Jones and Chandran (2008) state that 'the opposite of fragility is not stability, but resilience – the ability to cope with changes in capacity, effectiveness or legitimacy'. In political terms therefore, resilience is derived from capacity, resources, effective institutions and legitimacy in governance. It can therefore be argued that resilience at macrosystemic level, the ability to enact policy that supports children, families and communities is a key consideration in a socio-ecological approach.

Building Social Capital Through Bonding in Parenting Groups

Living in a deprived neighbourhood or what has been termed in some of the resilience research an adverse community environment (Wade et al., 2016; Schofield, 2018; Danielson & Saxena, 2019) is recognised as one of the most significant risk factors to health and wellbeing. The impacts of growing up in a deprived neighbourhood on education and employment, stress, poverty and social status are linked to low wellbeing and poor health outcomes (Poortinga, 2012). As is the case in the early studies of resilience in the child, not all communities have the same pattern of effect in the impact of deprivation and communities contain both risk and protective factors such as social capital (Danielson & Saxena, 2019). In order to better understand how the patterning of adversity and risk interacts with protective factors that may be at work in the community we can look at the different socio-ecological layers together with Szreter and Woolcock's (2004) definition of social capital involving 'bonding, bridging and linking'.

Reflecting on the data from parent interviews and focus groups, there was substantive evidence of the aggregation of social capital through bonding. Often the parents had participated in multiple parenting programmes in the Sure Start Centre with the same group remaining more or less intact:

> We have been together since we were pregnant. We did the pregnancy classes, did the baby classes, we are now doing the toddler classes and then some of us will be back to do the pregnancy classes again. (*laughs*)
>
> *(Parent, South River)*

> It's kind of a run on from previous programmes not a run on but an add-on. And we have done others together so we are comfortable with the people we are doing it with as well.
>
> *(Parent, North River)*

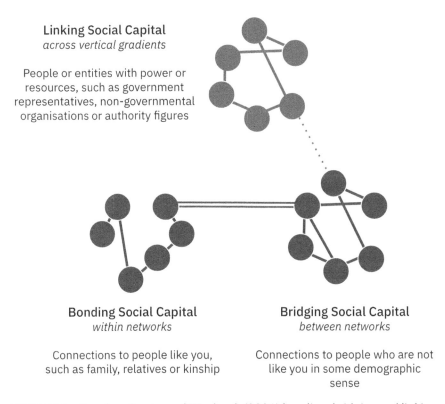

FIGURE 12.1 Based on Szreter and Woolcock (2004) bonding, bridging and linking

For parents with a second or third child programme, participation was also cyclical:

> After Ava was born I did the breastfeeding group, did the baby massage, baby aqua and this group till she was 6 months, then we had to leave, we had to graduate her (laughs) then we did the Amazing babies programme which lasted almost 9 months. Now I'm back again with this new wee one.
>
> *(Parent, North River)*

Much of the research on the effectiveness of parenting programmes in building resilience focuses on the effect size of a single programme (Schweinhart et al., 1993; Webster-Stratton et al., 2011; Reynolds et al., 2001). Although it was a small sample size, of the parents involved in the group parenting programmes, focus groups ($n = 28$), over 70% ($n = 20$) had participated in three or more previous programmes. Some had participated in five programmes by the time their children were two years of age. The participation in multiple programmes as a group points to the aggregation of social capital within the group itself, what Bourdieu describes as:

> the aggregate of the actual or potential resources which are linked to the possession of a durable network of more or less institutionalised relationships of mutual acquaintance and recognition.
>
> *(1986, p. 248)*

The social capital created in parenting groups also extended to the children who were aged between 18 months and three years. When the parents were reflecting on the impact on their children, they commented on children having made friends and being more connected:

> I knew that there was a change in Abbie, I realise what it was now, she has at least one good friend. When we are here, she would say to Maya, who is Danielle's wee girl, 'Don't you worry, your mummy is just having a cup of tea with my mummy'.
>
> *(Parent, Nurturing, North River)*

While this was clearly a strong and supportive experience for the parents who were taking part in the programme, it also raises questions that if the same group of parents are taking part in multiple programmes, connecting and linking, augmenting their social capital, what then happens with less connected parents in the community who are not in the room?

The uptake of multiple programmes by a smaller number of parents who are aggregating their social capital carries the risk of making the gap even wider for those parents who find it harder to engage with services. An identified challenge for Sure Start services is targeting 'hard to reach' parents. The term is itself contested, with key questions being the diversity of parents who don't access services (Boag-Munroe & Evangelou, 2012) or as to whether it is services, not parents, which are 'hard to reach' (Wilson, 2020). Parents in the focus groups were asked as to the possible reasons for others not connecting with group support:

Joanne: Their own perceptions. People who are not comfortable to go and meet other people. There are a couple of people I would try to get to come to courses. I would be at them 'why don't you?' trying to introduce them to everything, thinking that one thing will stand out and they will do it, but . . .
Orla: I think some people have a lot of support.
Fiona: No, I know people who just sit at home and don't do anything.

There was also a particular recognition that younger parents in the 18–25 age group did not tend to access group based parenting support. In the case study, less than 5% ($n = 4$) of the parents interviewed in all the neighbourhood groups were in this age group:

Joanne: I suppose if I think too on my group first time around, most of us were in our mid-thirties there weren't many younger mammies and by the time you get to that age you would have a bit more confidence to go.

Michaela: I think a lot of the people who come to classes are usually a wee bit older. We seem to find it easier. There are very few, like 18–25 year old mums.

Orla: Is that true, I didn't notice.

Although bonding social capital is primarily enacted in geographically defined communities, the 'inward focus' of bonding can also be based on other factors such as ethnicity or class (Hogg, 2006) and the different positionings of parents within the same neighbourhood are very evident here. Additionally, the limitations of inward facing social networks that reinforce homogeneous groups can be seen where the bonding of one group of mothers reinforced over the shared experience of multiple programmes may contribute to the exclusion of younger parents in need of support.

Bridging the Divide Between Parents and Professionals

Within the parenting groups, another effect observed was the capacity of midwives and health visitors to make the connection through to other professionals in the mesosystem. This brokering of communication between parents and other professionals can be seen where social capital garnered in the group is further augmented by the professional knowledge capital of midwives and health visitors. The role of the parenting group facilitator in supporting parents' interface with less accessible professionals, for example doctors and allied health professionals was a notable theme in the data. This further problematises the question as to whether in fact it may be some professionals rather than families who are 'hard to reach' (Wilson, 2020). The dynamic observed at work within the parenting programmes is that professional facilitators, often qualified midwives and Health Visitors sharing knowledge capital with parents, enable parents to be more powerfully positioned in their communication in the field thus building resilience:

> Letting you know you can talk to a health care professional like a person, not just like a number. It's your child and you know everything about your

child so that's why I felt, I don't have to just go by what the doctor said, I could say 'I want this done for my child now'. That's what I ended up doing and my son is now getting sorted.

(Parent, Nurturing Programme, North River)

In terms of individuals and families less likely to access group programmes, home visiting was described as a key factor in reaching families who were less likely to avail of centre-based services, who are also likely be the families most in need:

Another reason why home visiting is important is that people where children are most at risk are the last people to go to a centre seeking parenting support. We have seen this so many times, areas where you can't get in, but once the Family Visitor has got in to the home, the parent might say 'that's really good what I'm learning here' and suddenly you are overwhelmed with parents wanting home visiting because they know they are not being targeted.

(Starting Strong Programme Manager)

This capacity to access families in more need was also mentioned within a home visiting programme led by community facilitators rather than the midwives or health visitors who frequently led the centre-based groups:

Sometimes I can get into houses the Health Visitor can't get in to, the Health Visitor will tell me that she has been there six times and can't get in. I have had occasions when the parent has texted me to say that they are in the granny's house across the street and the Health Visitor was there earlier and they didn't let them in.

(Starting Strong, Family Visitor)

This leads to an important issue to reflect upon in relation to resilience through building social capital which is that statistically the majority of children and parents in neighbourhoods in the case study do not access programmes either home or setting based. A number of Neighbourhood and Sure Start Managers referred to families who were not accessing services:

The experience of families and particularly for families who are at the hard end of the economy and that the hard end sometimes of communities, people with learning disabilities or with their own health issues, people living in domestic abuse situations, addictions, I think they would see very little connection. They may see Sure Start as maybe somewhere they went once or twice, or somebody came out to the house and gave them a wee goodie bag but it actually isn't making a lot of difference at all in terms of their experience of life or their child's experience of life unfortunately. And I think that's a huge challenge.

(Sure Start manager, South River)

This manager goes on to describe the smallness of a programme intervention against the scope of families' problems, as well as acknowledging the difficulty of really understanding someone's experience:

Who are we to offer the 10-week solution to their problem? You really need to stand in their shoes try and think about where they are coming from. When we have angry parents, which doesn't happen a lot, it has been really useful for us to step back and try to work out where she is at, why is this parent coming at us like this? What is it that she is feeling? And it's like 'I'm annoyed that youze did not do something, you let me down', even though our expectations may not have been the same.

(Sure Start Manager South River)

One strategy employed in South River was the initiative of an experienced community-based midwife, a tuned-in professional who refuses the terminology of 'hard to reach':

I saw that with one of our midwives, when she would talk to other community midwives, she would do an awful lot of work for us and the way that she would put it across I suppose it's kind of in a different sort of way, she would say 'give me your bothers, anybody that you are worried about, have concerns around they are in our area, I can take them, I have got a bit of time I could support them that wee bit more'. . . . 'Give me your bothers' it's like a far better term than 'harder to reach' and all those sort of things.

(Sure Start manager South River)

The issue of language is important here in terms of how the deficit policy discourse of 'hard to reach', or the 'intergenerational cycle of adversity' is navigated in communities.

The Neighbourhood manager in North River also acknowledged that many of the families who do finally reach the Family Support Hub services for those most in need have never accessed support before. Here again, relationships and trust has priority over programmes:

It's about who is not attending rather than who is attending. A lot of the families who have come to the Family Support Hub have never participated in Starting Strong or Sure Start, or some had but hadn't stayed with it. . . . I don't offer no programme, it's building the trust and relationship first. Practical needs need sorted first and there are few family programmes. The most vulnerable have multiple issues debt, marital problems, domestic violence that need worked through first. This is time and resource intensive no one gives you resources to build trust you are dictated by outcomes, quick wins, results. You can't put a timescale on a family.

(Neighbourhood manager, North River)

So, the process of participating in programmes augments social capital for parents, particularly the bonding of those who participate in multiple programmes. This may be problematic however in relation to more marginalised parents who may become even more marginalised by these processes. These parents are unlikely to be 'programme ready' and need significant investment in building trust and relationships prior to programme participation. In contrast with the parents who accessed help to interface with doctors or allied health professional, parents who don't have access to this type of social capital were described as in often 'fight mode' with professionals and agencies.

We have clients that totally love their kids but they have been through the care system themselves and they are so protective. They are in fight mode, they are just fighting to survive but that is not what is appropriate when you are dealing with agencies. We have to sometimes go on in there with them as advocates as they are constantly in fight mode.

(Neighbourhood Manager, North River)

So interactions with the care system as children leave parents in 'fight mode'; however, the necessary habitus to navigate the system is by moderating that resistance, bonding with other parents and bridging the system through professional allegiances.

Bridging With Statutory Services and Commissioners

The struggle with statutory bodies does not however end at the interpersonal level with families and community groups also documented struggles with commissioning and funding services. Having discussed supporting parents in 'fight mode', a Neighbourhood manager spoke of her own struggles in communication with the statutory bodies in the attempt to develop a home grown Early Intervention programme, 'Little Talkers'. The ironies of the situation are all too apparent here as the community organisation were prohibited by the Health Trust from using the words 'speech' or 'language' in relation to the programme, 'Little Talkers', an early communication campaign for the area:

We were basically told by the Trust that we should have nothing to do with speech, language or communication, we were not the professionals. It should be left to the Trust. As a community organisation we had employed former Trust staff, qualified Speech and Language therapists who were working privately on the 'Little Talkers' campaign. We were told by the Trust not to use the words 'speech' or 'language' in any of our communication. I had to redraft the whole action plan which the whole community had come together to develop early years communication in our area.

(Neighbourhood Manager North River)

Here, the statutory body not only has control of the knowledge capital in relation to the evidence base of programmes and the power of commissioning, but it also controls this by controlling the discourse itself, restricting the use of the words 'speech and language' to external programmes run by professionals in the field and prohibiting their use for home grown programmes. This challenge is reflected not only in North River but also across the different neighbourhoods, where positioning within the field of power with a lack of the legitimated knowledge capital also has implications for economic capital:

If you are working with the health board they are just hung up on evidence based programmes and when you are trying to grow your own it is difficult, you get such a lot of opposition. The 'Little Talkers' they are doing in North River, we were very interested in that but they just didn't see the benefit. I think they need to be a bit more open to what the community are bringing forward. We can work with local people and see what benefits local people. I think they need to be a bit more open to home grown stuff. We look a lot to what is working in North River and our plan for next year is to start the Little Talkers programme here. To me it is great but they are not getting the recognition because it is community based. Community based is not recognised or valued.

(Neighbourhood Manager East River)

Interestingly, the solidarity and programme-sharing here is across neighbourhoods that would previously have been deeply politically divided. East River itself is a working class interface community, which has experienced deep political divisions and North River is a working class Nationalist Republican community which also has intra group tensions. The tension documented actually cuts through traditional political demarcations centring around where community-based approaches.

This solidarity and sharing of community-based home grown programmes is an interesting example of 'bridging' in Szreter and Woolcock's (2004) framework. Bridging social capital denotes relationships of mutual respect and solidarity between individuals and groups who are not alike. In this way the sharing of programmatic resources and knowledge base between neighbourhoods across the sectarian divide and indeed resistance in the face of statutory commissioning demonstrates a possible factor in community resilience in a divided society. VanderPlaat (2016) in her invitation to explore resilience through a sociological lens in builds on earlier work by Ungar (2008, 2011) and others to challenge the mainstream view which excludes disruptive voices or behaviours such as street culture as manifestations of resilience and see these as alliances between those who share the experience of adversity. While acknowledging that 'fight mode' goes against the rules of the game of what counts as resilience, it is interesting that a type of fight mode was being utilised by community leaders as they battled for recognition of home grown programmes. The bridging of the sectarian divide and constructing of heterogeneous alliances and an alternative knowledge capital against the dominant statutory discourse on early intervention is a particularly interesting phenomenon at the exosystemic level of the case study. The construction of resistance as resilience with a focus on the shared assets, particularly when it involves the bridging aspect of building social capital also has potential to challenge mainstream discourse which contributes to a deficit view of communities.

Linking – Building Resilient Governance

Having considered in the case study the mesosystemic dynamics between parents and professionals, the exosystemic interactions between community leaders and statutory commissioners, it is useful to expand the consideration of the case study to the macrosystem. The macrosytemic level is important also in terms of the final part of Szreter and Woolcock's (2004) triadic social capital model of bonding, bridging and linking. Where bridging and bonding are horizontal connections, linking social capital is a measure of how vertically connected individuals and communities are with governance structures and political institutions (Szreter & Woolcock, 2004; Poortinga, 2012).

If we recall Jones and Chandran's (2008) definition of political resilience as derived from capacity, resources, effective institutions and legitimacy in governance, it suggests that a key question from the socio-ecological perspective is how resilient are the institutions of governance in Northern Ireland? By tracing the key policy areas relevant to building capacity and resilience in childhood at macrosystemic level, a pattern of inaction and policy stasis is apparent. Critical interdepartmental strategies such as the Child Poverty Strategy (Northern Ireland Executive, 2016) and the Children and Young People's Strategy have languished in political inaction (Northern Ireland Commissioner for Children and Young People, 2020). The impact of ambitious policy innovation such as the Early Intervention Transformation Programme 2014–2020 (Department of Health, 2020) has struggled to achieve its promise due to the environment of political stalemate. Success of this major initiative is modestly claimed at microsystemic level in 'successful support for 2,000 families producing improvement in child behaviour, routine and family dynamics' and at the exosystemic level where 'relationships and co-operation have been strengthened across a wide range of stakeholders'. However, during the period of investment of £30 million over a six year period, a large proportion of which came from a non-governmental partner, the structures of governance and policy making were in suspension for over half of this period meaning that the sustainability of any policy impact is considerably compromised.

The reinstatement of the NI Assembly after a three year suspension was consolidated in the policy endorsement of *The New Decade, New Approach Deal* (2020) which sets out to tackle 'urgently needed local political oversight and decision-making' by enabling the restoration to full operation of all the institutions of the Good Friday Agreement. Among the priorities set out in the 'New Decade New Approach' document were three commitments focused on children and family policy: to develop and implement an Anti-Poverty Strategy; to implement an action plan to address links between persistent educational underachievement and socio-economic background and develop a Childcare Strategy to deliver extended, affordable and high-quality provision of early education and care initiatives for families with children aged 3–4. However at the time of writing these commitments have once again languished in inaction, with the NI Assembly once again suspended in 2022 in disagreement over the outworkings of Brexit and the Northern Ireland protocol. It appears that fundamental to building resilience following political conflict is to build resilient and effective institutions that can enact policy commitments and restore legitimacy in governance.

Conclusion

The expectations of political change following the Peace Agreement in Northern Ireland were enormous, with claims made that structural reform would be transformative and address the impact of conflict and adversity in the lives of children, families and communities. Instead, policy reform has been stalled and subsumed in a wider political struggle. The resilience of the power sharing executive has been tested and found wanting with politicians locked in the rhetoric of the past and unable to prioritise the future of Northern Ireland's children. At community level and in the case study explored here, bonding and bridging social capital and building resilience are evident in the connections between parents and in the interactions with supportive professionals and community leaders. However, the process of bonding carries some concern that close knit community networks can exclude as well as connect.

Connections were also evident between neighbourhoods and across the sectarian divide where quite literally the bridging of social capital is enacted. The aspect of Szreter and Woolcock's (2004) framework that is much less in evidence is the linking at macrosystemic level connecting social capital and trust building within wider political structures of governance. Crucially, it is at the macrosystemic level as well as in children, families and communities that resilience must be built.

References

Anthony, E. J. (1987). Risk, vulnerability, and resilience: An overview. In E. J. Anthony & B. J. Cohler (Eds.), *The invulnerable child* (pp. 3–48). Guilford Press.

Arthur, P. (2001). *Special relationships: Britain, Ireland and the Northern Ireland problem*. Blackstaff Press.

Boag-Munroe, G., & Evangelou, M. 2012. From hard to reach to how to reach: A systematic review of the literature on hard-to-reach families. *Research Papers in Education*, 27(2), 209–239. https://doi.org/10.1080/02671522.2010.509515

Bourdieu, P. (1986). The forms of capital. In J. G. Richardson (Ed.), *Handbook of theory and research for the sociology of education* (pp. 241–258). Greenwood Press.

Bourdieu, P. (1990). *The logic of practice*. Stanford University Press.

Bourdieu, P. (2004). *Science of science and reflexivity*. University of Chicago Press.

Braun, V., & Clarke, V. (2006). Using thematic analysis in psychology. *Qualitative Research in Psychology*, 3(2), 77–101. https://doi.org/10.1191/1478088706qp063oa

Bronfenbrenner, U. (1976). The experimental ecology of education. *Educational Researcher* [Online], 5(9), 5–15.

Bryman, A. (2008). Of methods and methodology. *Qualitative Research in Organizations and Management* [Online], 3(2), 159–168.

Burawoy, M. (Ed.). (1991). The extended case method. In *Ethnography unbound: Power and resistance in the modern metropolis* (pp. 271–290). University of California Press.

Danielson, R., & Saxena, D. (2019). Connecting adverse childhood experiences and community health to promote health equity. *Social and Personality Psychology Compass* [Online], 13(7).

Denzin, N. K. (2017). Critical qualitative inquiry. *Qualitative Inquiry*, 23(1), 8–16.

Department of Health. (2014). *The early intervention transformation programme*. Retrieved September 1, 2022, from https://www.health-ni.gov.uk/articles/early-intervention-transformation-programme

Department of Health. (2020). *Early intervention transformation programme infographic*. https://www.health-ni.gov.uk/publications/early-intervention-transformation-programme-eitp-infographic

Fairclough, N. (1995). *Critical discourse analysis: The critical study of language*. Longman.

Furlong, M., & McGilloway, S. (2015). The longer term experiences of parent training: A qualitative analysis. *Child: Care, Health & Development* [Online], 41(5), 687–696.

Gardner, F., Leijten, P., Melendez-Torres, G. J., Landau, S., Harris, V., Mann, J., Beecham, J., Hutchings, J., & Scott, S. (2019). The earlier the better? Individual participant data and traditional meta-analysis of age effects of parenting interventions. *Child Development* [Online], 90(1), 7–19.

Hogg, M. A. (2006). Social identity theory. In P. J. Burke (Ed.), *Contemporary social psychological theories* (pp. 111–136). Stanford University Press.

Horowitz, D. (2001). The Northern Ireland agreement: Clear, consociational, and risky. In J. McGarry (Ed.), *Northern Ireland and the divided world: Post-agreement Northern Ireland in comparative perspective* (pp. 89–108). Oxford University Press.

Jones, B., & Chandran, R. (2008). 'From fragility to resilience: Concepts and dilemmas of statebuilding in Fragile States', Report prepared for the Organisation for Economic

Cooperation and Development (OECD) by the center on international cooperation at New York university and international peace academy, New York: OECD.

Lather, P. (2016). Post-face: *Cultural Studies of Numeracy*. *Cultural Studies ↔ Critical Methodologies*, *16*(5), 502–505. https://doi.org/10.1177/1532708616655771

Lijphart, A. (1975). *The politics of accommodation: Pluralism and democracy in the Netherlands*. University of California Press.

MacLeod, J., & Nelson, G. (2000). G programs for the promotion of family wellness and the prevention of child maltreatment. *Child Abuse & Neglect*, *24*, 1127–1149.

McGarry, J., & O'Leary, B. (Eds.). (2004). Introduction: Consociational theory and Northern Ireland. In *Essays on the Northern Ireland conflict: Consociational engagements* (pp. 1–61). Oxford University Press.

Merriam, S. (1998). *Qualitative research and case study applications in education*. Jossey-Bass.

Merriam, S. (2009). *Qualitative research: A guide to design and implementation*. Jossey-Bass.

Mitchell, P., & Wilford, R. A. (1999). *Politics in Northern Ireland*. Westview Press.

Moriarty, G., & McClements, F. (2020). Governments reach deal aimed at restoring Stormont by weekend. *Irish Times*.

New Decade, New Approach Deal. (2020). *Restoration of devolved government in NI*. https://assets.publishing.service.gov.uk/media/5e178b56ed915d3b06f2b795/2020-01-08_a_new_decade__a_new_approach.pdf

Northern Ireland Commissioner for Children and Young People. (2020). *Statement on children's rights in Northern Ireland 2*. https://www.niccy.org/media/3691/niccy-socrni-2-main-report-web-nov-20.pdf

Northern Ireland Executive. (2016). *Delivering social change: The executive's child poverty strategy*. https://www.communities-ni.gov.uk/sites/default/files/publications/ofmdfm/child-poverty-strategy.pdf

Northern Ireland Office of the First Minister and Deputy First Minister. (2013). *Delivering social change*. https://www.executiveofficeni.gov.uk/articles/delivering-social-changeintroduction

Patton, M. Q. (1990). *Qualitative evaluation and research methods* (2nd ed.). SAGE.

Poortinga, W. (2012). Community resilience and health: The role of bonding, bridging, and linking aspects of social capital. *Health & Place* [Online], *18*(2), 286–295.

Reynolds, A. J., Temple, J. A., Robertson, D. L., Mann, E. A. (2001). Long-term effects of an early childhood intervention on educational achievement and juvenile arrest: A 15-year follow-up of low-income children in public schools. *JAMA*, *285*(18), 2339–2346.

Ruane, J., & Todd, J. (1999). *After the good friday agreement: Explaining political change in Northern Ireland*. University College Dublin Press.

Rutter, M. (2012). Resilience as a dynamic concept. *Development and Psychopathology* [Online], *24*(2), 335–344.

Ryan, S. (1995). *Ethnic conflict and international relations*. Dartmouth.

Schofield, T. J., Donnellan, M. B., Merrick, M. T., Ports, K. A., Klevens, J., & Leeb, R. (2018). Intergenerational continuity in adverse childhood experiences and rural community environments. *American Journal of Public Health (1971)* [Online], *108*(9), 1148–1152.

Schweinhart, L., Barnes, H., & Wiekart, D. (1993). *Significant benefits: The high/scope perry preschool study through age 27*. High/Scope Educational Research Foundation.

Szreter, S., & Woolcock, M. (2004). Health by association? Social capital, social theory and the political economy of public health. *International Journal of Epidemiology*, *33*, 650–667.

Ungar, M. (2008). Resilience across cultures. *The British Journal of Social Work*, *38*(2), 218–235. http://doi.org/10.1093/bjsw/bcl343

Ungar, M. (2011, January). The social ecology of resilience: Addressing contextual and cultural ambiguity of a nascent construct. *American Journal of Orthopsychiatry*, *81*(1), 1–17. http://doi.org/10.1111/j.1939–0025.2010.01067.x

VanderPlaat, M. (2016). Activating the sociological imagination to explore the boundaries of resilience research and practice. *School Psychology International*, *37*(2), 189–203. https://doi.org/10.1177/0143034315615938

Wade, R., Cronholm, P. F., Fein, J. A., Forke, C. M., Davis, M. B., Harkins-Schwarz, M., & Bair-Merritt, M. H. (2016). Household and community-level adverse childhood experiences and adult health outcomes in a diverse urban population. *Child Abuse & Neglect*, *52*(C), 135–145. https://doi.org/10.1016/j.chiabu.2015.11.021

Webster-Stratton, C, Rinaldi J., Jamila, M. R. (2011). Long-term outcomes of incredible years parenting program: Predictors of adolescent adjustment. *Child and Adolescent Mental Health* [Online], *16*(1), 38–46.

Wilson, R. (2010). *The Northern Ireland experience of conflict and agreement: A model for export?* Manchester University Press.

Wilson, S. (2020). 'Hard to reach' parents but not hard to research: A critical reflection of gatekeeper positionality using a community-based methodology. *International Journal of Research & Method in Education* [Online], *43*(5), 461–477.

PART 4
Connecting Ideas

13
REFLECTING ON WHAT WE KNOW AND BEYOND

Zoi Nikiforidou, Wilma Robles-Melendez and Babs Anderson

Everyone encounters challenges and risks as part of growing up. Young children face change, uncertainty and stressful circumstances that may affect their wellbeing at different levels and phases of their lives. Such interruptions might affect their sense of being, belonging and becoming, short term or long term. It is through resilience that someone can recover and maintain adaptivity (Garmezy, 1991). Thus, resilience becomes evident at different times in one's life (Rutter, 2007). Various risks and environmental changes can result in a child showing either resilience or lack of resilience. As Garmezy (1991) points out, all children experience stress at times, and therefore, resilient children are not 'heroic' compared to those children who in similar situations may show retreat, despair or disorder.

As identified in the chapters of the books, despite the multi-dimensional complexity of resilience, modern key theorists agree that there are two conditions apparent: the past or current presence of conditions that disrupt viability or cause threat and adversity and the achievement towards positive adaptation or development (Masten, 2014; Luthar et al., 2000). In each case, there are risk and protective factors involved, dependent on culture and broader personal and social constructs. Werner (1989) suggests that interventions need to address the balance of risk and protective factors at different stages in an individual's life. In naming a few, as indicated by Akgül and Yazici in Chapter 2, radical changes, poverty, social life barriers, family structure disorder, not meeting the child's basic needs and parental issues can be risk factors, whereas social structure, supportive classroom environments, close family relationships, addressing the child's personal special needs, family's attitude towards risk factors and bilingualism can be protective factors. Nevertheless, Akgül

DOI: 10.4324/9781003345664-17

and Yazici underline that several elements can operate as both risk factors and protective ones given the wider environment in which children grow and live.

Ungar (2013) emphasizes the interplay of individual characteristics and the environment (the individual's family, community and culture) in liberating or constraining growth or risk. Resilience can be enhanced by the structures around the individual, the services the individual receives and the way health knowledge is generated, in combination with the characteristics of individuals. He underlines that when designing interventions, it is important to understand the contextual, individual and cultural processes of each case (Ungar, 2013). Hence, resilience is not only a personal trait but also a product of the environment and the interaction between the child and the environment.

Nonetheless, children's agentic role in confronting and overcoming adversities is crucial. Children can develop or implement resilience when their self-efficacy, autonomy and risk literacy (Nikiforidou, 2017) levels are activated; instead of when they learn not to take responsibility, not to take risks and remain overprotected by worried adults in a culture of surplus protection and risk aversion. Hoyes in Chapter 3 discusses the need for a 'philosophy of resilience' instead of a 'philosophy of protection' (Gill, 2007) and proposes a 4Rs model. In addressing the balance of risk, rights and responsibilities in promoting children's resilience, 'trust' is positioned as a central tenant. Hoyes identifies trust in relation to the child's capabilities and strengths, and in relation to the adults who should provide an environment which is as safe as necessary, rather than as safe as possible.

Part 1, including Chapters 1–3, argues the multi-dimensionality of resilience at a theoretical level. Part 2 highlights the diverse nature of theoretical implications for practice. It shows the requirement for fully informed practice so that knowledge and understanding guide practitioner actions. In Chapter 4, Brosnan, Stallard and O'Donnell set their analysis of resilience in a specific context, that of the recent pandemic of COVID-19 and its impact on ECCE provision in Ireland. It poses the question as to whether the notion that children are naturally resilient takes full account of the challenges faced by young children and the strategies that may help them to overcome them, such as the supportive community experienced in high-quality ECCE provision. It also highlights the key importance of practitioner wellbeing in their belief in their ability to address these challenges and needs.

In Chapter 5, Moore explores a different context that of the parent and child's experiences within a purposeful situation of open active listening in validating relationships. It examines the importance of professional understanding of the interconnectedness of all aspects of the child's environment, so that this can influence and guide practitioner action.

In Chapter 6, Demetriou examines how positive relationships between young children can enhance resilience and the sense of personal wellbeing. Friendship adds to the individuals' sense of personal value and competence, with the knowledge that there is a bond of affection and care between each. They may also be regarded as a precursor of social competence, a blueprint for future relationships. The requirement for authentic active participation within the school community is one that can be actively promoted by practitioners for all children, those with disabilities and those without.

One overarching concept that can be usefully employed to examine resilience in its widest sense is Antonovsky's (1979) Sense of coherence (SOC).

> The sense of coherence is a global orientation that expresses the extent to which one has a pervasive, enduring though dynamic feeling of confidence that (1) the stimuli deriving from one's internal and external environments in the course of living are structured, predictable and explicable; (2) the resources are available to one to meet the demands posed by these stimuli; and (3) these demands are challenges, worthy of investment and engagement.
>
> *(1987, p. 19)*

For the first aspect, this highlights the confidence that events in the environment, both arising from within the individual and outside, are understandable. This is not to say that these are all entirely pleasant, but rather that the individual can understand why something is occurring. For a very young infant, this starts early but requires adult support, for example with an adult explaining to them that the reason they are distressed is because they are experiencing hunger. The infant does not understand the precise vocabulary but learns to associate the soothing tones of the adult as those which indicate the resources to address these needs will soon be made available. The third aspect, that of investment, is a natural attribute for a young infant and links to trust in the adults to support these investments of time and energy in order for them to obtain the resources they need, such as food.

Translated to early childhood provision and practice as examined in this part of the book, this relates to a young child being able to make sense of their experiences, recognizing that they are able to cope with these, and to put in place meaningful strategies that will enable a successful integration of new experiences into their existing schema within a positive world view. This requires a range of knowledge and understanding, skills, attitudes and values to form the basis of actions taken by the practitioner. These include personal awareness of the emotional challenges for the practitioner, the ability to seize teachable moments in order to support the child as advocated by Brosnan, Stallard and O'Donnell, positive active listening, validating the parent and child dyad as recommended by Moore and the recognition and promotion of friendships and positive relationships in a child's lived experiences as promoted by Demetriou.

The amount and type of support each child requires to achieve this successfully is necessarily nuanced, depending on individual characteristics and lived experiences within a specific cultural and geopolitical context and therefore different for each unique individual. This is dynamic and reflects the ongoing evolution of the complex human psyche.

A key role of the adult, be it family member, carer or early childhood practitioner, is therefore to facilitate the child's evolving understanding of this positive sense of self within their environment, so that they have belief in their own resources to meet challenging situations with resilience They also have trust in others, who will support them in their evolving sense of self. As is commonly held in early childhood practice, the child is agentic, yet the desire to protect from harm can impede the practitioner from fully acting on this belief, through a desire to keep children safe from difficult situations. Yet there is also a requirement, more encompassing than that for individual children and their families, for societies to invest in the wellbeing of the whole community, recognizing the essential fundamental connected nature of wellbeing and its outcomes of resilience for human populations.

Moving Into Action: Transferring Ideas Into Our Practice

Every day and every moment are an opportunity to instill in children a sense about the ability that lives within to overcome challenges. In times where society continues to be known for its uncertainty, early childhood education remains steadfast in its determination to safeguard children's wellbeing. Concerns about children's future continues to give precedence to the search for answers to practices that will effectively respond to the realities of the times, growing in complexity more than ever. This is what grounds the need for new perspectives to guide practices in early childhood classrooms and programs (Bartlett et al., 2021). To build and support resilience, we are in need of practices firmly anchored on the goal to achieve and sustain young children's wellbeing (Weir, 2017; Masten, 2001).

Throughout the preceding chapters, we have learned and made aware of the nature of resilience as a factor leading to support a child's wellbeing. Conscious about the role that resilience plays in an individual's experiences and responses, clearly points to the need for integrating resilience into everyday practices (Erdman et al., 2020). This is what is explored in this section, where we gather their tenets and suggestions to help early childhood practitioners bring resilience as a common principle in their practice. Gathered in Part 3 of this book, authors present views that connect children's successful development with research and practices that support the emergence of resilient behaviors, all within the reality of a continuously changing society. They make us aware of the fact that, notwithstanding the social, cultural and political challenges, practices in classrooms and programs for young children built on what the Convention on the Rights of the Child established to be 'in the best interest of the child,' can effectively prepare children to be resilient.

It Can Happen

Building resilience into early childhood practices is also centered on a rational understanding about the context where children are growing and developing in today. Only then can interventions and practices be determined to support and lead children to become resilient. An increasingly complex and globalized society, is what Broadfoot in Chapter 7, reminds us of as she calls attention to the social realities surrounding children today. This awareness is what according to Robles-Melendez, Capo and Robles in Chapter 11 is essential to objectively understand the urgency and need for conscious efforts leading to support children's resiliency. The presence of conflict, which in this century has emerged across multiple areas, the calls for attention to climatic changes, and the voices clamoring for socially just actions, are and form part of the social reality of the times where children are growing up. Even though the challenges seem to overwhelm society, there is hope. This is the message that McLeod, Boyd, Aniere and Axelsson share in Chapter 8, as they call us to instill hope as a perspective that can lead us to promote children's wellbeing. There is hope especially when considering that resilience is more than just a concept when integrated as a premise for empowering classroom praxis.

Preparing children to face and successfully address the challenges is not only a goal but also a reality that can effectively happen as an outcome of experiences in early childhood. This is what Watts reminds us in chapter ten, as she proposes a holistic approach to support children's wellbeing during the early years. She reminds us that holistically addressing wellbeing is a paradigm rooted in the fact that development is interconnected, therefore demanding efforts that consider and engage the child's experiences as a whole, where all influential factors are not only recognized but also regarded given their influence during the early childhood formative years. Resiliency, thus, cannot be seen as a separate effort but rather as one where all the interrelated factors are considered. This view calls on practitioners to know that experiences are related and influenced when the ecology of the child's reality is recognized. Children, families and communities are all holistically connected, a fact clearly calling for practices and efforts that mindfully address these realities and their influence on children. The need for consideration of the child's ecological realities is what Boyle prompts us to consider in Chapter 12 through a social capital perspective and its impact on efforts to create a resilient environment for the child.

At the heart of McLeod and colleagues' call for hope is the need for thoughtful understanding of children's needs. Only then, when their needs and experiences are considered, we will be able to foster their resilience. They remind us that the bridge into day-to-day practices is laid when our knowledge about the child is grounded in their realities both developmentally and as an individual. What practices to include, clearly, begin with experiences known to support and promote children's development. The ever presence and need for play is what Gibson & McNally bring to our attention in chapter nine, prompting us to reflect on the wellbeing of the child and the developmentally empowering role of play. In their discussion, one is reminded about the role that play has in building resilience across the spectrum of children's diversities.

Anchoring classroom practices on a pedagogy of care that incorporates a responsive and mindful relational approach is what is revealed as the parameter contributing to support and build resilience (Masten & Barnes, 2018). Such is also the approach that Robles-Melendez, Capo and Robles propose to permeate classroom practices. Moreover, they call for building a caring environment where the child will feel welcomed and supported. Creating this kind of environment challenges practitioners to consider the child's development and their personal stories so as to consciously define what is in their best interest. They remind us that caring practices are a powerful protective factor helping children to build their resilient spirit.

Altogether, the message brought by authors in Part 3 of this book clearly points out to the fact that mindfully and intentionally, integrating resilience into the praxis of early childhood education is a way to address and support children's wellbeing. The goal is clear and the need calls for future research and practices to explore resilience as a means of empowering and promoting a good quality of life in early childhood, at present and in the future to come.

References

Antonovsky, A. (1979). *Health, stress and coping.* Jossey-Bass.

Antonovsky, A. (1987). *Unravelling the mystery of health – how people manage stress and stay well.* Jossey-Bass.

Bartlett, J., Halle, T., & Thomson, D. (2021). Promoting resilience in early childhood. In L. Nabors (Ed.), *Resilient children. Springer series on child and family studies.* Springer. https://doi.org/10.1007/978-3-030-81728-2_10

Erdman, S., Colker, L., & Winter, E. (2020). *Trauma and young children: Teaching strategies to support and empower.* National Association for the Education of Young Children.

Garmezy, N. (1991). Resilience in children's adaptation to negative life events and stressed environments. *Pediatric Annals, 20,* 459–460, 463–466.

Gill, T. (2007). *No fear: Growing up in a risk averse society.* Calouste Gulbenkian Foundation.

Luthar, S. S., Cicchetti, D., & Becker, B. (2000). The construct of resilience: A critical evaluation and guidelines for future work. *Child Development, 71,* 543–562.

Masten, A. S. (2001). Ordinary magic: Resilience processes in development. *American Psychologist, 56*(3), 227–238. https://doi.org/10.1037/0003-066X.56.3.227

Masten, A. S. (2014). Global perspectives on resilience in children and youth. *Child Development, 85,* 6–20.

Masten, A. S., & Barnes, A. (2018). Resilience in children: Developmental perspectives. *Children, 5*(7), 98. https://doi.org/10.3390/children5070098

Nikiforidou, Z. (2017). Risk literacy: Concepts and pedagogical implications for early childhood education. *Contemporary Issues in Early Childhood, 18*(3), 322–332. https://doi.org/10.1177/1463949117731027

Rutter, M. (2007). Resilience, competence, and coping. *Child Abuse and Neglect, 31,* 205–209.

Ungar, M. (2013). Resilience, trauma, context, and culture. *Trauma, Violence, and Abuse, 14,* 255–266.

Weir, K. (2017). Maximizing children's resilience. *APA Monitor on Psychology, 48*(8), 40. https://www.apa.org/monitor/2017/09/cover-resilience

Werner, E. E. (1989). High-risk children in young adulthood: A longitudinal study from birth to 32 years. *American Journal of Orthopsychiatry, 59,* 72–81.

INDEX

Note: Page numbers in *italics* indicate a figure and page numbers in **bold** indicate a table on the corresponding page.

Adams, John 41
adaptive skills, strengthening 36–37, 40, 44, 116
addiction **28**, 30, 202
adulthood 38, 100, 117, 122, 150, 163, 166
adverse childhood experiences (ACEs): early experiences **18–19**, 72, 182, 184, 187
adversity: adaptability 179, 187, 195; early **18**, 98, *106*, 107; effects of 104, 117, 184, 198, 203, 206, 213; extreme 36, 72, 90; recovery from 35, 62, 96
advocate 3, 7, 89, 122, 150, 176, 178, 195–196, 204, 215
Aistear 53, 55, 148
Akgül, Esra 213
alcohol/drug use 78–79, 86
American Psychological Association 5, 11
analysis process 12–14; *see also* data analysis
anger 131–132, 203
Aniere, Catrina Luz 136–137, 217
Anning, Angela 75
Anthony, E. James 195
anti-phobic effects 37, 169
Anti-Poverty Strategy 207

anxiety 37, 41–42, 52–53, 62, 99, 132, 143
APA *see* American Psychological Association
Arabic language **20**, *85*, 140, 142
Aristotle 132, 134
Arnold, Cath/Pen Green Centre Team 75
aspiration **24**, 80, *83*, 89
Assi, R. 29
assumptions 98, 131; questioning of 41, 114, 133–134
athletic skills 97
attitude: of family regarding risk factors 14, *27*, **28**, 30–32, 213; negative 43–44, 98–99; positive 103, 137, 190, 215
attractiveness 97
attributes 44, 97, 100–101, 104, 115, *124*, 186
autism: communication challenges 147; resilience and 152
autistic adults 151–152
autistic children: compliance 150–151; early intervention 149–150; play, support of 147–150, 153
autistic play 148, 152–153
autonomy **16–17**, *27*, 30–31, 39, 214
Axelsson, Suzanne 136, 139, 217

Baby Massage 85, 199
Baker, Jess R. **20**
Ball, Mog 75
Barnes, Andrew J. 116
Barroso, Julie 12
Bath, Caroline 74
Beers, Courtney **15**
behavior: challenging 80, *81*; positive **17**, 90; purpose-oriented **27**, 30; resilient 6, 10, 179–181, 185, 192, 216
belonging, sense of **19**, 103–104, 107, 131–132, 139, 160, 171–172, 190, 213
Bernard, Bonnie 11
Bertram, Tony 74
Bethell, Christina 182
Better Regulations Commission 44
bilingualism 14, *27*, **28**, 30–32, 213
Blenkinsop, Sean 135
bonding 122; *see also* social capital
Bourdieu, Pierre 196, 200
Bourn, Douglas 143
Boyd, Diane 217
Boyle, Clionagh 217
Bradburn, Norman M. 11
Braun, Virginia 77
British Columbia: First Peoples Principles of Learning 132; Ministry of Education 132
Broadfoot, Harriet 217
Bronfenbrenner, Urie 75–76, 87, 99, 195
Brosnan, Maja Haals 214–215
Bullock, L.M. 96
bullying 149
Burgman, Imelda 101, 104

Capo, Berta 188, 217–218
caretaker 38–39
caring circle 185
Centre on the Developing Child (CDC) 35
challenges 6; adapt to 5, **15**, 116, *124*, 179, 187, 190; insecurity 176, *177*, 183–184; overcoming 4–5, 11, 104, 178–179, 183, 187, 190, 216
Chan, Kevin Ka Shing 121
Chandran, Rahul 198, 206
character building 36–37
child abuse 73, 96, 159, 202
Child Poverty Strategy 196, 206
Childcare Strategy 207

childhood experiences: adverse **19**, 30, 72, 179, 182; education 75, 117, 123, *124*; parental **28**, 30, 32, 213
childism 62
children: adaptability **15**, 52, 54, 57, *124*, 187, 190; basic needs as unmet 14, **19–20**, *27*, **28**, 29, 32, 72, 85, 118, 213; building resilience 58, 178, 180, 199, 201, 207, 217–218; challenges faced 4, 89, 96, 176, *177*, 184, 214; competence 38–39, 43, 96, 99, 142 (*see also* social competence); as competent *36*, 38, 43, 100; empowerment 4–5, 7–8, 89, 114, 125, 139, 176, 181, 184, 186; freedom 38–40, 43; high-risk 97, 101; as invisible 63, 73–74; listening to 58, 74–75, 131, 142, 170; lived experiences 72, 76, 87–88, 121, 123, 190, 215; marginalized 177, 181; as resourceful 55; speaking without words 138; special needs, addressing 14, **27**, 30, 32, 213; stressors 51, 61, 102, 115, 117–118, 120, *124*; as victims 38, 99, 149, 177, 184; vulnerable 38, 44, 51, 55, 96, 177, 182, 192, 195
Children and Young People's Strategy 206
children with disabilities: copying skills 104; friendships 96, 100–104, *106*, 107; heterogeneity 102; resilience 95–96, 98; social skills 103–104; strengths of 97
children's voices 74–75, 133, 163–164
children's centres 73, 75
Ciccetti, Dante 72
Clark, Alison 84
Clark, Victoria 77
Coba-Rodriguez, Sarai **23**, **25**
coding 12, 86
cognitive development 11, 31, 101, 121, 141, 180
collaboration **16**, 61, 87, **88**, 152, 189, 191
communication: open **18**, **27**, 30; between parents/professionals 14, 201; skills 100, 147, 149–150, 187; social 149–150, 153–154
community: adverse, environment 198; assets 6; -based approaches 136, 172, 205; belonging and 103, 131; building 165, 172; children's

engagement with 117–118, *124*; of the classroom 184, 189, 190; or compassion 125; connectedness 160; contextual factors 3; contributions to 118; disabling 99; ECE 114, 119–120, 122, 147, 161, *162*, 164–165, 167, 183, 214; everyday, experiences 56, 58, 79; facilitators 200, 202; groups 204; holistic educational context 162; infrastructure 197; isolation from 54; leaders 206, 207; midwives 203; Palestinian Refugee Camp 139–140; peers and 100; promoting resilience *186*, 196, 205–206; protective factors 198; reflexive pedagogies 130; relationship with others in 102; school **16**, 215; Traditional Indigenous Owners 137–138; whole 122, 205, 216; whole education 119

compassion: connection with wellbeing 114, 121; in education 113, 119; environment of 122; experiencing 120–121; importance of 121

competence: in children 38–39, 43, 96, 99, 142; development of 39, 43, 101, 142; family 30; social 100, 103, 215

confidence: feeling of 41–42, 215; lack of 132, 140; *see also* self–confidence

conflict 135, 140, 176–177, 180, 183–184, 197–198, 207, 217

connectedness 6, 30, 113, 120, 122–123, *124*, 132, 160, 167

consciousness: archaic 167–168; human 163, 167; integral 171; magic 168; mental 171; mythic 169

construct 4–5, 7, 148, 189

control: blocking control **27**, 30; loss of 141; perceived 36, 40, 149, 187

Cope, Vicki 77

coping skills 5, 7, 95, 98, 103, *106*, 107, 152

Cosden, Merith 97, 102

courage 120, 131

Covell, Katherine 39–40

COVID-19 51; "children are grand" theme 54; challenges 183; environmental changes 53, 58; implications 52–53, 59, 177; just a virus 52, 59; restoring wellbeing 58

Creche (nursery) 80, *81*, 85

cultural custodians 135, 137–139

Cumming, Tamara 52

Cunningham, Hugh 39

curriculum 35, 38, 52–55, 57, 59–60, 102, 139

data: analysis 13, **15–16**, **18**, **20**, **22**, **24**, **26**, 77; implications 54, 56–58, 71, 198

data collection: systematic 197; thematic analysis **25**, 77, 83

databases 12–13

deep listening 130–131, 133, 135–136, 138–139, 143

Demetriou, Kyriakos 214–215

developmental: benefits 36; growth 184–185; outcomes 4, 7, 29, 41, 159, 168, 182, 192; psychology 102, 105; support 30, 148, 151, 189

DfE (Department for Education) 132

dialogue 75, 87, 125, 140, 142

disability: deficit-focused 98; learning 97, 104, 202; stigma 96, 98, 102, 105

discourse: policy 196–197, 203, 205; wellbeing 7, 90, 117, 130, 135, 160

Distefano, Rebecca **16**

distress 120, 122–123, *124*, 131, 178, 183, 215

diversity: acceptance of 107, 147, 153; cultural **24**, 180

doctoral research 73–74, 89

Doll, Beth 104

domestic violence **28**, 29, 182, 204

Dunn, Judith 120

dysfunction **19**, **27**, 31

early childhood: child wellbeing 71–72, 77, *84–88*, 89; classrooms 178, 189, 216; education 113, 117–118, 159–160, 191, 216, 218; educators 4, 8, 52, 147, 150, 152–153, 178; environment 75, 99, 117; experiences 10, **19**, 28, 30, 72, 78; practices 5, 217; programs 3; right to play 38, 148, 152–153; rights and responsibility 35–36, 39–40, 44

early childhood education (ECE): community 114, 117–118, 120, 123; compassion 121; complex in nature 118, 122; environment of 125, 148–152; policy 113

Early Childhood Education and Care (ECEC): educational changes during the pandemic 51–52; pedagogies 54–55

early education: alternative narrative 113, 123, 125, 131; environment

123, *124*; family resiliency model 160; resilience awareness 159–160, 168
Early Intervention Transformation programme 196–197
Early Years Foundation Stage (EYFS) 43, 114, 118
Early Years Practitioners (EYP) 83, *85–86*, *88*
ECE *see* early childhood education
ECEC *see* Early Childhood Education and Care
education: higher 80; remote/online 53, 187; *see also* COVID-19
educator: burnout 60–61; childhood (*see* early childhood); demands-resources model 60; during/after lockdowns 54–55, 181; wellbeing 51–52, 61
Eismann, Emily A. 188
emotional: security 5; wellbeing **21**, 61, 75, 84, 121, 131
emotions: positive 12, 61, 63, 116, 121, *124*; reactions to 41–42
encouragement 42, *86*, 117
England's Early Years Foundation Stage (EYFS) 43, 114, 118
enjoyment 131; *see also* joy
Erdemir, Ersoy **24**
ERIC (database) 13
ethics 52, 74, 84, 130, 134–135, 185
Evans, Erica 84
expectations **21**, 39, 63, 99, 102, 203, 207

family: centres 73; religious traditions **23**, 27, 29; structure 14, 28–29, 32, 213; support 29, 71, 77, 79; *see also* social services
Family Support Hub 203
Family Support Practitioner (FSP) 83, *85–86*, *88*
fear: excessive 37–38; managing 37, 45, 64, 140, 170
Fee, Robert J. 96, 102
Feldman, Ruth 101
Fettes, Mark 135
Filed, Frank 72
flourish 72, 114, 132
focus groups **20–21**, 71, 77, 83, 197–200
freedom 38–40, 43, 79, 131, 133, 161, 166
Freire, Paulo 130–131, 135
Friedman, Samantha 152
Froebel Trust 162

Froebel, Friedrich 161–163, 165, 166, 169, 172
Froebelian pedagogy 161–162
fulcrum 36, 44

Garmezy, Norman 99, 213
gender: equality 140, 143; role 102
Gewirtz, Abigail H. 59
Gibson, Jenny Louise 149, 153–154, 218
Gill, Tim 36–37, 45
global citizenship 113–115, 123
Good Friday Agreement 207
good life 132–133, 135
Goodley, Dan 96, 99, 102
GoPro (camera) 163, 170–171
grandparents **27–28**, 29–30, 56, 139
Guralnick, Michael J. 103

Handley, Gill 39
happiness: feeling of 11–12, 167; individual/personal 63, 105, 131–133
Harris, Kathleen I. 104
Harvard University 35
Hatley, Jenny 143
Head Start **22–23**, 75
health: mental (*see* mental health); physical 36, 42, 85, 101–103; public 54
Henderson, Elizabeth 75
Hickham, Caroline 131
Hinton, Veronica 96, 102
Hochschild, Arlie Russell 63
holistic: education 159–163, 167, 172; pedagogy 160–161, 165–166; relations 163, 167, 171; wellbeing 5, 114–115, 123, 131
homeless/homelessness **16**, **22**, 27, 29–30
Howe, R. Brian 39–40
Hoyes, Samantha 214
human: connection 113, 115; development 122, 161; nature 119, 216; rights 38, 118

illness 96–97, 102
implications: educational 4, 7; emotional resilience 114, 116–117, 120–121, *124*, 125; health 37, 159; pandemic, long-term 53–54
inclusion 12–14, 31, 105, 148, 150
Indigenous: ancestors 133, 137; children 130, 135; communities 132–133, 136;

cultures 135; sustainability knowledge 136–137
Indigenous Elders "Tshenut" 133, 135, 137
individualism 39
influences 37, 59, 72, 75, *76*, 88, 99, 121, 133, 165, 181
initiatives 8, 11, 75, 203, 206–207
interactions: biocultural 160; family/caregiver 6, 73, 100, 170, 187–188, 207; one-on-one **23**; peer 100, 107; playful 105; professional 4, 6, 41–42, 61–62; social 53, 100, 103
intersectionality 6
intervention: holistic 167; intentional 6, 178; program **24**, 105, 196–197, 204, 206; resiliency 159, 195–196
Islamic traditions 139
isolation 51, 53, 55, 60, 64, 87, 97, 150, 160, *188*
Ives, Christopher D. 115

Jalong, Mary Renck 53
Jarrett, Robin L. **23**, 25
Jennings, Mark **19**
Jickling, Bob 135
Johnson, Jeanette L. 55
Jones, Bruce 198, 206
joy 56–58, 132, 142–143, 161
judgement 37, 141, 168

Kahn, Maria 39
Kasser, Tim 133
Kavedžija, Iza 119
Kennair, Leif Edward Ottesen 37
Keyes, Corey L.M. 11
Khambati, Nisreen 187
Kids on Country programme (Western Australia) 136–137, 139
kindergarten **23**, **26**, 30–31, 161
King, Gillian 100
Kleppe, Rasmus 42–43

Laevers, Ferre 131
Lansdown, Gerison *76*
Layard, Richard 120
Lee, Nick 38
Lee, Patrice D. 72
Levinas, Emmanuel 134
Lightfoot, Sara Lawrence 62
Lin, Kuan-Ling **23**
Lindon, Jennie 37–38
listening: culture *7*, 71, 75, 84, 130, 134, 136, 143; skills 133–134, 140, 215
literature review 12–14

Little Talkers progamme 204–205
love **18**, **27**, 30, 99, 132, 134, 139, 166, 204
Lumsden, Eunice 74
Lundy Model 77; Child Participation 75, 86, 87, 89
Lundy, Laura *76*, 86
Luthar, Suniya 72
Lyndon, Helen 74

Mason, John 134
Masten, Ann S. *6*, 10, 59, 73, 96, 98, 116, 195
Mather, Nancy 97, 101
Maturana, Humberto 134
McDowall-Clark, Rory 39
McLeod, Naomi 217
McNally, Sinéad Máire 218
media **27**–**28**, 29–30, 37, 41, 163
medicalisation 98
mental health issues **28**, 30, 132
Merriam, Sharan 195
midwives 201–203
Miljevic-Ridicki, Renata **21**
Millennium Kids Inc. 137
Mistral, Gabriela 185
Moher, David 14
Moore, Alison 214–215
morals 80
Morrison, Rachel 101, 104
Moss, Peter 131–132

Narvaez, Darcia 132
Naser, Shereen C. 39–40
nature, connection with 163–164, 166–168, 171
Neighbourhood Renewal 197
Nesterova, Yulia 135
neurodiversity 147, 150, 153
nightmares 56
Nikiforidou, Zoi 37, 40, 42
Noddings, Nel 132
normal/normality: development 98; experiences 56–59; feelings of being 62–63; new normal 64
Northern Ireland: Executive's Child Poverty Strategy 196; Office of the First Minister and Deputy First Minister 196; policymaking 197
nurture 4, 116, 121, 130, 133–134, 142, 176, 184–185, 187

O'Brien, Catherine 132–133
O'Donnell, Natasha 214, 215

Index **225**

O'Toole, Catriona 119
OECD (Organization for Economic Cooperation and Development) 61
Ofiesh, Nicole 97, 101
open-listening: convergence of meaning 134; rights-based *7*, 71, 74–77, 84, 88–89, 133
Other, respect for 130
othering 38
outcomes: developmental 4; negative 35–36; positive 35, 71, 90, 152, 159, 195

P4C *see Philosophy for/with Children*
Palestine 130, 136, 139–140, 142–143
pandemic *see* COVID-19
paratelic/telic states 41–42, 44
parent: in fight mode 204, 206; hard to reach 200–201, 203; issues 14, **27**, 28, 30, 32, 213; lived experience 76; participants 77; voice 86; young mothers 73, 78
parenting programmes *81*, 85, 198–199, 201
participant: general findings 77–80, *81–83*, 84–85; interviews 52, 54–60; narratives *81–83*; perceptions 60, 62; research **15–16**, 18, **20**, **22–26**; summary discussion 83, 86–87, 89
Pascal, Chris 74
Pedagogy of Hope 130, 134–135
peer: acceptance 102, 150; pressure 37, 39
Pelka, Daniel 74
personality trait/characteristic 37, 41, 102, 180
Philosophy for/with Children (P4C) 130
Philosophy with Children 141–142
physical: development 55, 97, 178; environment 53; play/activity 36; wellbeing 11, 42, 57, 85, 101–103
play: activities 97, 105, 149; defined as 148; social 151–153; spectrum view 148
policy: change 98; discourse 196–197, 203
political: change 207; issues 185; resilience 206
Pollard, Elizabeth L. 72
Portraiture (software program) 71, 89
positive: emotions 12, 61, 63, 116–117, 121, *124*; relationships 95–96, 100, 103–104, *106*, 107, 116–118, 121, 190, 214; wellbeing 135, 178

poverty: challenges of 176, *177*, 178, 181; effects of on health 198; as risk factor 14, **27**, 28–29, 96
practitioner: co-regulation practices 153, 215; early childhood 4, 42–43; perspectives 71–72, 76–77, 83, 87; risk/rights role 41, 45; support services 73–75, 89; trust building 44
pregnancy 78, 198
preschool: children **20–24**, 59, 101, 139; family trips 162–163, 165; transition to 29
prevention 10, 98
pride *83*, *191*
prison 78–79, *81*
Pritchard-Rowe, Emma 151
problem-solving skills 42, 95
professional: medical 98; perspective 71
programme: educational 136; intervention 105, 196; parenting 198–201; participation 199, 202–204
programs and services 6–7
ProQuest (database) 13
protection: child's need/right to 38, 76, 77, 99, 121; parental 31, 214; philosophy of 35, 214
protective factors: caring 187; findings 14, **18**, **25**, **27–28**, 186; resilience and wellbeing 5, 30–32
psychopathology 10, 98

quality of life 7, 100, 120, 218

reassurance 64, 80, *85*
reflections 83, *85*, *86*, *88*, 123, 163, 165
refugee **24**, **29**, 29–30, 130, 136
Reivich, Karen 95
relationship: building 51, 79, 104, 119, 138, 190–191; family 14, **27**, 30, 32, 213; positive 95–96, 100, 103–104, *106*, 107, 116–118, 121, 190, 214
research: meta-synthesis 10, 12, 14, 29, 31; methodology 73, 90, 196; scientists 10, 138; summaries **15–26**; traditional 96, 98
resilience: affiliative brain 301; autism and 152; behaviors 6, 179–181, 185, 192, 216; building 36–37, 63, 179–181, 184–185, 187–190, 192, 199, 201, 206; capacity for 180; circle of support 176, 185, *186*, 187; complexity of 4, 6, 213, 216; concept of 4–5, 11, **21**, 35, 37, 148, 179, 182, 206; counterbalancing

factors 36–37, 43; dynamic process 72, 115, 122, 159, 179; emotional 113–117, 120–121, *124*, 125; governance 197–198, 206–207; invulnerable child 195; research 10, 90, 99, 179, 195, 198; resources 102; see-saw scale 35 (*see also* fulcrum); understanding of 57, 98

response: appropriate 42, 55, 134; collective 41, 44; to COVID-19 52, 171; emotional 169; non-verbal 74; to risk 104; stress 119

reversal theory 41–42

rights and responsibility 35–36, 38–40, 44; miseducation of rights 39

Rinaldi, Carlina 134, 143

risk: aversion 37, 214; erosion of responsibility 44, 52; factors 11, **27**, 28–31; literacy 37–38, 42, 214

risky play: adult role 41–42; definition of 35–36; participation in 38–39; risk-benefit 36, 41

Robles, Eric 217

Robles-Melendez, Wilman 217

role model 42, 117, 138

Runswick-Cole, Katherine 96, 102

Rutter, Michael 11, 117, 195

Ryff, Carol D. 11

Saarinen, Aino 121

safe space 59–60, 133

safety: cotton wool child 37; legislation/litigation 37, 44

Sandelowski, Margarete 12

Sandseter, Ellen Beate Hansen 37, 41–42

scaffolding 42

Scharmer, C. Otto 133

Schön, Donald A. 134

Scopus (database) 13

screening process 13–14

SDGs *see* Sustainable Development Goals

selective hearing 134

self-advocacy 99

self-awareness 133–134

self-efficacy 36–37, 40, 44, 169

self-reflection 133

self-regulation **16–17**, 36–37, 40, 43, 122, 141, 149–154, 166

self-reliance 37

self-understanding 97

Senior Managers (SM) 83

Serious Case Reviews (SCRs) 74

Shatte, Andrew 95

Shirley, Dennis 61

siblings 56

Simovska, Venka 119

sleep deprivation 141

Smith, Ruth S. 97, 117

social: diversity 180; justice 40, 100, 181; life 14, **27**, 28–29, 32, 213; network 6, 150, 201; responsibility 39–40, 45; worker 73–74

social capital: bonding, bridging and linking 196, 198, *199*, 206

social services 4, 73–74

social structure: grandparents 30; media **23**, **27–28**, 29–30, 37, 41

Sokal, Laura 60

Sorin, Reesa 59

Stallard, Rhona 214, 215

Stay & Play *81*, 85

stressors 51, 61, 102, 115, 117–118, 120, *124*

support: children's resilience 35, 43, 55–56, 60, 195–196, 216; developmental 30, 45; family 29, 71, 73–74, 76–77, 86, 89, 167, 196, 203; practices 32, 185

Sure Start 75, 197–198, 200, 202–203

sustainability 113, 115, 123, 136–137, 207

Sustainable Development Goals (SDGs) 115, 118, 125, 130, 138–139

synchrony 101

Szreter, Simon 196, 198, *199*, 205–207

Tardif, Christine Y. 104

teacher: behavior **15–16**; early education **15**, **21**, **23**, 118–120, 122; effective/supportive 97, 103, 140–143, 161, 190; feedback 103; training 107

temperament 37, 97, 99, 187

tension 38, 133, 205

theoretical: framework 196, 214; lenses 75, *76*

Thomas, Trish 160

threat(s) 4, 11, 98, 176, 179, 184, 213

Tovey, Helen 35, 45

transitions (preschool/school) **15–16**, **23**, **27**, **28–31**

trauma: care 7, 11, 53, 142; early life **18–19**, 61, 159; intergenerational 30, 136; *see also* COVID-19

trust: atmosphere of 43; building 141, 191, 196, 204, 208

Tugade, Michele M. 117

UK (United Kingdom) 38, 44, 74
Ukraine 184
UNESCO *see* United Nations Educational, Scientific and Cultural Organization
Ungar, Michael 6, 100, 195, 206, 214
United Nations Convention on the Rights of the Child (UN) 3, 38, 138, 148, 178, 217
United Nations Educational, Scientific and Cultural Organization (UNESCO) 115, 123, 130–131
urban: landscape 141, 162–163, 168; low-income backgrounds **16**, **18**, **23**

values 6, 12, **20**, 80, 102, 135, 160, 215; *see also* ethics
VanderPlaat, Madine 195, 206
violence 96–97, 140, 176, 178, 182–184; *see also* domestic violence; war

Wallberg, Pamela 39
Waller, Tim 38
war 123, 143, 177, 184
Ward, Leonor Mercedes 133
Watts, Tansy 217
web of relations 115, 119
Web of Science (database) 13
wellbeing: *Bildung*, concept of 119; compassion and 114, 121; concept of 11, 71–72, 75, 77; COVID-19, restoring wellbeing 58; cultural link 136–143; definition of 11, 61, 71, 132; discourse 7, 90, 117, 130, 135, 160; early childhood 71–72, 77, *84–88*, 89; educator 51–52, 61; emotional **21**, 61, 75, 84, 121, 131; eudemonic perspective 11, 119; hedonistic perspective 11, 119; holistic 5, 88, 90, 114–115, 123, 131, 159; nurturing 130, 133–136, 143, 185; physical 11, 42, 57, 85, 101–103; positive 135, 178; resilience and 5, 30–32

Werner, Emmy 97, 117
Wiener, Judith 104
Williams-Siegfredsen, Jane 43
Wilson, Kaitlyn P. 149
Winfield, Linda F. 11
Wolmer, Leo 6
Woods-Jaeger, Briana A. **18**
Woolcock, Michael 196, 198, *199*, 205–207
World Health Organization (WHO) 118, 184
Wright, Travis **22**
Wyver, Shirley 44

Yazici, Dila Nur 213–214

Zhao, Yiran Vicky 149
Zolkoski, Staci M. 96
Zoom (online video format) 53